CONFLICT AND CRISIS
IN THE
POST–COLD WAR WORLD

ANGOLA AND MOZAMBIQUE

POSTCOLONIAL WARS IN SOUTHERN AFRICA

James Ciment

Facts On File, Inc.

For
The children of
Angola
and
Mozambique

Angola and Mozambique: Postcolonial Wars in Southern Africa

Copyright © 1997 by James Ciment

Facts On File, Inc.
11 Penn Plaza
New York NY 10001

Library of Congress Cataloging-in-Publication Data

Ciment, James.
    Angola and Mozambique : postcolonial wars in southern Africa / James Ciment
      p. cm. — (Conflict and crisis in the post–cold war world)
    Includes bibliographical references and index.
    ISBN 0-8160-3525-3 (alk. paper)
    1. Angola—Politics and government—1975–   2. Angola—History, Military.   3. Mozambique—Politics and government—1975–
4. Mozambique—History, Military. I. Title. II. Series.
DT1405.C56 1997
967.304—dc21   96-29643

Facts On File books are available at special discounts when purchased in bulk quantities for businesses, associations, institutions or sales promotions. Please call our Special Sales Department in New York at 212/967-8800 or 800/322-8755.

Jacket design by Robert Yaffe

MP FOF 10 9 8 7 6 5 4 3 2 1

This book is printed on acid-free paper.

CONTENTS

PREFACE: CONFLICT AND CRISIS IN THE POST–COLD WAR WORLD

The eminent British historian E. J. Hobsbawm has recently declared the end of the "short twentieth century," delimited by the two great Russian revolutions of 1917 and 1991. If that is so, then this series might be considered among the first histories of the twenty-first century.

Whatever date we care to assign the beginning of the new century, we carry into it a lot of baggage from the past. The Cold War may be over, but just as the two global struggles of the first half of the twentieth century left a legacy of troubled peace, so has the great confrontation of the second half.

Conflict and Crisis in the Post–Cold War World explores that legacy. Each conflict described in these volumes has been a place where the Cold War turned hot.

The confrontation between East and West, however, did not ignite these conflicts. Each one has a history that stretches back to long before the atom bomb was dropped on Hiroshima or the wall was built in Berlin. Most of them, in fact, are not products of the Cold War so much as they are legacies of the European imperial order of the last several hundred years and, in the case of Kurdistan, of a struggle that goes back a lot farther than that.

Similarly, these conflicts have had important indigenous and regional components. The great delusion of the Cold War, that all conflicts were essentially superpower confrontations by proxy, has been exposed in the post–Cold War era for the myth that it was. Ethnicity, religion and the animosity between settler and indigenous societies are, in varying measures, at the root of the very different conflicts examined in this series.

But that is not to let the Cold War off the historical hook. The struggle between Washington and Moscow exacerbated, extended and exaggerated each of these conflicts, and many more. Both East and West offered support in the form of money, weaponry, intelligence and military training to their favored clients. Worst of all, they provided an ideological force-field that deflected potential negotiations and peaceful solutions.

The books in this series examine the roles of pre–Cold War history, the Cold War, and indigenous and regional factors in these conflicts.

They are intended as introductory volumes for the reader acquainted with but not versed in the stories of these wars. They are short but comprehensive and readable reference works. Each follows a similar format and contains similar chapters: an introduction and overview of the conflict; its history; the participants, both those in power and those struggling against it; the issues, tactics and negotiations involved; and a final chapter as update and conclusion. (The volume on Israel/Palestine contains an additional chapter on the larger regional conflict between Israel and the Arab nations of the Middle East.) Each book also contains several maps, a glossary of names and terms and a bibliography.

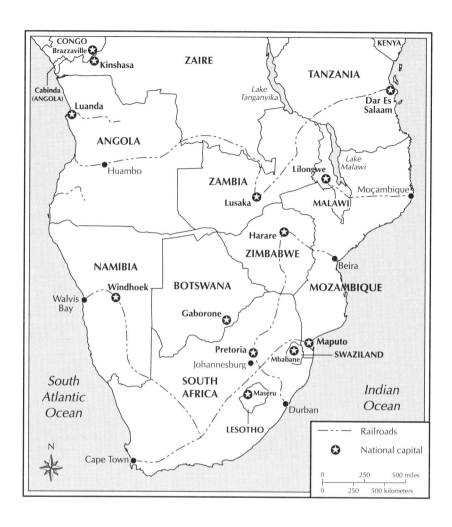

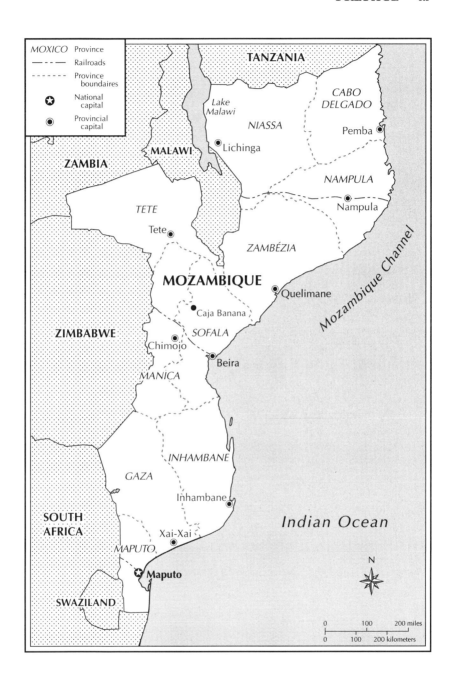

MOXICO	Province
—·—·—	Railroads
- - - - -	Province boundaires
✪	National capital
◉	Provincial capital

TANZANIA

ZAMBIA

MALAWI

Lake Malawi

NIASSA

Lichinga

CABO DELGADO

Pemba

NAMPULA

Nampula

TETE

Tete

MOZAMBIQUE

ZAMBÉZIA

Quelimane

Caja Banana

ZIMBABWE

Chimoio

SOFALA

Beira

MANICA

Mozambique Channel

INHAMBANE

GAZA

Inhambane

SOUTH AFRICA

Xai-Xai

Indian Ocean

MAPUTO

✪ Maputo

SWAZILAND

N

0   100   200 miles
0   100   200 kilometers

1

INTRODUCTION

THE THIRTY-YEAR WARS

Freedom is seen in a man's eyes.
> —Angolan proverb

You have to trust your feet.
> —Mozambican proverb

Sometime in 1994, during the height of Angola's so-called "second war," a food relief flight making its harrowing spiral descent into the besieged city of Huambo was shot down by rebel forces with a U.S.-supplied missile. The Russian-trained pilot somehow managed to crash-land the huge Antonov-class transport. Bleeding and bewildered, he crawled from the wreckage as bystanders shouted to him from a distance. He had unknowingly come down in a mine field situated between rebel and government battle lines, and had taken only a couple of steps when he put his foot down on one of Angola's estimated 10 million antipersonnel land mines. Designed to maim rather than kill, the land mine crippled the pilot. While the two sides heatedly discussed a mini-cease-fire to rescue the man, he bled to death.

When future historians tally the costs of the Cold War, they might very well begin in southern Africa. The Cold War may have been cold in the First and Second Worlds of the Northern Hemisphere, with confrontations, blustering and threats, but it was all too hot in the Third World, especially in Africa. This volume examines two such Cold War battlegrounds: Angola and Mozambique, two former Portuguese colonies on two different coasts of southern Africa. Both fought wars with their former European rulers, both were suddenly liberated, and then both immediately plunged back into foreign-sponsored internal conflict.

But Cold War politics alone are not responsible for the maelstrom that has engulfed Angola and Mozambique. In fact, as far at the latter is concerned, the Cold War was a secondary factor. Both countries had the unfortunate distinction of having three of the great post–World War II struggles play out on their soil: Europe's (in this case, Portugal's) rear-guard defense of nineteenth-century colonialism, the confrontation between West and East, and the aggressive defense of apartheid.

As in much of Africa, a wave of anticolonial activity and organizing swept Angola and Mozambique in the 1950s. Unlike the rest of the continent's peoples, however, Angolans and Mozambicans were ruled by Portuguese masters who would not yield to the "winds of change."[1] Having exhausted the possibilities for peacefully challenging Lisbon's fascist-inspired colonial policy, Angolan and Mozambican patriots launched guerrilla campaigns in the early 1960s. Though they enjoyed limited success in the field, the struggles put enough of a strain on Portugal's limited military and economic means to help bring about its Carnation Revolution in 1974–75.

The new government in Lisbon, dominated by socialist politicians and left-wing military officers, declared an end to the country's 400-year presence in Africa and withdrew within a year. As hundreds of thousands of skilled and unskilled Portuguese residents fled the colonies, Lisbon handed power over to the largest guerrilla organizations in each country, without elections, guidance, capital or concern. Virtually unchallenged, the revolutionary and socialist Mozambique Liberation Front (FRE-LIMO) took power in July 1975. In Angola, however, things were more complicated and bloodier. Three major guerrilla movements contended for power: the leftist, pan-Angolan Popular Movement for the Liberation of Angola (MPLA); and two ethnic-based parties, the National Front for the Liberation of Angola (FNLA) in the north and the Union for the Total Independence of Angola (UNITA) in the south.

Despite hastily patched-together accords, war broke out in the months before Angola's independence, with each organization trying to establish itself as the legitimate government of the oil-, diamond-, coffee- and cotton-rich country. Each side had its own patrons. Cuba and the Soviet Union intervened on the part of the MPLA, the FNLA enjoyed the support of Zaire, the United States and the People's Republic of China and South Africa launched an invasion to put UNITA leader Jonas Savimbi in power. After six months of fighting, the MPLA emerged triumphant. The FNLA collapsed, and Savimbi led the remnants of his UNITA supporters deep into the bush of southern Angola to prepare for the next round.

Although it was spared the independence disaster of Angola, Mozambique proved less lucky during the rest of the decade. Committed to supporting its compatriots fighting against the white regime in neigh- boring Rhodesia, Mozambique turned the screws on that landlocked country through the strict enforcement of international sanctions, which included denying Rhodesia access to Mozambican railroads and ports. The minority government in Rhodesia responded by launching the National Mozambican Resistance (MNR, later and better known by its Portuguese acronym, RENAMO), an organization consisting of disaffected FRE-LIMO officers and former lackeys of the Portuguese. For the next four years, RENAMO engaged in a war of terror against the Mozambican peasantry and in the destruction of the nation's infrastructure.

The 1979 British-brokered transition to majority rule in the newly renamed Zimbabwe witnessed the end of the Rhodesian phase of the war in Mozambique and the inauguration of the Pretoria-led one. With its greater resources and determination, South Africa greatly augmented RENAMO's ability to wreak havoc. Indeed, South Africa's aims were not so much to overthrow the Frelimo government—though this was undoubtedly what RENAMO's leaders had in mind—but to render the country ungovernable and its economy unworkable. The policy, known as "total strategy," was a resounding success. After another twelve years of war, a period in which both Soviet communism and apartheid collapsed, FRELIMO was forced to recognize and sue for peace with an organization it considered to be nothing more than foreign-created and -backed "bandits."

The conflict in Angola took a different but even more costly and deadly path. After a few years of relative peace, the country was again plunged into war when a revived UNITA, heavily armed and periodically supported by South African military invasions, established control over much of the southern Angolan countryside, homeland of leader Jonas Savimbi's Ovimbundu people. The war, which ranged from insurgency-style fighting to great open land battles involving tanks, long-range artillery and jet aircraft, lasted until the Bicesse (Portugal) peace accords were signed in 1991. Tactics, however, were not the only element of the war that underwent a dramatic transformation. So did the geopolitics of the conflict.

Until well into the decade, UNITA's main supporter was South Africa. But at the battles of Mavinga and Cuito Cuanavale (in southeastern Angola), the South African Defense Forces (SADF) were routed by a combined Cuban/MPLA force and were forced to retreat. In 1988, South Africa, Cuba and Angola signed the U.S.-brokered New York accords, calling for South Africa to relinquish its illegal colony in neighboring Namibia in exchange for a Cuban pullout from Angola.

Meanwhile, in Washington, Savimbi's fortunes were faring better. In 1986, the Reagan administration persuaded Congress to overturn the Clark Amendment, a 1976 law that banned all U.S. military aid to the parties in Angola. Within two years, the U.S. had become UNITA's main patron, annually pumping as much as $250 million in arms to the Angolan rebels. Despite the immense financial resources at its command, the Angolan government, like its Mozambican counterpart, was forced to negotiate a peace treaty—which included demobilization, new joint armed forces and multiparty elections—with an organization it had long considered a puppet of South Africa and the United States.

Angola's misfortunes, however, were not yet at an end. If the "first war" (as Angolans label the conflict from independence to the Bicesse accords) had a multitude of causes, the second had just one: Jonas Savimbi. An ambitious and uncompromising man, Savimbi expected to win the 1992 elections. That may be why nobody, including the understaffed UN force in the country, bothered much about UNITA's apparent refusal to demobilize. But Savimbi didn't win and charged fraud. As postelection violence grew, the UNITA leader rallied his still-mobilized troops and launched the "second war," a particularly vicious conflict, involving lengthy urban sieges, that saw more people killed in two years than had died in the previous twenty.

ANGOLA IN THE MID-1990s

The war in Angola is over, at least for now. In November 1994, the MPLA and UNITA signed the Lusaka (Zambia) accords. Though modeled on the Bicesse accords, Lusaka is a more flexible agreement, setting goals and establishing a framework for dialogue rather than a rigid deadline for demobilization and elections. Sporadic fighting between UNITA and MPLA forces continued for approximately a year, though it was largely localized and did not lead to the kind of renewed nationwide warfare that followed in the wake of the 1992 elections.

Current negotiations are proceeding, but very gradually. And as far as the once-burned United Nations Angolan Verification Mission (UNAVEM II) is concerned, that's fine. Demobilization is the most immediate problem. It took exactly one year from the signing of the Lusaka accords before the first MPLA and UNITA troops showed up at the cantonments established by UNAVEM. Given that the "second war" was a result of UNITA's failure to demobilize, along with UNAVEM's understaffed and limited mandate in 1991–92, all parties have been willing to allow demobilization to proceed at its own pace, albeit with occasional prodding by the international community and the UN. Nevertheless, in September 1996, the UN reported that fully 80 percent of UNITA troops had moved to demobilization centers and turned in their weapons. In addition, five UNITA generals have joined the new joint army in Luanda. Less encouraging have been the arms flights from Zaire to Savimbi's current headquarters at Negage in northwest Angola and conducted "under the UN's eyes."[2]

Despite the slow pace of demobilization, other long-range problems are currently being discussed, including elections and the establishment of the joint MPLA/UNITA-staffed army, though all sides have yet to agree on any of the details. Power-sharing remains the key issue. UNITA wants a serious preelection role in the government; the MPLA wants to keep it to a minimum. Two issues continue to obstruct the peace process. Savimbi has yet to make it clear what his role in a new government might be. Thus far, he has rejected joining the government for fear that his move to the capital would result in the collapse of his rebel movement. Under the current construction, Savimbi may serve in a governing coalition while retaining his leadership position in UNITA. The second obstacle is diamonds. Northern Angola is rich in the gem-quality stones, and much of this territory remains under UNITA control. The Lusaka peace process calls for all diamond production to be turned over to Endiama, the state monopoly, but UNITA soldiers and officers have balked at the idea. There has been talk of turning UNITA's diamond interests into a privately run corporation.

Meanwhile the UN wants to avoid another embarrassment and to make sure that the catastrophic 1992 winner-take-all style election is not repeated. Unlike the international organization's first mission, which tried to buy peace on the cheap, the UN is committing some 7,500 troops and almost a $1 billion to UNAVEM II, though it has talked of leaving in early 1997.

For the Angolan people, the suffering goes on. Hundreds of thousands of refugees remain in camps in neighboring countries. An estimated three million are still internally displaced, largely living in the overcrowded *musseques* (slums) and shantytowns of Angola's coastal cities. Angolan transport and travel remain crippled. UNITA patrols still control most of the nation's roads and refuse to allow passage lest the MPLA army take advantage of the openness to launch an offensive.

Five million, 10 million, 15 million, nobody is sure how many land mines lay in wait for the unsuspecting farmer and villager. Sowed at random, land mines were used by UNITA (and, to a lesser extent, the MPLA) to terrorize civilians and render farming and transport impossible. They have worked. Much of Angola's richest agricultural areas remain dependent on international food aid, though, unlike during the war years, much of it is now delivered more cheaply on mine-cleared main roads, rather than by costly and limited air transport.

MOZAMBIQUE IN THE LATE 1990s

The war in Mozambique is over, and it seems for good. Between the signing of the Rome accords in October 1992 and the elections in October 1994, Mozambique's two armies effectively demobilized under the UN's Mozambique Task Force (UNOMOZ) auspices, and a joint military command was established for the new integrated army. The disastrous events in Angola cast a sobering shadow over all parties involved in the Mozambique peace process. Thus, while demobilization fell a year behind schedule and elections had to be pushed back by the same, both FRELIMO and RENAMO demonstrated patience and discipline, a surprise to many who thought RENAMO might spin out of control and degenerate into independent banditry. For its part, the UN evinced a much greater commitment to the Mozambique mission that it had to Angola's, spending several times the amount of money and sending about 20 times the number of troops.

While the UN declared the October 1992 elections free of fraud and intimidation, a number of independent observers say that RENAMO used explicit and implicit threats against voters in areas under its control, a factor which helps explain RENAMO's relatively strong showing in parliamentary races. Still, FRELIMO emerged the winner, controlling a bare majority in the assembly and winning the presidency by a wide margin. To its credit, RENAMO leaders accepted the results, after a last-minute preelection boycott by its presidential candidate and long-time leader Afonso Dhlakama.

The elections, of course, have not settled all political disputes in the country, especially at the local level. Since the end of 1994, there have been a number of confrontations between RENAMO leaders and *regulos* (traditional and colonial era chiefs) on the one side and FRELIMO appointed administrators on the other. Some of them have turned violent. RENAMO claims that the majority FRELIMO is freezing it out of the government, while FRELIMO claims that the former rebels are unwilling to accept the democratically expressed will of the people.

Party politics is only one, and the lesser, of many problems facing the Mozambican people. Of far greater importance is the state of the economy. The country is virtually bankrupt; well over half the GNP comes from international aid. To get this aid, the government has had to accept political interference by the larger nongovernmental organizations (NGOs), who have established independent administrative networks within the country, and a drastic restructuring imposed by the World Bank and the International Monetary Fund (IMF). The latter has produced runaway inflation and led to strikes by industrial workers, health care professionals, and even soldiers. Meanwhile the government is placing its economic hopes on a $300 million British and American oil exploration project. In late 1996, the Paris Club of bilateral creditors agreed to forgive $400 million of the $600 million that Mozambique owed its members. This still leaves over $4 billion in outstanding international obligations.

While virtually all of Mozambique's several million refugees have now returned to the country (the exception being the several hundred thousand Mozambicans in South Africa who, for economic reasons, may never return permanently), this has exacerbated other problems. Like

Angola, Mozambique is littered with millions of unmapped land mines. An expensive and time-consuming task, mine-clearing operations cannot keep pace with the influx of refugees and internally displaced persons eager to return to their land-mine-laced farms and villages. Tens of thousands of returning combatants, including an estimated 10,000 child soldiers of RENAMO, add to the crisis.

Nature has added to Mozambique's current woes. Serious flooding in early 1996 displaced over 200,000 people and led to a widespread outbreak of malaria. Thousands of tons of emergency food and medicine was flown in by international relief agencies, though the disaster has set back the country's reconstruction efforts.

COUNTRY PROFILES

ANGOLA

> AREA: 481,381 square miles (1,246,700 square kilometers)
> POPULATION: 10,069,501 (July 1995 estimate)
> GNP: $6.1 billion (1994 estimate)

Geography, climate and resources

Angola has a relatively simple geography. A 50-mile-wide coastal plain along the South Atlantic Ocean gives way to a vast interior plateau that stretches eastward to the Zairian and Zambian borders. The highest reaches of these uplands, roughly two to three thousand feet above sea level, are in the west-central part of the country and are often referred to as the central highlands. While the war has had devastating effects on the Angolan people, it has helped preserve the environment. Angola suffers only minor problems of soil erosion, desertification, and deforestation.[3]

Angola's climate is tropical, with year-round semiarid conditions prevailing in the south. In the center and north of the country, the climate varies between cool, dry winters (May to October) and hot, rainy summers (November to April).[4] Angola is bordered by Zaire to the north and east, Zambia to the southeast and Namibia to the south. The enclave of Cabinda, separated from the rest of the country by the Congo River and a corridor of Zairian territory that ranges from 10 to 50 miles across, is bordered by Congo on the northeast.

Angola is gifted with immense mineral resources, including oil reserves in the northwestern corner of the country and Cabinda. Industrial and gem-quality diamonds are mined in the northeast. Approximately 2 percent of the land is currently farmed. Another 23 percent of the country is meadow and pasturelands, forests cover 43 percent, and much of the rest is bush or desert. Angola's main internal river is the Kwanza, while the

Congo forms part of the northern border. Neither river is navigable beyond the western fall line of the internal plateau. Angola has a 1,000-mile coastline. Its two main harbors are at Luanda in the north and Lobito in the center.

Demographics

As in many African countries, Angola's population is young. Almost half are under the age of 15. Birth, infant mortality and death rates are all high. Overall, the country has a population growth rate of 2.68 percent, roughly average for sub-Saharan Africa, but generally slightly higher than the Third World. Life expectancy is approximately 44 years for men and 48 for women. Male literacy is around 40 percent, while about 30 percent of women can read and write.

Angola's population is largely rural, with approximately 80 to 90 percent of the people involved in agriculture. Luanda is the capital and largest city, with a population of 2 million. (This figure, largely inflated by the war, may shrink during peacetime.) Other major cities include Huambo in the central highlands and Lobito on the central coast.

Virtually all Angolans are of African descent, though there is a small (about 10 percent) but highly influential minority of mestizos (mixed-race people) in the main cities. Europeans (largely of Portuguese descent) and Asians (mostly Indian) account for about 1 percent. Angola's major religions include animist faiths (about 50 percent of the people), Catholicism (about 40 percent) and various Protestant sects.

Like most African countries, Angola is ethnically and linguistically diverse. The largest ethno-linguistic group is the Ovimbundu, who represent about 37 percent of the population and inhabit the central highlands, though large numbers migrated to the north during the late Portuguese era. The second largest is the Kimbundu, with about 25 percent of the population. Most Kimbundu live on the coastal plain. The other major group is the Kikongo. With about 13 percent of the population, they inhabit northern Angola, though most of this important African ethnic group live in neighboring Congo and Zaire. Mestizos and minor ethnic groups make up the rest of the population. While Angola has several official languages, Portuguese serves as the lingua franca of trade, government, the military and education, though less than half of all Angolans speak it with any fluency.

The economy

Depending on one's perspective, subsistence agriculture or oil is the most important element of the Angolan economy. While approximately 80 to 90 percent of the population is engaged in the former, it only makes up 15 percent of the GNP, largely from the small fields of commercial crops (mostly coffee and bananas) that many peasants tend on the side. Oil, on the other hand, accounts for 60 percent of the government's revenues and nearly 90 percent of its exports. Diamonds and limited exports of coffee, bananas and cotton make up the rest.

Outside the oil sector, Angolan industry is in poor shape. Much of it is devoted to food processing and light manufacturing, with most industrial concerns situated in Luanda and its environs. Approximately 10 percent of the population works in industry. If oil revenues are subtracted from the total, Angola's GNP has, by some estimates, fallen by half since independence. Inflation, in 1994, averaged 20 percent a month, unemployment stood officially at 15 percent (with high rates of underemployment) and per capita income at $620, moderate by the standards of sub-Saharan Africa but distorted by oil income. The country's external debt in 1994 was approximately $12 billion.

Angola has several key transport corridors to the interior. The most important is the Benguela railway, which runs along the coast from Lobito to Benguela, then to Huambo, the Angolan east, Zaire and Zambia's copper belt. The Benguela railway is the latter country's most important link to the sea as well as Angola's only transnational railway, and hence was a target for UNITA saboteurs.

MOZAMBIQUE

AREA: 309,494 square miles (801,590 square kilometers)
POPULATION: 18,115,250 (July 1995 estimate)
GNP: $1.9 billion (1994 estimate)

Geography, climate and resources

Like Angola, Mozambique is an immense country, nearly twice as large as California. A narrow plain, gradually widening toward the north, stretches along its 1,543-mile coastline, giving way to a low plateau that makes up most of the rest of the country. Several mountainous regions along the Zimbabwean and Malawian borders boast moderate peaks ranging from about 6,000 to 9,000 feet in elevation. Cutting the country approximately in half, the Zambezi River is Mozambique's most important waterway and the Zambezi valley its most productive agricultural region. At least twenty-five other rivers, including the Limpopo, run from the internal highlands to the coast. War-induced migration to the coast has caused limited environmental damage to the nation's string of coastal lagoons, shoals and islets.

Stretching from 10 to 27 degrees south of the equator, Mozambique has both tropical and subtropical coastal regions. Its interior highlands enjoy moderate temperatures and cool, dry winters. All regions of the country are divided into wet (November to April) and dry (May to October) seasons, based on the Indian Ocean's monsoons. Like much of southern Africa, Mozambique is subject to extremes of weather, including occasional cyclones and lengthy droughts such as the one that hit the region in the late 1980s and early 1990s.

Unlike Angola, Mozambique is largely devoid of mineral resources, though recent explorations in the south have led to exploratory gas wells. The nation's main natural resource is its fertile land, especially along the Zambezi, and its low-lying, marine-life-rich coastal waters.

Demographics

Mozambique is as young a country as Angola. Approximately 45 percent of its people are under 15 years old. Its birth, death and infant mortality rates are all high, resulting in a population growth rate of nearly 3 percent per annum. Male and female life expectancies are 47 and 51 years, respectively. Literacy rates are quite low, at 45 percent for men and 21 percent for women. Approximately 90 percent of the Mozambican people live in the countryside. Maputo is the capital and largest city, with approximately one million people. Other important cities include the port of Beira in the central region and Nampula in the north.

Since independence and the mass exodus of Portuguese and Indians, Mozambicans have been overwhelmingly of African descent, with mestizos, whites and Indians together comprising about 1 percent of the population. Ethnically, Mozambique is extremely diverse with some nine major groupings (depending on who's counting), including the Tsonga, Shona and Ndau in the south and center, the Lomwe and Makua just north of the Zambezi, and the Yao and Makonde in the north. Most of these ethnicities are shared with other countries—South Africa to the south, Zimbabwe, Zambia and Malawi to the east, and Tanzania to the north.

Estimates vary as to how many Christians and Muslims inhabit the country. The population is between 10 and 20 percent Muslim, particularly along the coast and in the north, and 20 to 30 percent Christian, a majority of whom are Catholic. Between 50 and 60 percent follow indigenous faiths, though many Christians mix their faith with traditional worship.

The economy

Mozambique is among the poorest countries in Africa and indeed the world. A substantial portion of its GNP is provided by international aid, though that has been falling in recent years. Approximately 90 percent of the population is involved in agricultural production, much of it at the subsistence level. The war and the continued presence of land mines have kept food production in recent years to 75 percent of colonial levels. Many small farms and a few large plantations are responsible for Mozambique's main export crops: cashews, cotton, and, recently, vegetable farming for the South African market. Fishing is a major source of food and revenue. Shrimp alone accounts for 40 percent of Mozambique's exports by value.

While Mozambique lacks oil, it has tremendous hydroelectric resources. The Cabora Bassa dam on the upper Zambezi is one of the largest in the world, and once generated much of the country's electricity. Though the electricity grid was heavily damaged during the war, current repairs will reconnect the dam to the South African and Zimbabwean grids. Once one of the most industrialized countries in sub-Saharan Africa, Mozambique's current production is in poor shape, operating at 20 to 40 percent of capacity. Both inflation and urban unemployment stood at 50 percent in 1994. The country's external debt is over $4 billion.

Mozambique's many rivers, and Portugul's emphasis on interior-to-coast railway building, have left the country without a major north-south transport system. On the other hand, rail connections from the coast to the interior are, despite wartime sabotage, good. Major rail lines connect Maputo to Johannesburg and the mines of the Transvaal, and Beira to the Zimbabwean capital of Harare.

PARTICIPANTS

ANGOLA

Government

Since independence, Angola has been ruled by the MPLA. Founded in 1956, the pre-independence MPLA included whites, mestizos and blacks of varying political stripes. Most were urban; many were European-educated intellectuals. Though the MPLA was founded in Luanda, its founders had often spent many years out of the country. Few came from peasant or rural backgrounds. The party's racial diversity and urban origins were a source of outside criticism. Many Angolans felt that the MPLA, with its urban and elitist background, had little understanding of and connection with the vast majority of Angolan people, who earned their living in subsistence and small-scale commercial agriculture. From 1961 to 1979, the party was led by a Lisbon-trained medical doctor named Agostinho Neto. After his death, power was assumed by José Eduardo dos Santos, a Soviet-educated oil engineer. Elected in Angola's first multiparty elections in 1992, dos Santos serves as president of both Angola and of the MPLA.

The MPLA's ideological sources were diverse and included the Stalinist Portuguese Communist Party, the Third World counterdependency nationalism of Algeria's National Liberation Front, and Amilcar Cabral's African-based Marxism. In power, the MPLA proved to be mildly socialistic and intensely nationalistic in its politics and economic policies. This, too, subjected it to much criticism, both inside and outside the country. Other Angolan nationalists, such as Savimbi, accused it of imposing radical programs on a traditional-minded peasantry and saddling the country with new colonial masters from the socialist bloc.

Rebels

Two separate nationalist movements have contended for power with the MPLA. The first was the FNLA. Founded in 1957 as the Union of the Peoples of Northern Angola (UPNA), it soon dropped the regional element of its name. In 1961, it took its current name. Despite the name changes, the party remained largely based among the Kikongo people of northern Angola. Because the majority of the Kikongo lived outside the country, the party established its headquarters in the Congo (now Zaire) after that nation won its independence from Belgium in 1960.

The FNLA's ties to Zaire were significant. Holden Roberto, the FNLA's leader since its inception, was a close ally of Zairian dictator Joseph Mobutu (later Mobutu Sese Seko). After the early uprisings of 1961, tens of thousands of Kikongo settled in the Zairian capital of Leopoldville (now Kinshasa) and elsewhere in Zaire, where many prospered as traders and commercial farmers. This economic base and Roberto's close alliance with the anticommunist Mobutu gave the party its conservative political and economic outlook. The FNLA was often faulted both for its ethnic exclusivity and for its unwillingness to establish a permanent base within colonial Angola.

During the war of Angolan independence, Roberto and the FNLA launched an invasion of northern Angola with the help of the CIA and the Zairian army. But the organization was unable to take the capital by independence day and was soon shattered by a combined Soviet-armed force of Cuban and MPLA soldiers. Roberto went into European exile and the organization largely disappeared until the 1992 elections, when it re-formed as a political party. Its showing was extremely weak; the party did not win a single seat in the new assembly.

Angola's other main rebel organization, UNITA, has been longer-lived. Its founder and only president, Jonas Savimbi, an Ovimbundu Angolan who received an advanced degree in political science from the University of Lausanne (Switzerland), had once been a foreign minister for the FNLA but dropped out of that organization because of its unwillingness to settle in Angola. In 1966, Savimbi founded UNITA and quickly established an in-country base in Ovimbunduland in central Angola. UNITA has been viewed by many outsiders as little more than an organizational expression of Savimbi's own politics and ambition. Unlike the MPLA's consensus-oriented leadership, Savimbi rules UNITA autocratically, allowing little room for dissenting opinion even among the top leadership. Thus, UNITA's politics are largely Savimbi's and, as such, have changed dramatically over the years. An early self-described Maoist, Savimbi embraced a fierce anticommunism during the 1980s and evinced a commitment to multiparty democracy in the 1990s. Critics argue that this tacking with the geopolitical winds reflects Savimbi's opportunism rather than ideological conviction.

Foreign

The thirty-year war in Angola has lured a number of African and international powers. During the war of independence, Zaire, China and the United States backed the FNLA, South Africa (and, more ambivalently, Zambia) supported UNITA, and Cuba and the Soviet Union got behind the MPLA. Needless to say, each became involved for its own reasons. Zaire's Mobutu feared a radical regime on his western border for several reasons, but most especially because he did not want to see control of the critical Benguela railway fall into ideologically hostile hands. Despite diametrically opposed political systems, Chinese and U.S. support had a common denominator, anti-Sovietism.

For its part, South Africa wanted pliable leaders in its neighboring frontline states who would not criticize the apartheid regime too severely and would allow it to economically dominate southern Africa.[5] Savimbi seemed to fit the bill. Zambia's conservative president Kenneth Kaunda, like Zaire's Mobutu, was concerned about his nation's access to the sea and worried that an MPLA-controlled government in Angola might use the Benguela railway to exact political and economic concessions.

On the MPLA's side, foreign support was equally complicated. Despite Western leaders' opinion that Cuba was simply following Moscow's bidding in Angola, the alliance was a more subtle one. Moscow was at a stage in the mid-1970s where it felt ready to challenge U.S. hegemony in the Third World, while Fidel Castro was more interested in promoting Cuba's leadership in Africa through solidarity with ideologically conducive regimes. Thus, for a time, Havana's and Moscow's interests coincided.

The continuing commitment of South Africa, the U.S. and Zaire to anti-MPLA forces (with the disintegration of the FNLA, this left UNITA as the only viable option) and the Soviet Union and Cuba to the MPLA during the post-independence period reflected a situation in which none of the parties was willing to concede victory to its opponents. Every escalation by one side would trigger an equivalent move by its adversary, thereby upping the ante through the late 1980s. After the great land battles of 1987–88, a chastened South Africa and victorious Cuba pulled out under a U.S.-brokered peace agreement. The U.S. and the Soviet Union, however, continued to arm their respective clients, though Moscow's support for the MPLA fell off with the retreat and collapse of the Soviet Union in the late 1980s and early 1990s. U.S. support for UNITA continued through the peace treaty of 1991; it wasn't until the advent of the Clinton administration and Savimbi's decision to go back to war after losing the 1992 elections that Washington formally recognized the MPLA government in Luanda.

MOZAMBIQUE

Government

Founded in 1962, FRELIMO was Mozambique's only serious guerrilla movement during the Portuguese era, and it has ruled the country since independence. Like those of the MPLA, FRELIMO's original members were mostly educated and urban-based; many had lived in exile since the late 1950s, and the organization was in fact founded in neighboring Tanzania's capital of Dar es Salaam. FRELIMO launched its first guerrilla attack against Portuguese forces late in 1964.

During its early years, FRELIMO was riven by factionalism—mostly because northern chieftains resented the radicalism of the southern leaders and the fact that much of the fighting was going on in their territory. After several military setbacks, FRELIMO adopted a peasant-based approach to national independence and attempted to establish liberated zones within the country where the economy, social infrastructure and politics would be based on revolutionary principles. This approach was disputed by the northerners, who, with the connivance of Portuguese security, assassinated FRELIMO founder and president Eduardo Mondlane in 1969.

Under Mondlane's successor and protégé, Samora Machel, a nurse educated in Lourenço Marques (later Maputo), the organization established itself as the only viable successor to the Portuguese, who handed the colony over to FRELIMO in 1975. During its first decade or so of governing, FRELIMO pursued a centrally administered, state-planned approach to economic development. It established a much-celebrated rural health-care and education system. It also declared itself a Marxist-Leninist party and outlawed all other political organizations in the country. But since the mid-1980s, under international and RENAMO pressure, the country has shifted to multiparty democracy and market-oriented economics. Machel, who died in a mysterious plane crash in 1986, was succeeded by Joaquim Chissano, a former medical student, who was confirmed as president in Mozambique's first and only multiparty elections in 1994.

Rebels

Unlike UNITA or the FNLA, RENAMO has virtually no indigenous roots. Instead, the organization was founded by Rhodesia's Central Intelligence Organization (CIO) in 1976. In an effort to punish Mozambique for its strict application of international sanctions against Rhodesia's white minority regime, the CIO recruited a small number of disaffected FRELIMO officials and Mozambican expatriates. With funding from Rhodesia and former Portuguese colonists, RENAMO launched a campaign of terror and destruction against the civilian population and infrastructure of Mozambique.

With the fall of white rule in Rhodesia, RENAMO was adopted by the apartheid regime in South Africa. With its greater resources, Pretoria was able to turn RENAMO into a nationwide force, though most of the organization's activities were in the central Mozambican provinces, where anti-FRELIMO sentiment ran highest. In 1992, RENAMO signed the Rome peace accords with FRELIMO. This ended the war and called on RENAMO to reform itself as a political party.

From its inception in the 1970s, RENAMO has eschewed ideological declarations, though during the 1994 parliamentary and presidential campaign, it began to enunciate a vague pro-democracy, pro–free market platform. Most outside observers have taken a dim view of the party. They say RENAMO is, at best, a power base for the Ndau-speaking people who dominate party ranks, and, at worst, a mere vehicle for the personal ambitions of the leadership.

Foreign

Unlike Angola, Mozambique was not a Cold War battleground. The Soviet bloc and China supported FRELIMO with limited shipments of arms, while Western interference was largely restricted to economics. After Mozambique's failure to make payments on its external debt in 1984, it was gradually forced to adopt an economic restructuring program based on World Bank and IMF models. In addition, the country's heavy dependence on aid left it vulnerable to the demands and prerogatives of the larger NGOs.

On the other hand, Mozambique was a major battleground in the fight over apartheid. Following the 1978 collapse of the liberal, detente-oriented John Vorster administration in Pretoria, a new hard-line government under P. W. Botha came to power. The new administration pursued a policy it called "total strategy." This involved the destabilization of neighboring African regimes, particularly those with a radical domestic program and a strong anti-apartheid foreign policy. While South Africa's official reason for supporting RENAMO was to get Mozambique to stop supporting the ANC, most observers say there was a more important, hidden agenda. South Africa wanted to force Mozambique into Pretoria's political and economic orbit and to demonstrate the validity of its own white rule. By rendering Mozambique politically ungovernable and economically unviable, it hoped to show the world that blacks were incapable of self-rule and that the West needed South Africa to protect Western interests in southern Africa.

FRELIMO's only allies were fellow frontline states Tanzania and Zimbabwe, both of which contributed significant military contingents to the war against RENAMO, out of solidarity with Mozambique and to protect themselves. Zimbabwe, in particular, was highly dependent on Mozambique's railways and ports, both of which were targets of RENAMO sabotage.

ISSUES

ANGOLA

Just as the participants in the thirty-year Angola war changed over time but maintained roughly the same battle lines (the West and its allies on the one side and the socialist–Third World alliance on the other), so the immediate issues changed but not the long-term ones. Obviously, the immediate issue of sovereignty and self-rule that marked the struggle between Angolan nationalists and Portuguese colonists disappeared with independence, just as defense of Namibia faded as an issue with South Africa's 1988 agreement to relinquish its illegal colony the following year.

Still, the underlying issues remained the same. The U.S. and NATO supported their ally Portugal out of fear of Soviet expansionism and the communist domino effect in southern Africa. Washington therefore promoted any organization, either the FNLA or UNITA, that it felt could keep Angola from falling into Soviet hands at independence. When that failed, Washington supported UNITA and South Africa as a way of keeping the MPLA off-balance and making the Soviet Union pay heavily for its support there. Similarly, Moscow did not want to concede its hard-earned place in southern Africa to the U.S.

As for the forces within Angola, critics disagree on the issues that divided them. Some say the conflict was due to personal ambition and ethnic hatred, with others arguing that the MPLA and UNITA represented diametrically opposed views of what Angola should be. The MPLA claimed it wanted to promote a radical restructuring of the social, economic and political landscape. With the notable exception of the oil sector, which it left in the hands of Western corporations, it largely followed a Soviet and Cuban model for this: state economic planning, state-run cooperative farms and industries, and a one-party government. The latter had an African twist to it, however, in that the MPLA, like other one-party regimes on the continent (ranging from self-described radical to conservative ones), claimed that multiple parties exacerbated ethnic animosities fomented during colonial times by European imperialists like the Portuguese.

For his part, Savimbi elaborated an ambiguous and often contradictory vision of a peasant-based, tradition-oriented, capitalist Angola. The conflict between these two visions of Angola often played out at the local level. The MPLA sent administrators to rural areas to carry out the policies of government planners in Luanda and to coerce peasants onto the state-run cooperatives (in war-torn areas, this was often done for defensive purposes as well as political and economic ones). UNITA, on the other hand, attacked the cooperative farms and scattered peasants across the countryside. It also backed the traditional chieftains, helping them drive MPLA administrators out. The MPLA, while it worked with some chieftains, claimed most had been appointed by the Portuguese and were thus anti-revolutionary.

Ethnic strife played a role in the conflict, but not nearly as important a one as Western journalists implied. True, UNITA was almost exclusively an Ovimbundu organization, while the MPLA was dominated, though to a much lesser degree, by Kimbundu-speaking people. Portuguese imperial policy, sometimes intentionally and sometimes not, had provoked conflicts between the two groups, which political leaders like Roberto and Savimbi took advantage of. But, as scholar William Minter points out, Angola's ethnic groups have not evinced the kind of hatred and violence toward one another that is so evident in other internal conflicts, such as the one in the former Yugoslavia.[6]

MOZAMBIQUE

Most students of Mozambique, even those hostile to FRELIMO, find it difficult to say what RENAMO stood for during the war and, indeed, what it stands for today, other than its own self-interest and, during the war, the interests of the white-minority regimes of Rhodesia and South Africa. RENAMO claimed it stood against FRELIMO's one-party rule and anti–free market policies, though it continued to fight after FRELIMO introduced market-oriented policies in the mid-1980s and multiparty clauses in the 1990 constitution.

FRELIMO, during its early years in power, was indeed a radical regime. It declared itself the Marxist-Leninist vanguard party of the revolution and outlawed all others after 1977. In addition, it embarked upon a villagization program that established cooperative farms and villages where peasants were expected to plant commercial crops for export. While it paid higher prices for the produce than the Portuguese had and lured peasants with enhanced health and education facilities, it offered little in the way of consumer goods in exchange. Many peasants saw the new policies as a continuation of the old, and thus productivity fell. Some observers claim these policies were the source of RENAMO's support. Others, though admitting there was a rise in anti-FRELIMO sentiment in the countryside, point to RENAMO's forced recruitment practices (see "Tactics," below) as the only reason peasants served the rebels. Ironically, since the elections of 1994, FRELIMO as the majority party has imposed more market-oriented policies and RENAMO, as the opposition, has steadily denounced them.

Ethnic antagonism has played an even smaller role in Mozambique than in Angola. While FRELIMO has long been dominated by southerners and RENAMO by the Ndau-speaking people of the central provinces, neither side has played up the ethnic component, though the war has led to some indirect ethnic-based violence. Living in regions of continuous RENAMO control, the Ndau have largely escaped the depredations of the rebels.

TACTICS

ANGOLA

Angola's decades-long war has encompassed virtually every form of modern warfare, from guerrilla raids to tank-led infantry assaults. During the war against the Portuguese, much of the fighting entailed small-scale hit-and-run attacks on isolated outposts and convoys, mostly by MPLA guerrillas. The Portuguese responded with counterinsurgency tactics adapted from their American allies' methods in Vietnam. These included helicopter-borne assaults and the establishment of garrisoned villages. Portugal was largely successful in keeping guerrilla warfare away from the centers of population.

During the war of independence, the fighting escalated into conventional-style military campaigns. In the north, FNLA, Zairian and MPLA troops were not familiar with direct infantry attacks and so the Cuban and MPLA use of mortar and artillery fire eventually drove the rebels and Zairians out of the country. Elsewhere, the MPLA faced an even larger UNITA/South African assault. But having defeated the FNLA and Zaire, the combined MPLA/Cuban army was able to reinforce the southern front. While South Africa was not militarily defeated, the Vorster administration was divided between hard-line military officers and the détente-oriented foreign ministry. As fatalities, costs and protests grew (both in South Africa and internationally), the diplomats won the day and South Africa withdrew.

For several years, UNITA retreated to the bush to regroup and rearm under South Africa's aegis. By the late 1970s, the guerrillas were launching attacks against isolated MPLA outposts and cooperative villages. In 1981, South Africa invaded again, ostensibly to drive out Namibian rebels, but more likely to help UNITA fend off MPLA attacks and establish a liberated zone for the rebel organization. Pretoria returned in 1983, 1985 and 1987–88. The last invasion, a campaign to drive the MPLA from southwestern Angola, backfired dramatically when the MPLA and the Cubans launched a huge pincer movement, backed by tanks and MiGs, that trapped thousands of South African troops inside Angola.

Between these various invasions, UNITA conducted a campaign of terror and destruction in southern and central Angola, backed by South Africa and, after the U.S. ban on aid to UNITA was lifted by Congress in 1986, by Washington as well. UNITA especially targeted cooperative villages, driving peasants out and forcing them to farm for UNITA or work in their camps as porters and the like. Land mines were sowed extensively to prevent troop movements and render MPLA areas unfit for farming, travel and transport. The rebels also went after the Benguela railway, which they rendered impassable by the early 1980s. After South Africa's withdrawal in 1988, UNITA used even more desperate measures, including denying food aid to areas of UNITA control in order to exact concessions from the MPLA and the international community. The MPLA countered with air attacks on UNITA camps and the continued forced villagization of the rural population.

During the so-called "second war" after the 1992 elections, the conflict took on yet another form. Until 1992, UNITA had been unable to hold on to any sizable towns. Having purposefully failed to demobilize during the months leading up to the elections, UNITA used its military edge to capture major cities in the south and central highlands, including Huambo. It took control of some 70 percent of Angolan territory, including parts of the oil-producing region in the northwest and the diamond mines of the northeast. The MPLA's counteroffensive involved lengthy sieges of provincial capitals occupied by UNITA. Many such cities were destroyed by MPLA and UNITA artillery, MPLA bombing, and street-fighting in 1993 and early 1994.

MOZAMBIQUE

The pre-independence struggle by and against the Portuguese resembled that in Angola, except that FRELIMO did not have to fight off assaults by rival groups as the MPLA did both before and during the independence period. After independence, however, the war in Mozambique took on a depressing and destructive pattern. RENAMO avoided direct confrontations with FRELIMO troops, preferring instead to ransack villages, sabotage the infrastructure and terrorize the civilian population with rape, abduction, slave labor, torture and murder. Both FRELIMO and RENAMO practiced forced recruitment, but RENAMO took it to new depths. According to both Mozambican and international human rights sources, RENAMO forcibly recruited child soldiers as young as twelve, often making them torture and murder relatives and neighbors.

For several years, FRELIMO failed to respond adequately to the threat. The leaders in Maputo were convinced that the peasantry was so strongly behind the revolution that rebellion was impossible. The only threat FRELIMO perceived was a direct invasion by South African forces. Since FRELIMO knew it could not possibly stop such an attack, it demobilized much of its army, removed the more aggressive officers from colonial times and put its faith in diplomatic efforts to prevent South African hostilities. Only in the early 1980s did FRELIMO elect to beef up its army and put its best guerrilla officers back in command.

The changes, say most observers, were a case of too little, too late. Not only was the government too financially strapped to mobilize an effective force, but the insurgency had taken on a life of its own. As RENAMO undermined government authority, it grew stronger and FRELIMO grew weaker. Only as the level of support from South Africa declined under the F. W. de Klerk administration, and the Mozambican peasantry rallied behind a quasireligious, anti-RENAMO military movement known as the Naparama (after the region of Mozambique where it began), was RENAMO forced into retreat and a negotiated settlement.

NEGOTIATIONS

ANGOLA

In a war as long and varied as Angola's, it should not seem surprising that there have been as many negotiations (usually unsuccessful) as there have been. Fully five sets of formal negotiations have taken place between 1975 and 1994.[7] The first led to the January 1975 Alvor (Portugal) accords, a Portuguese-brokered pre-independence agreement calling for a cease-fire among the warring Angolan factions and a power-sharing arrangement that would lead to elections after Angola's official independence day, November 11, 1975. The accords broke down after several months when the factions went back to war.

The second formal set of negotiations took place in 1984 in Lusaka. Mediated by Zambia and the United States, the Lusaka talks led to an agreement calling for Cuba and South Africa to withdraw their troops from a demilitarized zone in southern Angola. While the agreement was broken by the 1985 South African invasion, it paved the way for the more permanent 1988 New York accords. Based on the Reagan administration's so-called "linkage" policy, the New York agreement called for a full, though gradual, withdrawal of Cuban troops from Angola in exchange for an end to South Africa's illegal occupation of Namibia. All parties involved honored the accords to the letter. By 1990 and 1991 respectively, Namibia was independent and the last Cuban troops left Angola.

The Bicesse (Portugal) accords of 1991 were supposed to end the war between UNITA and the MPLA. Brokered by Portugal, Russia and the U.S., Bicesse included provisions for the full demobilization of UNITA and MPLA forces, the creation of a joint-army command, and multiparty elections. Several factors doomed the accords. First, the UN did not commit the personnel and money necessary for such a large operation. In addition, the mandate of UN forces was extremely limited, not allowing them to interfere even in the face of human rights violations and political coercion of voters by one side or the other. Second, the agreement fixed a rigid timetable. Despite the fact that demobilization fell behind schedule (largely due to UNITA violations), the UN insisted on declaring the establishment of a joint command 48 hours before the elections. Third, none of the parties to the agreement considered power-sharing arrangements for the post-election period. In a context as volatile as Angola in 1992, the UN's own experts concluded later, the winner-take-all format was probably misconceived.

The most recent set of negotiations, concluded in Lusaka in November 1994, were intended to end the post-election fighting between UNITA and the MPLA. While the UN insisted that the Lusaka accords were based on the Bicesse agreement, that applied only to their format. That is to say, they addressed the same issues, but by including a power-sharing agreement, they negated the stipulation of the earlier accord that said the winning party in the 1992 elections (the MPLA) would be the governing power in Angola and the losing party or parties would form the opposition. In another variation on Bicesse, the Lusaka accords did not try to determine the pace or details of a final agreement. Instead, they simply established a cease-fire and set up a framework for further talks on power sharing, demobilization, creation of a new army, and elections. The UN also committed itself to a longer-term and more expensive peacekeeping process.

MOZAMBIQUE

Three sets of negotiations leading to agreements have punctuated the long Mozambican war. The first, the 1979 Lancaster House (Britain) accords, ending the insurgency against Rhodesia and establishing a majority-rule Zimbabwean government, did not directly involve Mozambique, though FRELIMO offered its good offices to the British mediators. But the accords were important to Mozambique nonetheless. With the demise of the white government in Salisbury, FRELIMO hoped to undermine the Rhodesian-backed RENAMO insurgency. As noted above, the plan failed when South Africa took over the reins.

In October 1984, South Africa and Mozambique negotiated the Nkomati accords. These called for each country to withdraw aid from the other's rebel movements. Maputo would not allow the African National Congress (ANC) to operate on its soil and Pretoria would discontinue supplying RENAMO and stop allowing it to use South African facilities. While experts disagree on when South Africa decided to violate the letter of the Nkomati accords, there is little question that it never intended to honor them in spirit. In the months leading up to the agreement, South Africa transshipped at least six months' worth of armaments to RENAMO. Then, during an attack on RENAMO's headquarters at Casa Banana in September 1985, FRELIMO uncovered incontrovertible evidence that South Africa was continuing to supply the rebels with arms. P. W. Botha was forced to admit that FRELIMO's accusations were true, though he said orders to violate the accords had not come from his office.

Beginning in late 1989, FRELIMO and RENAMO began to nego-tiate an end to their war under the auspices of the United States, Italy and the Vatican's Sant'Edigio religious brotherhood. For almost three years, the two sides hammered out an agreement that involved issues similar to those taken up by UNITA and the MPLA at Bicesse: demobilization, creation of joint armed forces and multiparty elections. Also like the Bicesse process, the Rome negotiations were about confidence building, including recognition of each other's legitimacy and security assurances for the RENAMO leadership to come out of the bush and re-form as an unarmed political party.

The Rome accords, signed in October 1992, were shadowed by renewed fighting in Angola. All parties agreed that conditions on the ground, rather than timetables formalized in the accord, would dictate the pacing of demobilization, army reform and elections—the latter, in fact, being postponed for a full year when the pace of demobilization slackened. For its part, the UN committed to a major force in Mozambique. These modifications seem to have done the trick. Mozambique has thus far avoided the catastrophic postelection violence of Angola.

NOTES

[1] Oliver, Roland, *The African Experience: Major Themes in African History from Earliest Times to the Present* (New York: HarperCollins, 1991), p. 239.

[2] *The Economist*, September 14, 1996, p. 43.

[3] Large animal life has not been as fortunate. UNITA was singled out by several environmental organizations in the 1980s for widespread ivory poaching and big-game hunting.

[4] Angola and Mozambique lie below the equator and so their seasons are the opposite of those of the Northern Hemisphere's. For simplicity's sake, however, all references to seasons in this book will refer to the Northern Hemisphere calendar, unless otherwise noted.

[5] The so-called frontline states, that is, the front line with the apartheid regime, included Angola, Botswana, Lesotho, Swaziland, Mozambique, Tanzania, Zambia, Zimbabwe and, after its independence in 1989, Namibia.

[6] Minter, William, *Apartheid's Contras: An Inquiry into the Roots of War in Angola and Mozambique* (London: Zed Books, 1994), pp. 103–105.

[7] All of the following negotiations and treaties will be referred to by the location where they occurred or were ultimately signed.

2

THROUGH INDEPENDENCE
(TO 1976)

The blacks in Africa must be directed and moulded by
Europeans . . . The Africans by themselves did not know how to
develop the territories they have inhabited for millennia.
—Portuguese Colonial Minister Marcello Caetano

It is the miserable Portuguese government that has mortgaged and
sold the colonies and even their own country.
—Angolan president Agostinho Neto

BEFORE THE PORTUGUESE (TO 1482)

In the winter of 1884–85, Europe's leaders convened in Berlin to divide the continent of Africa among themselves. The politicians and generals who met in the German capital considered many things: African resources, existing European settlements, and above all the avoidance of imperial conflict. But there was one thing they felt needed no consideration—the Africans themselves.

The Europeans squared the circle. They laid a grid over existing populations that, over a long period of migration, trade, strife, diplomacy and environmental adaptation, had established their own patterns of sovereignty on a continent with a land mass nearly three times that of Europe. Thus, every European colony, and the nations later established within those colonial borders, contained populations of disparate ethnic and linguistic backgrounds. As former Tanzanian president Julius Nyerere once commented, Africa's national borders have to be held sacrosanct because they are so absurd.[1] Angola and Mozambique are no exception.

The rift valleys of East Africa are, of course, where humans first evolved, but for the purposes of this study, patterns of African settlement need not be examined that far back in time. The most significant development in African prehistory concerns the vast migration of iron-smelting Bantu-language peoples from their original homeland in present-day Nigeria outward across central and southern Africa 2,000 years ago. Their superior technology and the food surpluses produced by village agriculture allowed them to push the preexisting Pygmy and Khoisan (Bush) peoples entirely out of present-day Mozambique and into the far south of what is now Angola.

Like the vast movement of Indo-Aryan peoples in southwestern Asia and Europe several thousand years earlier, the Bantu migrations left a host of disparate ethnic and linguistic groupings across much of southern Africa. In Angola, these groupings included the Kikongo in the north, the Kimbundu along the central coast and the Ovimbundu on the central plateau; numerous subgroups sparsely populating the south and southeast. In Mozambique, Lomwe- and Macua-speaking peoples inhabited the north, Shona speakers settled along the Zambezi River in the center of the country, and the Tsonga populated the south.

This neat diagram of precolonial Angolan and Mozambican peoples, however, is subject to debate. As European boundary-makers imposed their own order on political Africa, so European ethnologists imposed a conceptual map. Politics, culture and personal loyalties, says historian William Minter, "rarely fitted neatly into the sharp lines drawn between 'tribes' " by European Africanists. "None of these [ethnic] groups," he adds, "corresponded with precolonial political units, nor did the labels necessarily match what the people called themselves."[2] The use of related Bantu languages didn't fit neat labels either, as dialects shifted slightly from village cluster to village cluster across a given linguistic territory until they became mutually incomprehensible at the extremes.

On the eve of Portugal's encounter with southern Africa in the late fifteenth century, Angola boasted several substantial kingdoms, including the Kikongo and the Kimbundu.[3] In Mozambique, the Mutapa, descendants of the great Zimbabwe empire of the eleventh to fourteenth centuries, mined gold and raised cattle in the highlands of the interior, though the heartland of the kingdom was situated in modern-day Zimbabwe. In addition, several flourishing Islamic city-states represented the southwestern outposts of a vast trading empire that encircled the Indian Ocean from Indonesia to Mozambique.

THE PORTUGUESE ERA

SETTLEMENT AND SLAVERY (1483–1885)

In their slow and painstaking quest for an oceanic route to Asia, the Portuguese first reached Angola in 1483. Over the next twenty years, Portuguese goods, culture and religion gradually penetrated the realm of the Kongo during the reign of King Nzinga, who grudgingly converted to Catholicism in 1491 but was never considered a safe ally by the Portuguese. In 1506, the king was eased out of power by his son, Nzinga Mbemba, with encouragement from the Portuguese, who offered a devil's bargain. Their insatiable appetite for slaves undermined the king's authority and bred dissension. Mbemba was unable to stop the trade, and his ambitions and kingdom—at least as a formal political entity—died with him.

Mozambique faced a different fate, at least for a time. Disputes with Spain over the newly "discovered" lands of America and Africa delayed the Portuguese arrival in Mozambique until 1498. In a strategy pursued throughout the Indian Ocean littoral, Portugal used its superior naval capabilities and seaborne cannon to oust Islamic traders both from their island-based trading cities of Sofala, Pemba and Moçambique and from the trade routes to the gold fields and ivory sources of the Mozambican interior.

Nevertheless, Portuguese penetration of the African mainland was minimal until the twentieth century, limited largely to the environs of Luanda in Angola and, in Mozambique, to a thinly spread presence in the fertile Zambezi valley. As late as the turn of the century, there were still less than 10,000 Europeans in Angola, and there were just 27,000 in Mozambique as late as World War II. "Until recent decades," historian Gerald Bender notes of Angola, "most Africans have had little or no association with whites."[4]

While the physical presence of the Portuguese was minimal and highly localized, their cultural impact on Angola and Mozambique was more profound and far-reaching. Like their Spanish counterparts in the New World, the Portuguese conquistadores of Angola and Mozambique inter-married with local women—primarily Kimbundu in Angola but of diverse ethnicities in Mozambique—producing a small but very influential Creole population of Afro-Portuguese or, as they were known in Mozambique, *muzungu*.[5] According to historian David Birmingham, the Afro-Portuguese of Angola "became the commanders of local armies, the interpreters in the finance houses, the leaders of the caravans of textile porters into the interior, the planters on incipient agricultural estates, the teachers and catechists in the up-country [trade] fairs, the ox-riders who were crossing the continent on the paths later used by European missionaries and explorers."[6]

In Mozambique, says historian Malyn Newitt, "the Afro-Portuguese families . . . were to dominate Mozambican affairs locally until the twentieth century."[7]

The Afro-Portuguese were the main agents of mercantile penetration into the interiors of Angola and Mozambique, owners of the largest plantations (known in Mozambique as *prazos*) and a bulwark of Portuguese colonialism. According to Newitt, their presence was the principal reason the Portuguese maintained even a tentative hold on their colonies in southern Africa.[8] Still, not too much should be made of the Portuguese component of Creole culture, even though many spoke Portuguese. The Creoles were in appearance and custom a predominantly African people.

They were usually indistinguishable in appearance from the non-Creole African population, and they saw themselves in largely African terms. For example, while the Portuguese stipulated that the *prazos* were land grants from the crown, much like the Spanish *encomiendas* of Mexico, the Afro-Portuguese considered them akin to chieftaincies. "It is one of the much misunderstood curiosities of Portuguese colonial rule that apparently little in the way of European 'civilisation' or technology was introduced into Africa over a continuous period of four to five centuries," writes Newitt.

> The reason is that the *muzungus* adopted an African way of life, farming, mining, traveling, ruling and fighting according to African custom, because they ultimately had to fit into patterns of inheritance, land use and reciprocal obligation that would satisfy their African kin and their African retainers and clients.[9]

The Afro-Portuguese were true colonial middlemen. They both resisted the more intensive European colonization of the late nineteenth century and were "the agents through which conquest and domination were eventually achieved," says Newitt. They were "one of the pathways whereby Portuguese language and culture were transmitted to the population," and they provided singular leadership in the nationalist movement that eventually broke the hold of the Portuguese in the mid-twentieth century.[10] In short, they prevented both a stronger colonial presence in Angola and Mozambique until the end of the nineteenth century as well as obviated the establishment of powerful indigenous political entities.

More devastating still for African political unity was the transatlantic slave trade, which was an integral part of the Angolan economy from the 1500s. According to Africanist Roland Oliver, fully a third of the roughly 12 million Africans shipped to the New World between the fifteenth and nineteenth centuries came from south of the equator, with a large proportion from the territory that makes up modern-day Angola.[11]

Four centuries of slave trading devastated Angola. Beyond depopulating the country of its most productive members, it sparked a series of wars between the coastal Kimbundu and interior Kikongo, as well as conflicts between ethnic groups in what is now Zaire. No people was immune as the vagaries of war and access to European arms led to the enslavement of one group after another. The importance of the slave trade, which went into decline with the international treaties against it in the 1830s and 1840s and was eventually outlawed domestically in Angola in 1878, can be assessed by the collapse of the colony in the post-slaving era. "The end of the slave trade," notes Bender, "fulfilled the most dire predictions of the governors who had warned of economic doom."[12]

In Mozambique, the external slave trade had more ancient origins than in Angola, though the mass deportation of slaves from the mainland that marked the trade in Angola took longer to get started. The Islamic trading cities had shipped Mozambicans north since the tenth century, and the Portuguese took up the trade when they moved in after 1500. Nevertheless, Mozambique was geographically remote from the transatlantic slave market, and the Indian Ocean was relatively immune from the heightened demands of the commercial revolution until the French established sugar plantations on several islands off Madagascar in the mid-1700s. The new demand for slaves led to massive seaborne raids by Swahili-speaking marauders in the north of Mozambique and the invasion of the militarily formidable Nguni from the south, both of whom became major primary suppliers of Mozambican slaves.

While never coming close to the levels in Angola, the trade was still substantial, with roughly 10,000 people shipped annually in the late 1700s and early 1800s. International treaties and British pressure aside, the slave trade in Mozambique only went into serious decline with the fall in international sugar prices from the 1840s on, though it continued illicitly until the late nineteenth century. As Newitt notes, the industrial revolution came late to the Indian Ocean, producing first a demand for slaves, followed by a "growing interest in African markets and raw materials, and finally by the arrival of surplus capital in search of investment opportunities.

> Long before this occurred, however, the old structures of African and Indian Ocean production and commerce, which had easily accommodated themselves to the lazy mercantilism of the Portuguese, had broken down and been replaced by a more direct exposure to the forces of European capitalist enterprise.[13]

BOUNDARIES AND ADMINISTRATION (1885–1945)

If, by some magic, Portuguese and other European colonists had vacated southern Africa in 1875, their physical legacy would have been minimal. The European presence in the subcontinent, with the exception of the large Dutch settlement around the Cape of Good Hope, was confined to a few small coastal enclaves centered around English, French and Portuguese trading garrisons. Widely separated by lengthy stretches of coastline, with no land-based communication between them, the Europeans were prevented from penetrating the African interior by a hostile climate and formidable African foes. In fact, with the decline of the slave trade, the Portuguese presence actually shrank, with their inland garrisons and presence at the trade fairs of the interior largely a thing of the past by the mid-nineteenth century.

Several long-term and immediate events in Europe and Africa led to the "scramble" for Africa, that is, the partition of virtually all of sub-Saharan Africa into European colonies in the mid-1880s: advances in weaponry, new exploration that revealed temperate highland zones suitable for European colonization in the interior, and the discovery of vast gold and diamond deposits in the Transvaal of South Africa. In West Africa, expanding French and English settlements were creating imperial friction, and in Europe a newly consolidated Germany was demanding an empire of its own. Together, these developments made a continent-wide settlement increasingly imperative. But the catalytic event behind the partition concerned the Congo (now Zaire).[14] King Leopold II of Belgium had been on the lookout for a suitable colony since the 1860s and had sent British adventurer Henry Stanley to explore the Congo River Basin.[15] The presence of this new imperial force in the very heart of Africa was the immediate impetus for the Berlin Conference.

Of all the European players at the table in Berlin (there was not a single African in attendance), the Portuguese held the weakest hand. Not only was Portugal not a power in Europe, but its efforts to consolidate its hold on the interior of Angola and Mozambique had backfired. The nineteenth-century attempts to settle *degregados*, or exiled prisoners, in agricultural settlements drained the Portuguese treasury and intensified racial tensions among Creoles, whites and blacks. Thus, Portugal retained its colonies for essentially negative reasons. First, other European imperialists were largely uninterested in Angola or Mozambique (or other Portuguese colonies in Guinea-Bissau, São Tomé and Príncipe, and the Cape Verde Islands). More importantly, the Portuguese presence was viewed as a useful means to separate the colonies of the more aggressive imperial powers.

From the late nineteenth century through World War II, the Portuguese accelerated their efforts to extend administrative and economic control. These included new attempts at pacification, colonization, land appropriation and, most importantly, more effective means for exploiting African labor. While emphases on one facet of policy or another changed over the years, the general thrust of colonial consolidation weathered the abrupt political changes in the metropolis, as Portugal transformed itself from an ineffective monarchy to a chaotic republic in 1910, and then a military-backed fascist dictatorship under António de Salazar in 1926.

The tentative nature of Portugal's hold on Angola and Mozambique concerned administrators in Lisbon even before the ink had dried on the documents signed in Berlin. They feared that the continued power and sway of African and Afro-Portuguese chieftains in their territories might lead other European colonizers in southern Africa to insist on a repartition of the subcontinent. To obviate that possibility, the Portuguese conducted a thorough reassessment of their colonial policies in the 1880s and 1890s. In Mozambique, they tried to rein in the political power of the *prazos* even as they gave them more economic leeway. New laws were passed turning the *prazos* into individual freehold properties in an attempt to spur colonial settlement. But few Portuguese took up the offer, and much of the land that was distributed went to absentee joint-stock companies, usually controlled by British and French capital.

Moreover, the efforts to develop commercial plantations proved disastrous. The Moçambique Company, a concession owned by Portuguese and French investors, tried to wrest control over the agriculturally rich Zambézia from local chieftains. Unable to field forces up to the task, the concessionaires formed alliances with rival chieftaincies, producing a decade of anarchy and violence throughout much of central Mozambique. Angola was plagued by similar projects. Until the late nineteenth century, land appropriation by the Portuguese had been minimal, though laws on the subject were so vaguely worded that if any party had shown an interest, the land could have been had. In 1907, Portugal tried to formalize the process by setting aside tracts of land specifically for individual Africans and African communities, a policy that, by implication, left large sections of the country open to colonizers.

Renewed attempts to found agricultural colonies, this time settled by impoverished farmers from the metropolis, proved almost as big a failure as the earlier attempts with *degregados*. Huge subsidies for the farmers, including housing, furnishings, livestock, seeds, lands and even pensions, turned out to be so much money poured down the drain. Ambitious Portuguese émigrés made for Brazil or the United States, leaving the most uneducated and inefficient farmers for Angola. Nor did the colony possess the infrastructure necessary for commercial agriculture—not, at least, until the completion of the trans-Angolan Benguela railway in 1929. Lastly, the very subsidies granted to the settlers worked at cross-purposes to the aims of the program. Often provided in cash, they were worth more than most peasants had earned in Portugal. "Such dependence on the state," notes Bender, "made the *colono* more of a civil servant than an independent farmer."[16] The vast majority, of a very small cohort, gave up farming and flocked to Angolan cities.

There were some noble if paternalistic motives behind these efforts to introduce commercial agricultural colonies in Angola. The Portuguese viewed their "civilizing mission" in Africa differently than did the British, French or Germans. Conceptualized later as Luso-tropicalism, it envisioned Portugal as a multi-continental, multiracial nation where white settlers worked, lived and married with local peoples. The thinking behind the agricultural colonies, for instance, centered on the idea of colonial farmers imparting their expertise to Angolans, sharing the bounty of the land and extending Luso-tropical nationalism throughout the colony. Aside from the misplaced notion that impoverished and uneducated farmers from Portugal had anything to teach Angolans about farming in the tropics, the number of settlers was never sufficient to do the job.

Nor were the Portuguese settlers free from the racist attitudes that permeated other European societies in Africa. The equation behind Luso-tropicalism—Portuguese-speaking Brazil was a successful multiracial society (suspect as that notion now seems), therefore the Portuguese mentality was somehow free of racism—was unbalanced to begin with. Even Portuguese officials, says historian Gerald Bender, cited "the *colono* attitude that 'only blacks should work in Africa' as one of the principal causes for the failures in white settlement through 1934."[17]

As colonial settlers drifted into Angolan cities in the late 1800s, an additional and potentially more explosive racial problem emerged. By the beginning of the new century, a subtle, multifaceted transformation in the makeup of Angola's urban population and class system had emerged. First, there was the growing presence, though still minute, of a semi- and fully assimilated mestizo class, made up partly of the old Afro-Portuguese families but containing a new element of missionary-educated Africans.[18] Unlike the semitraditional Afro-Portuguese of the interior, the urban mestizos "seldom, if ever, identified with the Africans because for all practical purposes they were Portuguese in nearly every way except colour."[19] Second, both the increased number of settlers and, equally important, the declining ratio of men to women began to make a separate urban society and class of white Angolans and Mozambicans possible.

Almost as soon as the white population began to outnumber that of the mestizos around the turn of the century, the former began to pass laws oppressive to the latter. In 1901 and 1911, Angolan whites upgraded the requirements for entry into the upper and lower echelons of the colonial bureaucracy, making it more difficult for mestizos to fill these posts. Just before World War I, the authorities in Mozambique passed the Organic Charter, which stipulated a complex system of citizenship that largely denied that status to all but the most assimilated of Africans and Afro-Portuguese, whom they called *não-indígena*, or new natives.[20]

In effect, the Portuguese developed a catch-22 to prevent African entry into the middle class. Educational requirements for bureaucratic jobs, virtually the only non-manual labor available in the underdeveloped colonies, were raised, but no provisions were made for educating Africans. These exclusionary practices were made worse by the influx of poor white settlers—some with far less education than local mestizos—who began to fill virtually every vacancy in the colonial bureaucracy. Thus the mestizos, who had dominated urban life in Mozambique and Angola throughout the nineteenth century, were pushed several rungs down the social and economic ladder. Not surprisingly, the very earliest nationalist associations in Mozambique, largely composed of *assimilados* (assimilated Africans) and emphasizing a program of equality within a Portuguese empire, date from the early twentieth century.[21]

Still, while *assimilado* frustrations would prove critical in the subsequent development of Angolan and Mozambican nationalism, their numbers remained small. For the vast majority of Africans, over 98 percent of the population in the two colonies until after World War II, the struggle involved land and labor, an old story but one that took on increasing relevance with the expansion of colonial administrative control in the early twentieth century. "Prior to the second half of the nineteenth century," says Bender,

> most of the battles between Portuguese and Africans revolved around the slave trade, but following the Berlin Conference in 1885 Portuguese attacks were principally motivated by desires for territorial conquest and the subjugation of the African peoples.[22]

Due to its weak economy, Portugal had always been an anomaly among empires, a peculiarity that seemed more glaring as other European countries began to develop their African colonies. France, Britain and Germany saw their possessions as both a market for manufactured goods and an outlet for metropolitan capital investment. But Portugal had little of either. Thus, unlike other European empires, Portugal envisioned Angola and Mozambique not as outlets for surplus investment capital but as sources of it. And if colonists could not be enticed to develop the colonies, then the state would endeavor to exploit African labor more directly. In the process, it initiated large migratory shifts in the African population and created the foundation for a distorted colonial economy and infrastructure that would persist into the postcolonial era.

Slavery was formally ended in the Portuguese colonies in 1878, but forced labor persisted under other legal guises until 1961. In fact, even before slavery was officially outlawed, Portuguese administrators began erecting a legal edifice for already freed slaves and other Africans. A loosely worded 1875 vagrancy statute permitted local administrators to round up all "nonproductive" Africans as vagrants and thus subject to nonpaying labor "contracts." As Bender notes, "Determination of 'productivity' was usually left to local administrators, who had no difficulty finding enough 'vagrants' to meet the settlers' demands for free labor."[23] According to a British diplomat posted in Angola, "nobody regarded the contract labourers as anything other than slaves."[24]

By 1900, the Portuguese administration was insisting that taxes be paid in cash rather than in kind. This produced a steady source of income for the concessionary companies, the government and the *prazo* owners. As Newitt notes, "The Nyassa Company, which originally had grandiose plans for the capitalist development of its territory, soon saw hut tax receipts as its major source of income."[25] Originally designed to promote commercial agriculture by the peasantry, the tax soon produced a supply of "contract" labor for the concessionary companies, *prazos*, the government and South African mines, since delinquent taxpayers were forced to pay off their taxes and fines through forced labor.

The use of Mozambican labor in South African mines deserves special attention. Direct economic ties between the British and Dutch in South Africa and the Portuguese in Mozambique go way back, but the discovery of gold and diamonds in the Transvaal in the 1860s greatly accelerated the pace of economic integration, with Mozambique assigned the subordinate role as an outlet to the sea and a source of cheap labor. This use of contract and voluntary Mozambican labor in South Africa proved especially lucrative for Portugal. With South African connivance, Lisbon assessed approximately half of the miners' earnings in gold and deposited them directly into the Portuguese treasury, thus providing much needed capital for economic development in the metropolis.

While criticism of colonial labor law emerged in Portugal during the republican period from 1910 to 1926, it hardly affected practice. Only with the rise of Salazar and his New State doctrine were the laws changed. New "native" laws in 1926 and 1928 abolished the vagrancy clause and outlawed forced labor, but with loopholes so large they rendered the new laws a virtual dead letter. Salazar, a former university economist, was determined to modernize the Portuguese economy through a state-directed program of private development. Like the leaders of other fascist governments, Salazar was convinced that the then-current world economic order favored free trade advocates like Britain. Thus, along with eliminating Portugal's indebtedness to foreign capital, a goal helped mightily by Mozambican earnings in South Africa, he was determined to create a closed Portuguese imperial system. To that end, he extended Portuguese control over all concessionary companies in the colonies by 1942 and reversed Lisbon's prohibitions on industrial development in the colonies.

Moreover, Salazar extended metropolitan control over virtually every aspect of Angolan and Mozambican administration. New labor and investment codes micro-managed economic development, official state-run unions and employer associations were established, and administration spread to all parts of the colonies, putting to an end "the anachronism whereby many areas . . . were only visited spasmodically by bands of armed *cipais* [native police or soldiers] seeking tax and labour."[26] The changing economic and political order that began in the 1930s, and accelerated greatly in the three decades after World War II, would have a profound effect on the liberation struggles that began in the early 1960s.

Two Angolan commodities, coffee and cotton, did much to alter the ethnic makeup, class structure and political ideology of the colony. In the north, Portuguese and foreign investments in coffee plantations effectively displaced large numbers of Kikongo farmers, tens of thousands of whom fled to Zaire, where the urban and rural economies were more vibrant. Many of these farmers were commercially adept, having grown coffee for the international market on their small holdings, and they formed a successful class of small entrepreneurs there. This experience would eventually lead many of the Zairian Kikongo to reject the socialist program of the Popular Movement for the Liberation of Angola (MPLA), opting instead for the business-oriented politics of the Kikongo-led National Front for the Liberation of Angola (FNLA). Over several generations, the Kikongo adopted the French language of Leopoldville (now Kinshasa), making it more difficult for Angolan nationalism to take root.

In the agriculturally rich central highlands, the Ovimbundu underwent a somewhat different experience when many were pushed off their land to make way for British and Portuguese cotton planters. Some, of course, stayed to work, but others looked for lands along the newly completed trans-Angolan Benguela railway, which bisected their territory, or went north to work on the coffee plantations. This dispersal and fragmentation had a profound effect on Ovimbundu ethnic consciousness, say historians Christine Knudsen and I. William Zartman, and "largely explained their late entry into the nationalist movement."[27]

Moreover, the ethnic mixing produced lasting antagonisms. Doing the lowest-paid plantation work, and on plantations that had displaced Kikongo peasants, they were denigrated and ostracized by the northerners, both Kikongo and Kimbundu, who saw them as less sophisticated and more subservient. Thus, when the Ovimbundu did join the nationalist cause, they preferred their own ethnic organizations, Jonas Savimbi's Union for the Total Independence of Angola (UNITA).

Twentieth-century economic development had a very different impact on Mozambique, a fact that helps to explain the very different liberation struggle in that colony. While labor migration in Angola tended to fragment ethnic groupings, in Mozambique it served to unify them. For many Mozambicans, labor migration meant work in the South African mines. The industrial experience contributed to a common ideological development, and, being at the bottom of the economic ladder and looked upon suspiciously by their black South African coworkers, the Mozambican miners developed a stronger Mozambican nationalism than their counterparts on Angolan plantations. Thus, Mozambique had a largely unified liberation movement that cut across most, though not all, ethnic and regional boundaries.

COLONISTS AND COMPETITION (1945–1961)

The Portuguese experience in Africa had always run counter to that of other European imperialists, and never was that fact more apparent than in the post–World War II period. As France and England gradually accepted and then prepared for the postcolonial era in the 1950s and 1960s, Portugal dug in its heels. True, France refused to accept the loss of Algeria until beaten in a vicious eight-year-long struggle, and even England considered clinging to its settler colony in Kenya. But both were largely trying to maintain the status quo. Portugal went further, resurrecting the rhetoric of the white man's burden and vastly accelerating its plans to settle colonists in Angola and Mozambique.

World War II had been good to Portugal and to Portugal's colonies. As a neutral country in a world at war, Portugal offered products, particularly hard-to-get tropical commodities, that were in great demand. Much of this productivity came from forced labor, as wartime demand and the lure of profits convinced colonial administrators to interpret labor laws loosely. Revenue tripled in Mozambique, while sugar and tea production set record levels. The postwar era saw the trend continue. "After the Second World War," says Newitt, "the relationship between Portugal and its colonies became closer than at any time in . . . history."[28] Roughly half of all of Mozambique's exports and half of its imports went to and from Portugal. Lisbon even relaxed its policies on colonial industrialization, and by 1974 Mozambique had the eighth largest industrial output in Africa. Angola experienced a similar boom.

Still, until the discovery and exploitation of oil in Cabinda in the 1960s, agriculture remained the mainstay of the two colonies' economies. The continuing postwar boom encouraged the colonial government to expand its unpopular program of forcing independent peasant farmers to grow commercial crops. As a Mozambican peasant explained,

> We didn't want to grow cotton, but we had to grow it; we wanted to grow cassava, beans and maize. If we refused to grow cotton, they arrested us, put us in chains, beat us and then sent us away to a place from where one often didn't come back.[29]

The expansion of commercial agriculture also entailed the accelerated establishment of large plantations, which were often financed by foreign capital under Portuguese management.

Despite the Salazar (and successor Marcello Caetano) regime's ongoing policy of settling white farmers on the land and establishing a network of black and white small commercial crop producers, the vast majority of Portuguese émigrés in the postwar period headed for the colonial cities. This flow of colonists was not the trickle of the prewar years, but a torrent of poor and middle-class Portuguese that continued right up to the 1974 coup, which brought down the Salazar/Caetano dictatorship and ushered in the independence of Portugal's African empire. Between 1950 and 1974, the number of white settlers in Mozambique quadrupled from around 50,000 to almost 200,000. In Angola, the corresponding numbers were 78,000 and 335,000.

The encouragement of colonial settlement in an era of decolonization was part of a larger Portuguese anachronism. The country was perhaps the last in Europe to undergo the wrenching changes of industrialization, experiencing the collapse of peasant agriculture and the migration to urban areas a full century after these had occurred in much of the rest of the continent. Unable to find sufficient employment in Portugal, many newly displaced peasants migrated to other European countries to find work on a seasonal and year-by-year basis. Their experiences in a democratic and prosperous Europe produced unrest and dissatisfaction with the Salazar/Caetano regime. But the government failed to adjust and move Portugal toward a closer relationship with the European community. Instead, it continued to subscribe to the Luso-tropical idea of Portugal as a transcontinental nation with a mission of bringing its Christian civilization to the Africans while, at the same time, delivering prosperity to the metropolis.

Unlike earlier colonists, the postwar cohort of settlers included a good number of skilled professionals, middle-class bureaucrats and business people. Still, the majority were the poorest of Portugal's poor, their emigration, as Salazar put it, "a logical solution to Portugal's problems of overpopulation."[30] Unlike other European colonies, where Africans performed much of the low-wage service work and filled the lower echelons of the colonial bureaucracy, in Angola and Mozambique, poor Portuguese colonists monopolized virtually all levels of employment in urban areas. Many in Angola lived at an economic level not much above that of urban Africans, making their homes in the same *musseques*, or shantytowns, of Luanda.

While Portuguese settlers had a long history of displacing *assimilados* and mestizos, the sheer volume of new immigrants angered urban Africans, who found themselves pushed down the economic ladder. The racism of the Portuguese didn't help either. For all Portugal's claims that its racial attitudes were far more enlightened than French and English ones, the reality was very different. Officially, the entire colonization program was founded on racist assumptions. "The natives of Africa," pronounced Caetano, "must be directed and organized by Europeans, but are indispensable as auxiliaries. The blacks must be seen as productive elements in an economy directed by whites."[31] Nor were the recently arrived settlers immune. "[It is claimed] that because of their own poverty and rural background," argued Mozambican nationalist Eduardo Mondlane in 1969,

> Portuguese immigrants were able to mix easily with people of the colonies and did not have an innate sense of superiority. This is not, however, substantiated by the experience of Africans in Mozambique. Portuguese settlers have often surpassed the government in their racialist approach.[32]

RESISTANCE AND REBELLION (1961–1974)

Always an imperial anomaly, Portugal was both the first European nation to colonize Africa and virtually the last to leave. Why, students of modern Portugal wonder, did Lisbon hang on to its African possessions a full decade after other Europeans had left? One answer can be found in the ideology and politics of the Salazar/Caetano regime, which imagined Portugal's destiny as a bridge between Europe and Africa and sought solutions to the contradictions that riddled Portuguese society and the Portuguese economy in colonial exploitation and white overseas settlement.

Another explanation lay in the continued imbalance of exports from and imports to the colonies, as well as forced remittances by Mozambican miners in South Africa, which continued to feed the Portuguese treasury even as the wars of liberation drained them. And, of course, Portugal experienced a fate similar to that of France in Algeria. A potent, unified and recalcitrant colonial constituency—Angolan and Mozambican whites and *assimilados* were given Portuguese citizenship in 1961 when the African territories were declared overseas provinces rather than colonies—had a disproportionate impact on Portuguese politics. Not only did they oppose decolonization, but they stubbornly resisted virtually any reforms in the colonial order that placed them, despite many of their dire economic circumstances, above the Africans. "The Portuguese never felt sufficiently secure (or threatened)," notes Bender, "to train and employ even a token number of Africans in responsible positions."[33]

Marxist analysis offers a slightly different take on the Portuguese predicament. Unlike England and France, which had the economic wherewithal to establish lucrative neocolonial relationships with their former colonies, the Portuguese feared that decolonization would yank Angola, Mozambique and the other colonial possessions out of the Portuguese sphere as better capitalized and more aggressive foreign firms moved in.

At the beginning of the 1960s, when the liberation movements began their armed resistance against Portugal, Angola and Mozambique were societies highly stratified by race and class. At the top were the white elite, largely administrators, businesspeople and planters. Beneath them was a middle class of professionals, merchants and civil servants, usually white, occasionally *assimilado*, and, in Mozambique, Indian as well. These groups were largely urban. In the countryside, where the vast majority of Africans lived, the populace was divided between small commercial farmers, subsistence farmers and agricultural laborers on the large estates.

The colonies also displayed a regional diversity. In Angola, the north and the central highlands were dominated by large plantations and smaller peasant holdings producing crops for export. Much of the rest of the country was devoted to subsistence farming. Mozambique was divided into three zones. The south and central provinces were dominated by plantation agriculture and commercial farming, some of it devoted to food crops for urban areas. The north, meanwhile, was dominated by subsistence farming.

Colonial cities were divided into two general districts: the so-called "cities of cement," that is, the downtown area and wealthier suburbs; and the "cities of sand," where the vast majority of Africans, mestizos and poor whites lived. In Angola, the urban economy was dominated by government, services and light industry. In Mozambique, these activities were supplemented by the ports, which served as outlets to South Africa and Northern and Southern Rhodesia (now Zambia and Zimbabwe), and by the tourist industry catering to South African, Portuguese and Rhodesian whites. Culturally and linguistically, the cities were a hodgepodge as well. A highly Europeanized settler and *assimilado* population was surrounded by majorities of native-speaking, semi-assimilated Africans. In the countryside, however, there was little Portuguese cultural impact.

The Portuguese talked much of their assimilationist policy in Angola and Mozambique, but did little. Based on the Brazilian experience, it would have involved the destruction of traditional societies, the inculcation of Portuguese culture and ultimately the integration of "detribalized," acculturated Africans into colonial society.[34]

The lack of effort to educate Africans and promote assimilation was neither accidental nor solely the result of Portuguese poverty. "Local administrators, bush traders, soldiers and *colono* farmers and ranchers had little interest in the assimilation of Africans," noted Bender of Angola.

> Instead they were principally concerned with collecting taxes, recruiting cheap labour, imposing the cultivation of cash crops, cheating peasant farmers and herders in commercial transitions, expropriating communal lands, and containing any protest which these and other similar activities engendered . . . Each viewed African progress as a threat to their livelihood and duties—in other words, to *their* own future progress. Any attempt to inculcate Portuguese culture and values or to treat rural Africans as equals was perceived by whites as jeopardizing the well-entrenched patterns of exploitation which had enriched so many of them.[35]

General Galvão do Melo, one of the seven army officers who overthrew Caetano in 1974, put it more succinctly:

> We benefited little from Africa and Africa benefited little from us. The Portuguese people and the African people remained unknown to each other: foreigners.[36]

Angola

Just as Belgian king Leopold II's efforts to colonize the Congo precipitated events leading to the consolidation of Portugal's hold on its African colonies, so Belgium's sudden evacuation in 1960 provided a catalyst for the armed revolt against Portuguese rule in Angola. In British prime minister Harold Macmillan's words, "winds of change" started sweeping across Africa when the French granted Tunisia and Morocco independence in 1956. The momentum shifted to sub-Saharan Africa with Ghana's independence from Britain in 1957. Bowing to black opposition, Brussels agreed to a four-year decolonization plan in Zaire in 1959, then unilaterally scrapped the idea and relinquished control on June 30, 1960. Belgium hoped sudden independence would force the Zairians to accept their tutelage, but civil war broke out instead. "Consummated in blood, assassination, fire, and intrigue," writes historian Daniel Spikes, "from the independence of the Congo was to be born the battle for Angola."[37]

The Portuguese reacted to these events anxiously. As pre-independence strife escalated, they tried to isolate Angola, which shared a 1,200-mile border with Zaire, by cutting off communications and transport links between the two colonies. But the action came too late. After rioting in Leopoldville in 1959, Belgian police evicted illegal residents, including thousands of Kikongo, who drifted back to their former homes in northern Angola. Then on June 8, 1960, Portuguese authorities arrested MPLA leader Agostinho Neto. When demonstrations followed, the Portuguese opened fire, killing 30 and injuring 200. As Spikes notes, "For the first time since the end of the wars of pacification [at the beginning of the twentieth century] the Portuguese military had been called into action against Angolans. It would not be the last."[38]

Discontent, of course, had been forming among Angola's blacks and mestizos for some time. "But misery in itself," notes Africanist Basil Davidson, "is no guarantee of effective protest, [which]

> depends upon the growth of a moral and political consciousness that change is not only necessary but also possible; and this in turns calls for effective leadership. For a long time there was none. What marked these slums was not the seething agitation of political discontent, but despair and self-abandonment to the harshness of a fate that seemed beyond repair. Drink and demoralization were the badges of their sorrow.[39]

In a pattern familiar to students of Third World decolonization, the first indigenous organizations to press for colonial reform were cultural ones, founded largely by *assimilados* influenced by cultural re-Africanization surfacing among Angolan students and exiles in Lisbon in the early 1950s. Their initial agenda, to confront Portuguese racism, soon evolved into a program of colonial liberation. Neto, arrested for his participation in the Communist Party, was in a Lisbon prison when a group of nine Portuguese, mestizos and *assimilados* founded the MPLA in Luanda in 1956. Three years after his 1959 return to Angola, Neto took over as head of the liberation organization. But as Davidson notes of these acculturated, intellectual founders of the MPLA, "they were a million miles from the backland villages. They had even forgotten their native tongues."[40]

Meanwhile, a separate liberation movement, with a very different leadership and agenda, was forming among the Angolan Kikongo in Zaire. Originally known as the Union of the Peoples of Northern Angola (UPNA) when it was founded in 1957, the group quickly dropped the regional affiliation to make its appeal more nationalistic. But as Spikes points out, the name change did not alter the group's reputation. "Just as charges of communism were to dog the MPLA," he writes, "accusations of tribalism were to hound [UPA founder Holden] Roberto. Neither would ever succeed in putting these founding suspicions to rest."[41] Where the MPLA was cosmopolitan, socialist and integrated, the UPA (which would change its name once again to the National Front for the Liberation of Angola, or FNLA, in 1961) was provincial, entrepreneurial, anticommunist and ethnically homogenous. When the liberation war broke out in 1961, the two organizations would find themselves fighting each other almost as much as they did the Portuguese.

The first armed conflicts in Angola, however, were led by neither organization but, rather, were spontaneous popular uprisings. First, there was the demonstration following Neto's arrest in June 1960, but that was largely an incident of unarmed protesters being gunned down by the police. The first real armed uprising ("armed" meaning *catanas*, or machetes, were used) occurred among Kimbundu cotton farmers in Malange province, about 400 miles southeast of Luanda. Protesting falling cotton prices, the peasants attacked Portuguese livestock and property, but abstained from attacking settlers. The Portuguese response was brutal: Some 7,000 Africans were killed by the military.

Largely ignored outside Angola, the incident only came to light after the Luanda uprising of February 1961 captured world attention. Rather than that in Malange, the violence in Luanda, in which hundreds of Africans attacked the city's prison with knifes and clubs trying to free militants about to be deported, marks the authentic beginning of Angola's war of liberation. While the MPLA later claimed credit for the assault, most historians conclude it was a largely unplanned affair. In either case, the immediate results were disastrous: Some 40 Africans and seven guards were killed, but no prisoners freed. Worse still, the attack fomented a brutal reaction among whites, who killed hundreds of unarmed blacks.

The following month, a separate revolt in the Kikongo coffee-growing region of the north, under the loose control of the FNLA, resulted in the deaths of several hundred Portuguese settlers. The colonial response was more brutal than that which followed the Luanda revolt. Thousands of Portuguese soldiers were brought to Angola and, with the help of local militia and white vigilantes, killed an estimated 20,000 Africans. Nor were the reprisals confined to the areas of guerrilla attacks or to known militants; "almost any African who had achieved some degree of education" became a target.[42]

The counterrevolutionary violence was effective. Starting in 1962, the FNLA largely confined itself to ineffective cross-border raids (from the newly independent Congo, now Zaire) on soft civilian targets, though it occasionally attacked isolated military outposts and convoys. By the mid- to late 1960s, the FNLA had deteriorated into a kind of organized crime syndicate, providing "protection" for Kikongo entrepreneurs in Zaire and smuggling goods into and out of Angola. Its strategy, says Spikes, became one of waiting out the Portuguese.[43]

More destructive for the anticolonialist cause, however, was the growing animosity between the MPLA and the FNLA. During the Kikongo uprising, the rebels had not only targeted Portuguese civilians, a tactic that the MPLA officially denounced, but went after *assimilados*, mestizos and non-Kikongo Africans as well. Then, in October 1961, UPA troops began to attack MPLA guerrillas as well. While MPLA guerrillas were more than able to defend themselves in the field, UPA/FNLA hostility often prevented them from even getting there.

The problem was a product of Zairian politics. Because of the harsh crackdown inside Angola, and especially inside the MPLA's stronghold of Luanda, the organization was forced to reestablish its headquarters in Leopoldville alongside Roberto's UPA/FNLA. But the MPLA was never welcome there. After the U.S.-sponsored coup against and murder of radical Zairian nationalist Patrice Lumumba in 1960–61, Zaire was ruled by right-wing U.S. protégé Joseph Mobutu (later known as Mobutu Sese Seko). Roberto's anticommunist politics, his thousands of Kikongo supporters—once again exiled in Zaire after the 1961 revolt—and his marriage to Mobutu's sister-in-law gave the FNLA an advantage. Theoretically, says historian William Minter, Roberto "could have taken the initiative towards unity.

> But Roberto had little inclination towards power-sharing, and little understanding of Angola beyond the Kikongo-speaking area of the north. Angolans from other parts of the country in the UPA leadership found themselves sidelined, and unity efforts with other groups repeatedly capsized on Roberto's intransigence.[44]

Still, despite the hostile atmosphere in Leopoldville, the MPLA's more inclusive nationalism was attracting followers. That fact, and its Marxist rhetoric, further alienated the MPLA from both Roberto and Mobutu. In 1963, the organization was exiled from Zaire and settled across the Congo River in Congo-Brazzaville. Now forced to traverse Zairian territory to attack Angola, the MPLA guerrillas were at an even greater disadvantage. Not until 1966, when they opened their eastern front from Zambia, did the MPLA effectively engage colonial forces again. While this was a boost for MPLA morale, it also placed the group in headlong confrontation with a new rebel movement, Jonas Savimbi's UNITA.

Savimbi, a Portuguese and Swiss-educated Ovimbundu, had initially joined Roberto's organization and become its foreign minister, but broke with Roberto in 1964 for a variety of reasons, including the organization's military ineffectiveness, its unwillingness to relocate inside Angola and—surprisingly, given Savimbi's later political orientation—because of the FNLA's virulent anticommunism.[45] In 1966, Savimbi formed UNITA, in large part because he felt the Ovimbundu, as the largest ethnic group in Angola, needed their own liberation movement and, say his critics, because he believed an Ovimbundu should rule Angola.

But just as charges of tribalism and communism haunted the FNLA and MPLA leadership respectively, so accusations of collaboration and opportunism dogged Savimbi. In 1974, the Paris-based journal *AfriqueAsie* published documents implicating Savimbi as a Portuguese "agent" who had agreed in the late 1960s to fight the MPLA and refrain from attacks on the Portuguese in exchange for UNITA authority in Ovimbunduland. While Savimbi denied the accusations and claimed the documents were forgeries, Minter and other historians say that details in the documents, as well as later confirmation by Portuguese officials, attest to their authenticity. Other secret Portuguese documents released after the war attributed nearly two-thirds of all guerrilla attacks to the MPLA and over a third to the FNLA, but just four percent to UNITA.

As the accusations against UNITA hint, Portuguese counterrevolutionary strategy employed a variety of tactics and was a mix of repressive measures and liberalization. In order to keep the struggles in its African colonies from international scrutiny, Portugal declared them overseas provinces, thus rendering the violence there an internal affair. In 1961, just six months after the initial uprising in Luanda, it extended citizenship to all indigenous people in the colonies, placed concession companies under closer governmental scrutiny, and established limited local self-rule for Africans. At the same time, the Salazar government tried to settle former soldiers on the land.

For the most part, however, Portuguese strategy emphasized the military option, employing antiguerrilla tactics adapted from Portugal's NATO partner the United States. These included antiguerrilla sweeps, the use of helicopter-borne troops, the establishment of village militias, napalm to deny guerrilla cover, and the resettlement of the peasantry who, it was feared, provided guerrillas with food, information and refuge. While the Portuguese claimed the resettlement centers offered the peasants safety from attack, better social services and wage work, many centers were, in fact, little more than forced labor camps for the benefit of white planters. As Bender points out,

> Control over the African population—the primary goal of resettlement—was attempted through the interaction of a variety of methods such as restricting and regulating their movements, creating a network of spies and informers, violence, and sowing distrust both among the villagers and between the villagers and the nationalists.[46]

Mozambique

The liberation struggle in Mozambique presents several parallels with that of Angola, including early spontaneous protests, an *assimilado* leadership, and Portuguese liberalization and military escalation. It also had one crucial difference: a unified African resistance.

As in Angola, Portugal's use of military troops against unarmed Mozambican peasants provided a catalyst for the armed rebellion. When farmers petitioned Portuguese administrators at Mueda in the northeast corner of the colony in June 1960, soldiers fired on the crowds, killing over 500 Africans. While the event went largely unnoticed in the international press, it had a galvanizing effect on many northern Mozambicans. As one Mozambique Liberation Front (FRELIMO) militant put it,

> I saw how the colonialists massacred the people at Mueda. That was when I lost my uncle. Our people were unarmed when they began to shoot. I was determined never again to be unarmed in the face of Portuguese violence.[47]

While early student movements formed in Lourenço Marques in the late 1940s, the Mozambican nationalist resistance began outside the colony after Portugal's International and State Defense Police (PIDE) penetrated and uprooted organizations inside Mozambique. Some of the liberation struggle's future leaders, including FRELIMO founder Eduardo Mondlane and current president Joaquim Chissano, worked and studied in America and Eastern and Western Europe. Others, like Mozambique's first president, Samora Machel, lived in the colonial capital in the early 1960s. For the most part, however, the various nationalist organizations that would come to form FRELIMO sprang up among Mozambican émigré populations in neighboring colonies, where they got caught up in the anticolonial mood and agitation sweeping sub-Saharan Africa in the late 1950s. Limited to exiles and intellectuals, and situated outside the country, "these early movements achieved little," says Newitt, "except the mere fact of existing, but for the first time they allowed a black Mozambican leadership to emerge and were a forum where the initial ideas about the future of the country could be tested."[48]

Cajoled by newly empowered African leaders like Nyerere in Tanzania, and inspired by the anti-Portuguese movements in Angola and Guinea-Bissau, three Mozambican groups came together in 1962 to form FRELIMO. Still, this unity was more name than fact. Like the MPLA and the FNLA leadership, FRELIMO's leaders, and Mondlane in particular, were accused of elitism, cronyism and racism (Mondlane married a white American). The charges against the leaders, however, were not just personal ones. They reflected the fundamental dilemma of all nationalist movements in African states with significant mestizo and white populations. Were they Africanist or multiracial?

Other questions such as the social and economic agenda, as well as the difficult subject of tactics (that is, peaceful or armed resistance) led to intense conflicts within the movement. While they rarely resulted in the kind of open fighting that marked Angola's war of liberation, they were not without casualties. In 1969, Mondlane was assassinated by a mail bomb planted by party dissidents with the assistance of PIDE. After a brief power struggle, FRELIMO's military head, Samora Machel, was chosen to replace him. Gradually, most Mozambican nationalists rallied to FRELIMO's increasingly militant and radical agenda, with only one group, COREMO, engaging in very limited military action against the Portuguese.

With spontaneous anticolonial violence and banditry on the rise throughout Mozambique in the early 1960s, the FRELIMO leadership decided to take the initiative. On September 25, 1964, FRELIMO launched its first attack against the Portuguese military, at Chai in northern Mozambique, after its initial plan, to attack the capital directly, was thwarted by a mass PIDE raid in December 1964, which led to the arrest of 1,500 FRELIMO activists and the near total destruction of the organization's infrastructure in the south. From that point onward, FRELIMO activities were largely confined to the northern and central provinces of the colony.

With ongoing wars in Angola and Guinea-Bissau, the Portuguese were stretched extremely thinly in the north and seemed to be taken by surprise. They made up for their initial setbacks, however, with a ruthless military and resettlement campaign of northern peoples, which thoroughly disrupted the economy there and had the added effect of sowing conflict between the local Makua and the largely southern leadership of FRELIMO. Debate over strategy produced profound divisions in FRELIMO, leading to virtual civil war in 1968–69. Ultimately, in what would prove a historic decision, FRELIMO leadership opted for a "soft" policy of political education and the establishment of social services in "liberated" areas, as well as opening up a new front in the Zambezi River valley to deflect northerners' complaints that the war was being fought on their territory exclusively. FRELIMO's overall strategy, as well as its decision to headquarter its organization in the country, helped to smooth over some of the differences within the group's leadership and between the movement and the peasantry.

Still, the Portuguese military maintained the upper hand through most of the conflict, pinning FRELIMO down in isolated regions of the north and central provinces of the colony. With the succession of Caetano in 1968, the military opted for a nationwide offensive, which initially caught FRELIMO off guard. A strategic withdrawal across Malawi and into Tete province, however, saved the organization and put Portugal on the defensive once again. Another Portuguese offensive in 1972, this time with the active collaboration of South African and Rhodesian forces, failed when FRELIMO surprised the Portuguese by moving south into more populated areas rather than retreating to the bush. Aided by the local population in Manica, which had a tradition of rebellion going back to the great Barue Kingdom uprising in 1916–17, FRELIMO launched attacks against the crucial Beira railway, Rhodesia's key transportation corridor to the sea.

As in Angola, the war in Mozambique was stalemated in the early 1970s. Neither rebel movement was likely to defeat the Portuguese militarily, while Lisbon was unable to pacify rural areas. A political shock was necessary to break the standoff.

INDEPENDENCE (1974–75)

COUP AND REVOLUTION IN PORTUGAL (1974)

Portuguese communists had always insisted that their nation's African colonies would be freed only after drastic political change had occurred in the metropolis. The communists had it half right. The 1974 coup, which overthrew the Salazar/Caetano dictatorship, speeded up the decolonization process immensely. But the coup itself was largely the result of the wars of liberation, which had drained the Portuguese treasury, military and populace.

In 1970, the European Economic Community granted Portugal its long-coveted associate-status membership. A way station on the road to full membership, Portugal's new affiliation required it to dismantle the regulations and tariffs that protected its colonial markets. But more than the specifics of European statutes, Lisbon's move toward admission represented a profound shift in the thinking of Portugal's business and governmental elites, away from the Salazarist vision of an intercontinental nation to one integrated with the prosperous industrial economies of Western Europe.

But the new orientation was not without its contradictions and setbacks. Paradoxically, as Portugal dismantled its statist economic policies, metropolitan investment in the colony grew and the colonial economies boomed as never before. Moreover, throughout the war, Portugal had invested heavily in Angolan and Mozambican infrastructure. This included developing the oil fields of northern Angola, as well as the massive Cabora Bassa dam project in Mozambique. "That one of the world's greatest civil engineering projects should have been undertaken in the dying days of colonialism in one of the remotest and most backward regions of Africa," comments Newitt, "is an astonishing aspect of Mozambican, indeed African history."[49] In fact, the dam was built for strategic as well as economic reasons. The huge lake that would form behind it was expected to act as a barrier to FRELIMO guerrillas, and the sale of electricity, largely to South

Africa, was expected to commit the apartheid regime to defending Portuguese rule in Mozambique.

This increasing commitment to and involvement in the colonial economies did not, however, come without a price for Portugal. On February 22, 1974, General Antonio de Spinola, deputy commander of the Portuguese armed forces and perhaps the most respected military man in the country, published his manifesto *Portugal and the Future*, in which he called for more open debate within the country, arguing that Portugal could not retain its colonies by military means alone. Spinola was not necessarily advocating decolonization; he believed, somewhat astonishingly, that the peoples of Angola and Mozambique would opt for a modified colonial relationship if given the chance to vote on it. His ideas got him fired.

Modest as Spinola's reforms were, they sparked outrage in the Caetano regime and agitation among dissidents. Among the latter were a group of 190 young officers who, in the summer of 1973, met to sign a petition criticizing the government for Spinola's dismissal and then formed the leftist Armed Forces Movement (MFA). The officers, most of whom had served in Africa, believed that Spinola's half-measures had been rendered obsolete by the racism of white settlers in the colonies, who had fully alienated Africans and were absolutely unwilling to accept or implement any political reforms.

When it became clear that Caetano did not have the backing of even the senior leadership of the military, the MFA went into action. On the night of April 24–25, 1974, it overthrew the dictatorship in a relatively bloodless coup that was "greeted with flowers and celebration" in Lisbon and a great deal of anxiety in Luanda and Lourenço Marques. The MFA immediately called for a national plebiscite within one year on Portugal's future political system and its relationship with its African colonies. Then it drafted Spinola as leader of a transition government. Spinola's lukewarm embrace of democracy and decolonization, however, alienated the MFA and the majority of the Portuguese people. Suspecting a pro-Spinola coup in the offing, the MFA forced Spinola to resign in September and installed another more amenable general in his stead. The radical democrat and anti-imperialist wing in the MFA were in the ascendant. The "Carnation Revolution" had won.

ANGOLA: THE WAR OF INDEPENDENCE (1974–75)

The Alvor accords

Like a strobe, the coup caught the three liberation organizations of Angola in various poses: the MPLA agitated and riddled with factionalism; the FNLA confident and well-entrenched in Kinshasa; and UNITA off guard and undermanned in the south. Each reacted to the coup in its own way. Neto railed against Spinola, Roberto displayed a guarded willingness to negotiate, and Savimbi voiced an eagerness to open any kind of dialogue with the Portuguese authorities.

Indeed, of the three movements, the MPLA appeared to be in perhaps the worst position to capitalize on the sudden changes in Lisbon. Not only were Neto and the Luanda leadership facing a challenge from Daniel Chipenda and his MPLA forces on the eastern front, but a group of radical dissidents within the Luanda wing had issued a manifesto criticizing Neto as too "presidential," that is to say, too imperious, too concerned with international opinion and too detached from the day-to-day struggle in Angola. The FNLA, on the other hand, seemed best prepared to assume power, having the backing of Zaire, the People's Republic of China—which soon sent 100 advisors to Kinshasa—and the United States. In the south, UNITA appeared poised to establish a solid base in Ovimbunduland, though Savimbi had bigger ambitions than that.

Meanwhile, Angola's whites were in a state of extreme agitation. On the night of July 10–11, 1974, a white taxi driver was found murdered, and whites rioted, shot at Africans and set fires in the *musseques*. With Portuguese authorities unwilling or unable to curb the violence, Africans began to organize self-defense militias. This reaction, in turn, set off six days of murder, arson and looting by both Africans and whites. The cycle of post-independence violence had begun a full two weeks before the last act of the liberation war, an MPLA attack on Portuguese forces in Cabinda.

While fighting among the various liberation groups was still several months away, the situation in both the capital and countryside rapidly deteriorated during the summer and fall of 1974. With the left increasingly ascendant in Lisbon and Luanda, officials began turning a blind eye to Soviet shipments of small arms to the MPLA. Thus, when whites again rioted in November, they were met by African self-defense committees, nominally controlled by the MPLA and armed with AK-47s. At the same time, a number of white farmers tried to occupy the town of Cela, 250 miles southeast of Luanda, in a last-ditch effort to foment an Angolan Universal Declaration of Independence, akin to the white Rhodesian UDI of 1965. In addition to the white uprising, there was a major peasant uprising near Malange, an MPLA military sweep of Cabinda, and the FLNA's so-called "silent invasion" of northern Angola. By November, says Spikes, "Angola was sinking into civil war."[50]

Not that negotiations had been entirely ignored. Because he was in the weakest military position of the three, Savimbi seemed keenest to arrive at a negotiated settlement and forestall what many believed was an inevitable civil war. Late in November, he met with Roberto, his old boss at the FNLA, to sign an agreement to coordinate their movements' activities. But at the last minute, Roberto insisted Savimbi draw in Chipenda as a way to break Neto's power over the MPLA. Savimbi, however, convinced Roberto that any agreement with the MPLA, minus Neto, was not worth the paper it was printed on.

Meanwhile, the Portuguese were desperately trying to arrange an agreement between the three factions, both to avoid civil war and to allow themselves a face-saving way out of the growing imbroglio. In January 1975, the Portuguese invited Neto, Roberto and Savimbi to the Lisbon suburb of Alvor. There, on January 15, the three signed an agreement that declared, in awkward diplomatic language, that all three movements were "the sole and legitimate representatives of the Angolan people" and that "full independence and sovereignty of Angola shall be solemnly proclaimed on November 11."[51]

The Alvor agreement also called for a transitional government consisting of one representative from each organization, with elections to be held for a national assembly shortly before independence. The celebrations held in Luanda at the end of January seemed to promise much. As "thousands of singing, chanting, ecstatic Angolans swayed rhythmically to the sounds of throbbing drums," writes Spikes, "they were held back by troops of three liberation movements who linked arms" to prevent a disruption of the inauguration of the transitional government. Sadly, this cooperation was not to last. As one Portuguese Angolan commented several months later, "Right afterwards . . . blood began to flow in Luanda."[52] In fact, it started two weeks later with an MPLA assault on the Chipenda faction's headquarters in Luanda, and a broader and more brutal purging of mestizos, whites and MPLA sympathizers in the Kikongo region in the north.

The war in the north

Tensions in Luanda that winter were not a strictly internal MPLA affair. Under the leadership of the militant Nito Alves, who later attempted a coup against Neto, the MPLA was organizing and arming the self-defense committees formed during the white riots of the previous year, under the rubric of the *podar popular* (people's power) movement. Fearing an MPLA takeover of Luanda, the FNLA attacked an MPLA office on March 23, leading to a night of give-and-take street fighting between partisans of the two movements. But the real opening shot of the savage war between the FNLA and MPLA occurred in Caxito. As the first major town on the road between Luanda and the FNLA stronghold in northern Angola, Caxito represented a crucial crossroads. On the day following the fighting in Luanda, FNLA guerrillas rounded up and massacred more than fifty recruits at an MPLA training camp.

With the situation growing increasingly fluid inside Angola, the superpowers and various African regimes began jockeying for influence. The CIA reestablished its lapsed contacts with the FNLA, while China sent advisers and arms. The Soviet Union and Cuba, longtime supporters of the MPLA, began to airlift arms via a Congo-Brazzaville airbase at Pointe-

Noire. Mobutu began setting up the infrastructure for an FNLA assault on northern Angola, while the South Africans sent out feelers to UNITA.

While the Soviets and Cubans had once been happy to keep a low profile, they grew increasingly anxious as Mobuto openly aided the FNLA. With rumors of an imminent assault by FNLA forces circulating through the now largely MPLA-controlled Luanda, the Soviets accelerated their shipments of arms. The Ford administration, preoccupied with the rapid demise of South Vietnam, barely responded to what normally would have been seen as a major Soviet provocation. Only the CIA seemed determined to make a stand, and, to that end, it continued to advise and work with both Roberto and Mobutu.

By late spring, events were moving at an accelerated pace. In May, Neto negotiated an agreement with the leader of the Katangese rebels, a 5,000-man guerrilla army exiled in Angola ever since their attempt to carve out an independent nation in the Zairian province of Shaba had failed in the late 1960s. While no great partisans of the MPLA, the Katangese were fiercely opposed to Mobutu, who, in turn, responded to this provocation by sending more troops to fight alongside the FNLA in northern Angola.

In June, Neto, Roberto and Savimbi met once again to try and salvage the peace process. Hailed as the "Summit of Hope," the eight-day-long meeting in Nakeru, Kenya resulted in an agreement to continue drafting the new Angolan constitution. But prefatory remarks in the communiqué told the real story, as each of the three organizations officially set down its accusations against the others. The general consensus of those observing the Angolan situation was that all three leaders looked on the Nakeru agreement as a way to buy time for further military preparations. Alvor, it seems, was all but a dead letter. Just two weeks after the signing of the Nakeru agreement, the FNLA, along with its Zairian allies and hired mercenaries, launched a new attack, capturing Caxito and threatening Luanda itself.

With the maneuvering and fighting between the FNLA and MPLA escalating, Savimbi and his relatively small UNITA force tried to stay outside the fray. The Ovimbundu leader's strategy involved both concilia-tory gestures to the other organizations and preparations for conflict. At the end of April, Savimbi flew to Luanda, visiting the capital for the first time in his life. According to Savimbi biographer Fred Bridgland, the UNITA leader "received an enthusiastic reception in a city regarded by the MPLA's leaders as their exclusive patch."[53] Neto tried to recruit Savimbi, but the latter refused. Worse still, when the *podar popular* committees heard about these negotiations with a man they considered a traitor, they massa-cred between 50 and 250 UNITA trainees at their camp in a Luanda suburb.

Even before the June attacks, Savimbi had desperately tried to estab-lish relations with any power willing to back him. He approached the CIA in Kinshasa and the Chinese in Dar es Salaam, but received little positive response. His desperation, says Spikes, "caught South Africa's eye."[54] At a series of April 1975 meetings with South African military and security officials in Lusaka, Savimbi began to establish the foundations of his long-term relationship with the apartheid regime.

The escalating hostilities did nothing to reassure white Angolans. Ever since Alvor, when it became clear that a white-dominated regime was no longer in the cards, thousands of Portuguese had been fleeing the country for Portugal, Brazil, South Africa and other destinations. Feeling sold out by their own government, angered by FNLA attacks on white property and lives, and threatened by the MPLA's anticapitalist rhetoric, decamping Portuguese settlers engaged in a widespread stripping and sabotage of property. On an August tour of the countryside east of Luanda, Neto tried to soothe white Angolans by telling them that the MPLA envisioned a multiracial future for Angola. But his speeches, laced with denunciations of settlers who had already abandoned the country, had the opposite effect. During a six-month international airlift organized in May, nearly a quarter of a million whites, mestizos and *assimilados* left the country.

Meanwhile, intense fighting between FNLA and MPLA forces continued through August, as did MPLA attacks on UNITA positions along the southern coast. By late August, however, a peace had fallen over both battlefields. This, however, had less to do with reconciliation than it did with preparations for the final confrontation that all sides predicted was coming as November 11 drew near. In fact, both the FNLA and the MPLA had drawn the same conclusion: Whichever group occupied Luanda on that day was likely to be the internationally recognized government of Africa's newest nation.

In early August, the CIA decided to go ahead with a plan to ship large quantities of arms to the FNLA, despite ongoing congressional scrutiny of past CIA operations, including its 1960–61 involvement in neighboring Zaire. As John Stockwell, the CIA agent in charge of the Angolan operation, wrote,

> During September and October, the CIA, with remarkable support from diverse U.S. government and military offices around the world, mounted the controversial, economy-size war with single-minded ruthlessness.[55]

At the same time, three ships embarked from Cuba with 1,500 troops and a major stockpile of Soviet-supplied arms. The first arrived in Luanda harbor on October 4, more than a month before the Portuguese were to officially relinquish the capital to whichever organization was in control.

The final showdown between the FNLA and the MPLA, however, had already begun. In mid-September, the MPLA counterattacked against Caxito, deploying a particularly effective World War II–vintage Soviet weapon, popularly known as Stalin's Organ but actually a rather inaccurate 122-millimeter rocket that exploded with a thunderous clap, which sent the green FNLA troops running back to the north in terror. The tide, however, was quickly reversed when Mobutu sent in elite battalions to assist the FNLA.

Meanwhile, the CIA advised Roberto to consolidate his hold over territory in the north first, but the FNLA leader would have none of it. "Burning with impatience and hungry for power," says one historian, "Roberto had decided to make his historic attack on Luanda the inevitable end game of the war."[56] For six weeks, he pushed hard at Luanda's defenses but was unable to take the city, though his advance units got as far as the suburbs. On November 10, the eve of Angola's formal independence, a combined army of Soviet-armed Cuban artillery units and MPLA infantry defeated the combined forces of Zairian artillery and FNLA infantry, sending them once again fleeing northward in a battle that came to be known as "Nshila wa Lufu" (the Road of Death). "[The FNLA] never recovered," says Bridgland, "retreating in ill-disciplined alarm from one town to the next, as and when the Cubans and MPLA decided on a methodical push forward."[57]

The war in the south

The FNLA was just one of three threats facing the MPLA. The others were UNITA and the increasingly militant and independent *poder popular* committees in the capital. Though in the midst of a life-and-death struggle with Roberto, Neto moved to take a firm grip on the capital. He ordered Alves, who had organized the committees, to disarm them. By mid-October, the committees had either been annihilated or placed under firm MPLA control.

Though geographically distant, UNITA potentially represented the greatest threat of all. By August, both UNITA and the scattered FNLA units in the south were receiving airlifted supplies from South Africa. This, however, was a preliminary testing of waters by Pretoria. Two months later, on October 16, the South African Defense Forces (SADF) launched a massive invasion of Angola from bases in South-West Africa (now Namibia). MPLA forces were no match for the well-trained and well-equipped South Africans and began to fall back. Within a month, the South Africans had penetrated to within 120 miles of Luanda.

Thus, on November 11, Angola's formal independence day, troops from three foreign countries (Zaire, Cuba and South Africa) and three Angolan armies (the MPLA, FNLA and UNITA) were fighting from one end of the country to the other, using weapons provided by three different superpowers (the U.S., the USSR and China). Given that context, it doesn't seem odd that the country marked its independence with three separate ceremonies: UNITA's in Huambo, and the FNLA's and MPLA's in different squares in Luanda, though these latter ceremonies had to be cut short for fear they would draw enemy fire. The surrealism of the day was capped by a speech from Admiral Leonel Cardoso, commander in charge of the last Portuguese troops in Angola. Lowering Portugal's flag at noon, he declared,

> In the name of the President of the Portuguese Republic, I solemnly proclaim the independence of Angola and its full sovereignty. It is up to the Angolan people to decide in what manner they will exercise it.[58]

By evening, the admiral and his men were already on ships heading out of Luanda's harbor. As one commentator notes, "the Portuguese brought five centuries of colonial rule to a pathetic, whimpering end."[59]

If anything, formal independence brought an intensification of the fighting. By mid-November, the Cubans decided they would have to bolster MPLA forces in the south to keep Luanda from falling. Known officially as Operation Carlota, the Cuban offensive in southern Angola effectively stopped the South African forces in their tracks, at least for a while. By early December, however, the South Africans had opened a second offensive from the east. Even the well-armed and disciplined Cuban troops were forced to pull back.

The war winds down

Despite their successes on the battlefield, the clock was running out on South Africa, UNITA and the FNLA. Although Pretoria was doing its utmost to bolster UNITA and FNLA forces and have them carry the fight, the fact of the matter was that the SADF was largely responsible for the military successes on the southern front. Not only were Angolan forces less well armed and trained, but troops from the two movements often fought with each other after the South Africans had moved ahead to the next target. Cuban commanders too complained about the lack of discipline among their Angolan allies, but they had two advantages. First, despite the contentious political leadership of the MPLA, its forces were not fighting amongst themselves. Second, and more importantly, Cuba and its Soviet backers had African and international opinion on their side.

Given its pariah status both on the African continent and in the international community, South Africa was forced to run its part of the war as surreptitiously as possible. On the other hand, the Soviet Union avoided bruising the sensibilities of a continent deeply wounded by European imperialists by utilizing the already enthusiastic participation of Cuba, another Third World country with Iberian roots. Thus, Eastern Bloc support for the MPLA was conducted openly and, as far as Castro was concerned, proudly and in the spirit of international Third World solidarity, since he was seen by many as the defender of a black nation under siege by South Africa.

Nor was Washington in a much better position than Pretoria. While Secretary of State Henry Kissinger supported the war, the CIA was largely running it, secretly coordinating its efforts with the South Africans and not-so-secretly funneling almost $100 million in military hardware to the FNLA. The covert action machine running the war from Washington and Pretoria operated with a high degree of precision, but was delicately balanced. South Africa's participation in the war rested on the covert okay it received from the United States, while U.S. participation depended on maintaining distance from the South Africans. Mobutu's Zaire was the crucial link. But the Zairian forces supporting the FNLA, though better trained and more disciplined than Roberto's, were not the SADF. Without U.S. support, they could not have carried the fight. Moreover, Mobutu was not the stablest of allies. It might only take one hint of defeat—like that on November 10—or talk that he was in league with the apartheid regime and he was likely to balk at the war's being conducted from his territory.

In short, the diplomatic and military edifice constructed by Zaire, South Africa and the United States was a house of cards; the slightest gust would bring it down. Such a blow came on November 22, when the *Washington Post* ran an article by Bridgland, a British confidante of Savimbi's and a journalist with a long history of writing favorable articles about UNITA. In the article, Bridgland unambiguously stated that South Africa was the real force behind the setbacks of MPLA and Cuban forces in southern Angola. The MPLA, of course, had made the same accusations, but few observers believed them. With the Bridgland revelations, says Spikes, "the whole world sat up and paid attention."[60]

The first to do so were the Africans. Through most of the war, the Organization of African Unity (OAU) had been on record favoring a tripartite FNLA, MPLA and UNITA transition government in post-independence Angola. But for a black African organization to be seen siding with or even neutral about forces that received support from the apartheid regime in Pretoria was anathema. Thus, in the wake of Bridgland's article, the momentum within the OAU quickly turned toward the MPLA. As Stockwell noted, "There was nothing the [CIA] could invent that would be as damaging to the other side as our alliance with the hated South Africans was to our cause."[61]

The reverberations of the Bridgland revelation, as well as MPLA propaganda displays of U.S. arms captured from FNLA troops, shook up U.S. politics as well. The CIA was not in good standing with the liberal, post-Watergate Democratic majority in Congress during the mid-1970s. For months, Iowa's Dick Clark, chairman of the Senate's African Affairs subcommittee, had been trying to block covert aid to the FNLA. With the Bridgland revelation, other senators began rallying to Clark's cause. In December, the Senate passed a rider to the year's defense appropriations bill outlawing any funding for Angola by a veto-proof majority.[62]

Meanwhile, with the collapse of the FNLA and the Bridgland revelation, Savimbi faced a diplomatic and military catch-22. To get a hearing at the all-important OAU emergency summit on January 10, 1976, when the organization would decide to recognize the legitimate government of Angola, he had to convince his fellow black Africans that he was not wholly a product of the SADF. On the other hand, with the FNLA out of the way, he faced the likely onslaught of Cuban and MPLA forces and needed all the help he could get from Pretoria. Savimbi tried to get around the dilemma by using his own forces to capture the remaining stretch of the important Benguela railway near the Angola-Zambia border. By the end of December, it was clear he had failed. Moreover, the newly invigorated MPLA had launched a major and ultimately successful offensive to rout both UNITA and South Africa from the central highlands.

With the Americans pulling out and fearing entrapment by Cuban/MPLA forces, the SADF pulled its remaining troops back to a narrow swath along the Namibian border. South African defense minister and future president P. W. Botha then vowed to keep them there until they had received assurances from Luanda and Havana that Cuban forces would not invade Namibia. Two months later, with no word from Luanda, the South African forces withdrew anyway.

South Africa's retreat seemed like a mortal blow to Savimbi, but it wasn't. Having expended his forces on the eastern Angolan offensive and with no South African or U.S. support forthcoming, UNITA was driven from its strongholds in the central highlands as well as the central Angolan ports of Benguela and Lobito. On February 9, 1976, the same day Cuban and MPLA forces occupied Huambo (Angola's second largest city and the "capital" of the Ovimbundu people), Savimbi began his famous "long march" into the southern Angola bush and vowed to fight on. With 3,000 guerrillas and their families, the cohort marched 2,000 miles in six months, all the while being harassed by MiG fighters. "The machine of war that Cuba and the Soviet Union have assembled in Angola is beyond imagination," he wrote to Zambian president Kenneth Kaunda, an erstwhile supporter,

> To prevent the total destruction of our forces we have decided to revert immediately to guerrilla warfare. . . . In Angola might has made right but I will remain in the bush to cry for justice.[63]

The cost of Angola's war of independence in lives and property was appalling. At the end of January 1976, with the war largely over, the Red Cross estimated that over 100,000 Angolans had died; Havana lost between 1,000 and 1,500 men, and South Africa less than 100. By March 1976, some 50,000 Angolans, mostly Ovimbundu, had fled to Zambia. Tens of thousands of Kikongo sought permanent refugee status in Zaire. The United States and the Soviet Union poured over a billion dollars in arms into Angola, approximately 90 percent coming from the latter. President Neto estimated the war cost Angola $6.7 billion in weapons purchases and property losses. The Angolan war of independence was easily the costliest and most destructive conflict in modern sub-Saharan history, though it would pale next to the horrors to come.

MOZAMBIQUE: PEACEFUL TRANSION, WHITE FLIGHT (1974–75)

Mozambique escaped the independence carnage of Angola for two obvious and related reasons: There was no liberation group of any stature or size capable of challenging FRELIMO, and thus no regional or international intervention in support of it.

As in Angola, the Portuguese coup came in the midst of war in Mozambique as FRELIMO conducted its last offensive into the central province of Zambézia. The coup incapacitated both military and civilian authorities, and led to the appearance of various groups, in both the white and regional African communities, demanding a say in negotiations over the future of the colony. Portuguese authorities in Lisbon, however, ignored them and opened bilateral negotiations with FRELIMO officials in June 1974. In September, the two sides signed an agreement handing over all power to FRELIMO upon formal independence in July 1975. Preoccupied with its own problems, Portugal was not in any position to make serious demands of FRELIMO. This acquiescence, as well as FRE-LIMO's radical agenda, disconcerted white settlers. In September 1974, a white uprising in Lourenço Marques led the South African military to move troops to the border. But when Prime Minister John Vorster refused to allow them into Mozambique, all hopes for a settler coup were quashed.

White anxieties were also fueled by the fact that the September agreement ignored the issue of post-independence property and civil rights. "It can only be considered a complete abdication of responsibility by both sides," comments Newitt,

> that conditions under which skilled Portuguese and Mozambican workers could have stayed on were not negotiated, and that no commercial or financial arrangements were made which would have guaranteed a continued harmonious relationship between former colony and metropole.64

While some of these important details were cleared up later, FRELIMO's decision to forgo post-independence elections provoked more concern.

Thus, despite the relative lack of violence in the transition period, Mozambique experienced the same white flight as Angola. Like Angola, settler flight and FRELIMO reaction created a vicious circle. "As the exodus gathered momentum," writes Newitt, further nationalization measures helped to create a snowball effect. The retreating settlers cashed whatever assets they could. Vehicles were driven out of the country, bank balances were emptied, consumer goods were purchased and taken along. Portuguese companies used a variety of devices to get their assets repatriated including sending money abroad as payment for phantom orders.[65]

Bitter and angry, whites also sabotaged property in various ways. Among other things, urban property holders poured concrete down the elevator shafts of high rises, and white farmers poisoned cattle.

The drain on Mozambique by white flight was not isolated to property losses. By independence, 180,000 of the 200,000 Portuguese in the colony had fled, largely to Portugal and South Africa. On the one hand, this flight was a blessing for the new country. It removed a potential fifth column and it obviated race conflict. But in the sum of things, the flight represented a debit. The new country lost the vast majority of its skilled technicians, administrators and professionals. The crucial port and railway sector alone lost 7,000 skilled workers. Moreover, some of the more embittered exiles came to provide, over the next 15 years, an international voice and political base for forces trying to destabilize the Mozambican economy and overthrow the FRELIMO government.

NOTES

[1] Vines, Alex, *Renamo: Terrorism in Mozambique* (Bloomington: Indiana University Press, 1991), p. 6.

[2] Minter, William, *Apartheid's Contras: An Inquiry into the Roots of War in Angola and Mozambique* (London: Zed Books, 1994), pp. 82–83.

[3] The official title of the Kimbundu monarch was Ngola, hence the name of the Portuguese colony founded on his territory. Mozambique's name comes from the name of the island on which the Portuguese established one of their first trading posts.

[4] Bender, Gerald, *Angola Under the Portuguese: The Myth and the Reality* (Berkeley: University of California Press), 1978, p. 27.

[5] Not all Creoles were descendants of the Portuguese. Some of the so-called Afro-Portuguese in Angola, including the van Dunems, a prominent political family after independence, were the descendants of Dutch traders and soldiers. And numerous *muzungu* in Mozambique were the offspring of Indian merchants from Goa, Portugal's enclave on the subcontinent.

[6] Birmingham, David, *Frontline Nationalism in Angola and Mozambique* (Trenton, N.J.: Africa World Press, 1992), p. 9.

[7] Newitt, Malyn, *A History of Mozambique* (Bloomington: Indiana University Press, 1995), p. 127.

[8] *Ibid.*, pp. 127–129.

[9] *Ibid.*, p. 128.

[10] *Ibid.*, p. 129.

[11] Oliver, Roland, *The African Experience: Major Themes in African History from Earliest Times to the Present* (New York: HarperCollins, 1991), p. 127.

[12] *Ibid.*, p. 69.

[13] Newitt, *History of Mozambique*, p. 245.

[14] Zaire, of course, is the Congo's official name since 1965. Originally known as the Belgian Congo, or Congo-Leopoldville, to differentiate it from the French Congo, or Congo-Brazzaville, the country was first called the Congo after independence. The name Zaire will be used throughout the text.

[15] Knowing the Belgian people did not share his imperial ambitions, Leopold engaged in one of history's first covert intelligence operations, using international organizations and missionaries as fronts to disguise his intentions.

[16] Bender, *Angola Under Portuguese*, p. 101.

[17] Cited, *ibid.*, p. 101.

[18] Since the late nineteenth century, English, Scottish and American missionaries had established schools and churches in various parts of Angola and, to a lesser extent, Mozambique. The education offered by these schools, and the alumni they produced, would have a profound effect on the nationalist movements of the mid-twentieth century (see chapter 3).

[19] Bender, *Angola Under Portuguese*, p. 53.

[20] For simplicity's sake, this class of people will be referred to in both countries by their popular term, *assimilados.*

[21] These include the Lourenço Marques-based African Guild in 1908 and the African Association of 1920 (see chapter 3).

[22] Bender, *Angola Under Portuguese*, p. 138.

[23] *Ibid.*, p. 139.

[24] Cited, *ibid.*

[25] Newitt, *History of Mozambique*, p. 373.

[26] Ibid., p. 453. The consolidation of metropolitan control would become a factor when independence came in 1974–75. Conditioned to look to Lisbon for direction, the whites of Angola and Mozambique contemplated but were never able to effectively execute a repeat of the Rhodesian phenomenon where the whites, fearing the British were about to hand over the reins of government to the black majority in 1965, announced a Unilateral Declaration of Independence.

[27] Knudsen, Christine and Zartman, I. William, "The Large Small War in Angola" in *Annals of the American Association of Political and Social Sciences*, September 1995, p. 133.

[28] Newitt, *History of Mozambique*, p. 468.

[29] Mondlane, Eduardo, *The Struggle for Mozambique* (New York: Penguin, 1969), pp. 85–86.

[30] *Ibid.*, p. 79.

[31] People's Press Angola Book Project, *With Freedom in Their Eyes: A Photo-essay of Angola* (San Francisco: People's Press), 1976, p. 12.

[32] Mondlane, *Struggle for Mozambique*, p. 56.

[33] Bender, *Angola Under Portuguese*, p. 201.

[34] Franz-Wilhem Heimer, a German anthropologist, conducted a survey of rural Angolan peoples in the 1960s and found that less than one percent could identify Lisbon as the capital of Portugal or knew that Mozambique was a Portuguese colony, while less than 20 percent showed even "reasonable" fluency in spoken Portuguese. Cited, *ibid.*, p. 221.

[35] *Ibid.*, p. 222.

[36] *Ibid.*, p. 224.

[37] Spikes, Daniel, *Angola and the Politics of Intervention* (Jefferson, N.C.: McFarland and Company, 1993), p. 19.

[38] *Ibid.*, p. 23.

[39] Davidson, Basil, *In the Eye of the Storm: Angola's People* (Garden City, N.Y.: Doubleday and Company, 1972), p. 146.

[40] *Ibid.*, p. 150.

[41] Spikes, *Angola and Intervention*, p. 14.

[42] Minter, William (ed.), *Operation Timber: Pages from the Savimbi Dossier* (Trenton, N.J.: Africa World Press, 1988), p. 6.

[43] Spikes, *Angola and Intervention*, p. 62.

[44] Minter, *Operation Timber*, p. 7.

[45] The FNLA always claimed Savimbi left because he was caught embezzling organization funds.

[46] Bender, p. 162.

[47] Cited in Mondlane, *Struggle for Mozambique*, p. 117.

[48] Newitt, *History of Mozambique*, p. 521.

[49] *Ibid.*, p. 528.

[50] Spikes, *Angola and Intervention*, p. 122.

[51] *Ibid.*, p. 128.

[52] *Ibid.*, p. 135.

[53] Bridgland, Fred, *Jonas Savimbi: A Key to Africa* (Edinburgh: Mainstream Publishing Company, 1986), p. 121.

[54] Spikes, *Angola and Intervention*, p. 148.

[55] Stockwell, John, *In Search of Enemies: A CIA Story* (New York: W.W. Norton and Company, 1978), p. 161.

[56] Spikes, *Angola and Intervention*, p. 250.

[57] Bridgland, *Jonas Savimbi*, p. 147.

[58] Spikes, *Angola and Intervention*, p. 261.

[59] Bridgland, *Jonas Savimbi*, p. 131.

[60] Spikes, *Angola and Intervention*, p. 276.

[61] Stockwell, *Search of Enemies*, p. 202.

[62] Because the Democrats had a veto-proof majority, Ford was forced to sign the bill into law in February 1976 in order to get the defense budget passed.

[63] Spikes, *Angola and Intervention*, p. 312.

[64] Newitt, *History of Mozambique*, p. 540.

[65] *Ibid.*, p. 551.

3

POST-INDEPENDENCE
(1976–1991)

[The US] must prevent an easy victory by communist-backed forces in Angola . . . The Soviet Union must not be given any opportunity to use military forces for aggressive purposes without running the risk of conflict with us.
—U.S. secretary of state Henry Kissinger

We have nothing to hide . . . we helped train and support RENAMO . . . [Some] would say it was wrong and reprehensible: but I have never considered it reprehensible to place my country's interests first.
—South African foreign minister Pik Botha

PEACE AND WAR (1976–1980)

Angola and Mozambique emerged from the immediate independence period politically polarized and economically crippled. War had devastated the Angolan countryside, particularly its most productive regions: the north and the central highlands. Moreover, the conflict left deep political and ethnic wounds that were barely given a chance to heal before the cycle of violence began again. Though spared the horrors of war, white flight from Mozambique had drained the country of assets and skilled personnel. Despite these setbacks, both the MPLA and FRELIMO attempted to chart a new social and economic order for their respective countries, based on a mixed program of Western investment (particularly in resource-rich Angola), state-provided social services and Marxist ideology. The two regimes also tried to consolidate their political grip and reach out to the international community. Both achieved some of their goals even as each was targeted by internal and external forces bent on their destruction.

ANGOLA

The MPLA: Policy and Power
Not surprisingly, given the bitterness of the conflict from which it had just emerged victorious, the MPLA made eliminating the opposition its first order of business. Both UNITA and the FNLA were outlawed; 13 FNLA

59

mercenaries, mostly Englishmen and Americans, were put on trial, and four executed. The MPLA also purged its own ranks. Two advisors to President Neto, Joaquim Pinto de Andrade and Gentil Viana, were arrested for having criticized the party and organized dissident coalitions within it. Elections were indeed held, but they were of the socialist bloc's up-or-down variety and confined to Luanda. Only about ten percent of the eligible voters bothered to participate.

At the same time, the government reached out to the international community. With its newfound political strength and control of key southern African railways, the MPLA government was able to force the lukewarm Kenneth Kaunda of Zambia and the openly hostile Mobutu Sese Seko of Zaire to make peace. Angola also benefited from a relatively benign international environment, especially for self-professed socialist nations. Both the U.S. and South Africa were in periods of foreign policy retrenchment, reevaluating major setbacks, the former in Vietnam and the latter in Angola. Both South African prime minister John Vorster and U.S. president Jimmy Carter wanted better relations with the Third World, though both would bow to more conservative and aggressive elements in their governments before the decade was out.

Meanwhile, the socialist bloc was in a confident mood. Southeast Asian communists had defeated the Americans and Marxist generals in Ethiopia had overthrown the pro-American emperor Haile Selassie, while in at least three of Portugal's former African colonies—Guinea-Bissau, Angola and Mozambique—left-wing governments had taken power. Nevertheless, the MPLA leadership was not anti-Western. They understood that the socialist bloc provided critical military support, but that it could not offer the capital necessary to develop Angola's tremendous resource potential, which included extensive oil and diamond fields, as well as some of the richest farmland on the continent. "Since coming to power in 1975," writes economist Shawn McCormick,

> the MPLA . . . exhibited a pragmatic willingness to establish constructive relations with foreign companies, especially those involved in the country's critical oil sector . . . [T]hat pragmatic streak has always contrasted strongly with the regime's formal commitment to Marxist rhetoric on a range of issues.[1]

The MPLA maintained there was no contradiction. Rationalizing its deals with Gulf Oil in the Cabinda oil fields, the government argued it needed the American firm's capital and technical expertise. "Gulf Oil has been permitted back," admit MPLA supporters,

> but it must meet minimum-wage requirements, provide day-care and education for its workers, and train workers for the highly skilled jobs of the oil industry. Through the formation of its own oil company, the People's Republic of Angola prepares for the time when it will staff and run its own oil fields.[2]

Radical critics say the MPLA sold out. Production, rather than worker control, was the main consideration, and this emphasis permeated every aspect of the MPLA's economic program. Limited government resources were lavished on Angola's agricultural export sector, while food production for local consumption languished. By 1979, Angola had to import one-fourth of its food and utilized less than five percent of its arable land. The industrial sector operated on the same principles, with production and bureaucracy emphasized over worker control and a share of the profits. Moreover, say critics, the rural state trading network established by the government after white traders fled maintained the worst of Portuguese practices. "Under Portuguese colonialism," notes historian Nicholas Cummings,

> the barter system meant that the peasants were forced to turn over a part of the crops they produced to Portuguese-run trading posts in exchange for rare consumer goods . . . priced way beyond their actual value. This is what has been adopted as the main system of exchange in the countryside today, with the only difference being that today the MPLA is running the state-owned trading posts.[3]

If most experts agree that Angola's post-independence agricultural policies were less than a success, the more sympathetic ones place the failure in historical context. Angola's tremendous agricultural productivity, says historian David Birmingham, was due to the high level of crop expropriation and taxation by the Portuguese. By abandoning such practices, the MPLA made a drop in agricultural productivity inevitable. Though, he adds, the government attempted certain radical measures, such as forcing the urban unemployed to work in the countryside, that, in retrospect, appear to have been economically counterproductive and socially divisive.[4]

The MPLA's troubles, however, were not confined to the economy. There was the matter of extending its political and administrative control over a largely rural country with immense and underpopulated expanses. Most students of contemporary Angola agree that the MPLA succumbed to bureaucratic excess, a result of its colonial legacy, wartime necessity, party ideology and Eastern Bloc advisors. But conclusions about the MPLA's local rural administration differs with each observer. Some argue that the MPLA attacked traditional leaders in the countryside, thereby alienating the peasantry. Others conclude that the MPLA worked too closely with these "corrupt" and "feudal" holdovers from the colonial era. Either way, most agree that MPLA leaders became too comfortable too quickly and, as a largely urban-based intellectual movement of whites, mestizos and *assimilados*, had little knowledge of or even concern for the 85 percent of the Angolan people who were rural peasants.[5]

These and other issues led to independent Angola's first major crisis, the May 1977 coup by former *podar popular* organizer and MPLA military leader Nito Alves. Alves and his supporters represented a mixed bag of interests. On the one hand, they spoke for trade unionists, slum dwellers and peasants who felt shortchanged by MPLA policies. On the other, they dabbled in extreme ethnic and racial rhetoric, accusing the MPLA of being un-black and therefore un-Angolan. The Alves coup also revealed divisions among the MPLA's Eastern Bloc allies. While later revelations indicated that the Soviet Union both knew of and failed to inform Neto about coup preparations, it was Cuban forces, barracked around Luanda, who ultimately came to the president's rescue.

Ultimately, the Alves coup was crushed, with severe repercussions for MPLA dissidents, many of whom were either killed during the coup or imprisoned afterward, and troubling long-term consequences for the MPLA itself. The harsh crackdown on political speech and activities did not improve Angola's international image and, it can be argued, played a role in both South Africa and America's increasingly hard line toward Luanda. It killed any chance of diplomatic recognition by the Carter administration, which had always been lukewarm toward the MPLA, and encouraged U.S. conservatives in their efforts to reestablish a military aid pipeline to UNITA.

UNITA: Back from the Dead

Before discussing the resurrection of Savimbi and UNITA, a few words about the FNLA's post-independence fate are in order. Roberto lived on in Zairian exile and then moved to France. His main supporters eventually reconciled with the MPLA and moved back to Angola. But a good number of his troops were recruited by the South Africans, who formed them into the 32nd Battalion (Buffalo Battalion) of the South African Defense Forces in South-West Africa (later Namibia), where they would play a key role in the South African/UNITA offensives of the late 1980s. Eventually, Roberto and the FNLA reconstituted themselves as a political party for the 1992 elections, but received a minuscule portion of the vote.

Savimbi and UNITA were another matter. True, both Roberto and Savimbi were the products of ethnic politics. But where Roberto was limited by them, Savimbi was able to overcome them. In other words, because both represented a minority within Angola, both required external support if they ever hoped to achieve national hegemony. Roberto, as it turned out, lived and died by that support; Savimbi could survive, though perhaps not win, without it.

For the first two years following his defeat by the MPLA and the retreat of his South African benefactors, Savimbi kept a low profile. Though conducting occasional raids to keep his cause in the public eye, Savimbi largely spent his time organizing UNITA from its bases deep in the Angolan bush, in a region of the country the Portuguese called Terras do Fim do Mundo (Lands at the Ends of the Earth). Journalists who dared the weeks-long march to Savimbi's headquarters at Cuelei in southern Angola were generally impressed by the discipline, enthusiasm and loyalty of Savimbi's troops. In February 1977, UNITA launched its first major raid against the MPLA, an attack on the small central highlands town, railroad depot and garrison of Mungo. Within two years, Savimbi's forces were capable of hitting the Benguela railway at any point along its more than 700-mile length and had virtually shut it down.

Historians disagree about the sources of Savimbi and UNITA's fortunes in the late 1970s. Some point the finger at the MPLA itself. According to Savimbi biographer Fred Bridgland, the MPLA effectively drove people into UNITA's arms. Its agricultural policies, including the establishment of state cooperatives, government-set production quotas on independent farmers, and low prices paid for commercial crops, were largely responsible for the widespread famine in the agriculturally rich central highlands, a famine with which the top-heavy MPLA bureaucracy seemed unable to cope. "You cannot impose a political programme that no one understands," Savimbi declared in 1979. "The Angolan peasant is not a statistic in some book of economic theories—he is not a machine. And if you attempt to treat him that way, he will reject you."[6]

Human Rights Watch/Africa offers a more dynamic analysis of UNITA's revival. The MPLA's policy of forcing villagers into cooperative farms and ignoring their traditional leaders alienated Ovimbundu peasants, but some of this regrouping, or villagization, was a response to UNITA attacks. As UNITA forces became more daring, the MPLA and the Angolan military expanded their policies, thereby disrupting the lives of even more peasants. For the most part, says HRW, peasants were in an unenviable position, caught between two hostile armies and forced to take sides. Not surprisingly, they usually chose to accept the leadership of whichever group ruled in their territory.

Meanwhile, the MPLA had made several errors in the international arena as well. One concerned the Katangese rebels of Zaire, who had sided with the MPLA in its post-independence struggle with Mobutu and Roberto. Relations between Kinshasa and Luanda, though tentatively patched up in 1976, remained tense. A major Katangese attack on their home province of Shaba, Zaire in May, 1978, an attack based in Angola with the tacit approval of Neto, strained Zairian/Angolan relations to the breaking point. To put counterpressure on Luanda, Mobutu renewed talks with Savimbi and offered his airports as conduits for aid from the outside.

Political events in Pretoria and Washington lent substance to Mobutu's offer. To many South African conservatives, the Angolan fiasco of 1975 had emboldened black South Africans and led directly to the Soweto uprising the following year. In a well-orchestrated political coup, military hard-liners led by Defense Minister P. W. Botha "brutally" drove Prime Minister John Vorster from office.[7] Of course, it was the military that had pushed for the Angola incursion, but they believed they had been sold out by Vorster. In a policy called "total strategy," laid out in a South African Defense Forces (SADF) white paper, the new government decided to back

UNITA as a way of taking pressure off Namibia—where guerrillas of the Southwest African Peoples Organization (SWAPO) were fighting for independence—and off South Africa itself.[8]

Meanwhile, a similar policy shift was occurring in Washington. Ever since Congress had banned CIA activities in Angola in 1976, a quiet dispute had been brewing between State Department liberals, who advocated a hands-off approach to Angola, and Zbigniew Brzezinski's National Security Administration, which wanted to back UNITA. As the Alves coup and the subsequent political crackdown in Luanda accelerated the process, the general rightward trend in U.S. foreign policy in the late 1970s emboldened Brzezinski's forces. While the events in Pretoria and Washington might seem beyond the control of players in Angola, a closer look reveals a different picture. Most observers of U.S.-Angolan relations have noted the discrepancy between Savimbi's adeptness at manipulating policymakers' opinions in Washington and the Angolan government's complete disregard for public relations. Savimbi, says Bridgland, had cleverly changed his rhetoric from the democratization of Angola to the struggle against communism, a theme close to the heart of Washington's rising conservatives.[9] It didn't take long for Savimbi's strategy to bear fruit. "His 1979 visit [to Washington]," writes media analyst Elaine Windrich,

> did result in the establishment of ties with the right-wing lobby groups and their media that were to play a key role in promoting the UNITA leader's cause during the 1980s. Since these organizations had also been campaigning for a Reagan presidency, and many of their members were to hold office in the Reagan administration, Savimbi was assured of the official support that would attract mainstream media attention.[10]

The pieces were thus beginning to come together for the escalation of Savimbi's war against the MPLA: a South African regime that saw its own defense as intimately linked to UNITA's success, an American political environment that saw Savimbi as a key player in the rollback of communism and a regime in Zaire willing to provide a black African cover for both. By 1980, says Bridgland, UNITA was reorganizing its military structure and strategy from guerrilla bands and hit-and-run raids to a conventional army and broad offensives northward. The growing military effectiveness of UNITA and the impact of renewed warfare on the people of southern Angola in the late 1970s was but a prelude of worse things to come for all Angolans in the 1980s.[11]

MOZAMBIQUE

FRELIMO: Policy and Power

FRELIMO came to power in Mozambique with several distinct advantages over its compatriots in the MPLA. It had no serious political rivals, no war of independence, no South African invasion. This good fortune was not entirely a blessing from without; FRELIMO, most observers agree, was endowed with exceptionally intelligent, humane and experienced leadership. Mozambique's first post-independence leader was Samora Machel, the son of an impoverished peasant family. This background, as well as FRELIMO's long-term commitment to in-country political and social organizing during the war of liberation, helped minimize the urban intellectual—rural peasantry cultural gap that plagued the MPLA and helped to create a culture of shared sacrifice among the FRELIMO leadership. During the first decade of independence, says historian Joseph Hanlon,

> FRELIMO maintained an attitude of common sacrifice; privilege was paired with puritanism. Ministers and high officials lived modestly and were manifestly honest. They did not abuse their positions; they were not getting rich and building grand houses.[12]

Having decided early on in the anti-Portuguese struggle that successful guerrilla warfare depended on establishing a solid working relationship with the peasantry and the development of health, education and other social programs in liberated zones, FRELIMO leaders both understood the problems of the peasantry and were deeply committed to solving them. From the very beginning, FRELIMO invested a goodly percentage of its meager resources on rural development. In 1982, the World Health Organization (WHO) singled out Mozambique as an example of a very-low-income country that had made "extraordinary" strides in rural health and education, having vaccinated 95 percent of the country's children within three years of independence and quadrupled the number of primary and secondary school graduates.[13]

Important as these accomplishments were, they paled in comparison to the task of postcolonial economic development. As in Angola, the Portuguese had left an economy skewed to the needs of a tiny urban elite and foreign markets. Mozambique had been a great generator of capital for Portugal, largely from the taxed earnings of migrant miners in South Africa, as well as the agricultural surpluses created by forcing peasants to grow commercial crops at below-market prices and underpaying workers on Portuguese and foreign-owned plantations. FRELIMO was determined to change all that. It modeled its industrial program on what seemed at the time to be the paragons of rapid industrialization: Eastern Europe and upper-tier developing nations like Algeria. Emphasis was placed on the production of basic consumer goods for the masses and centralized ultramodern factories, like the textile mills around the capital.

Reordering the agricultural sector represented an even bigger task. "FRELIMO," writes Hanlon, clearly could not continue the colonial policy which was very inefficient and would not generate the necessary economic surplus. In any case, peasants were not prepared to grow cotton nor work long contracts on plantations except under duress.[14]

To increase productivity, vast acreage abandoned by Portuguese farmers was turned into state farms and cooperatives. For FRELIMO planners, mechanization and irrigation were the sine qua nons of agricultural productivity and needed centralized planning and bureaucratic management. In addition, the consolidation of peasant holdings fit the government's social agenda. It was easier to provide health and educational services to concentrated settlements than geographically dispersed ones.

Colonial-era distortions were not confined to the economy, the FRELIMO leadership concluded. They also permeated the political and cultural life of Mozambicans. The Portuguese had appointed and ruled through traditional chiefs and clan leaders, known as *regulos*, who were often guilty of serving their colonial masters by enforcing exploitative land and labor policies. Many of these leaders also utilized their roles as quasi-traditional spiritual leaders to reinforce their authority. Informed by their Marxist outlook and embued with an antitraditionalist modernism, FRELIMO leaders believed that traditional authority had been perverted to colonial ends, as desperately poor and ignorant peasants clung to a system of beliefs that subjugated them to the whim of authoritative chieftains and offered them the false hope that magic equaled power.

In short, FRELIMO leaders believed the traditional political and spiritual order was the main obstacle to social and economic progress in the countryside and thus had to be ruthlessly uprooted. To that end, FRELIMO devolved all authority from the *regulos* to centrally appointed administrators and launched an educational/propaganda campaign against spiritual healers, whom they labeled, in an unfortunate choice of words, "witch doctors." "FRELIMO" had in effect cast the keepers of order and stability from the community," says journalist Jeremy Harding. "For many of them the shame was so great that they left their lands and disappeared for long periods, leading semiclandestine lives."[15] In addition, FRELIMO went after the more hierarchical faiths, in particular the Catholic church. Priests became politically marginalized and their schools and clinics nationalized.

Within a few years, Mozambique had created a unified and centralized educational and health-care system, and eliminated all tribal courts and councils. Shortly after independence, FRELIMO empowered peasant committees, known as "dynamizing groups," to do the work of dismantling the traditional political, social and economic order. By 1977, however, this peasant-style democracy was no longer in favor in Maputo. Many of the dynamizing groups refused to participate in production campaigns initiated in the capital. Many clung to their traditional leaders out of faith or because some of the *regulos* were genuinely concerned with the welfare of their people. Other groups such as the families or clans who profited from the proximity of their traditional lands to the newly created cooperative villages formed a new elite. Peasants who did not want to travel long distances, because of the growing insecurities caused by the National Mozambican Resistance (RENAMO), were forced by necessity to work these nearby lands. In short, says historian Alex Vines, "FRELIMO was attempting to stand Mozambique's history on its head."[16]

FRELIMO's rural policies are critical to an understanding of the causes of the 15-year-long war with RENAMO. Like any subject that has generated extensive scholarship, analyses of the Mozambican war fall into traditional, revisionist and postrevisionist categories. The traditional school, articulated by Hanlon and others, argues that FRELIMO's reforms "had substantial popular support. Real wages increased. Urban jobs were protected. State farms provided more favourable rural employment than had been available during colonial times. Successful communal villages offered a better life."[17] Admittedly, mistakes and excesses occurred, but these were largely incidental to the war. RENAMO was successful militarily only to the extent that it received foreign support.

Revisionists, such as anthropologist Christian Geffray, argue that FRELIMO's policies alienated much of the peasantry, who, he says, were forced to live on state farms and participate in foreign-export productivity campaigns that they rightfully saw as a continuation of Portuguese policies under a nationalist guise.[18] RENAMO, say the revisionists, recruited among dissatisfied peasants and thus was a genuinely indigenous movement. Postrevisionists, including many of the human-rights foundations, argue that the war in Mozambique was the result of both foreign intervention and FRELIMO authoritarianism.[19] As the war grew worse, so did peasant living standards, and hence receptivity to RENAMO blandishments increased.

But before turning to the origins of RENAMO, a look at FRELIMO's foreign policy in the first years of independence is in order. Unlike the MPLA, FRELIMO was acutely attuned to the political atmosphere in both Washington and Pretoria, and assiduously pursued good relations in both capitals. With détente-oriented Vorster and Carter, FRELIMO was largely successful, though the former cut work permits to Mozambican miners from over 110,000 in 1975 to under 33,000 in 1976. Mozambique also fostered cordial relations with the communist bloc, though it was forced to forgo Chinese support when it signed a friendship treaty with Moscow in 1977. Mozambique's most delicate international relationship involved neighboring Rhodesia. Almost immediately upon FRELIMO's coming to power, Mozambique began supporting Zimbabwean liberation forces, allowing them to operate from bases inside the country. It also enforced international sanctions against the white regime by closing its railroads and ports to the landlocked nation.

At the end of the decade, Mozambique became a crucial supporter of the British-sponsored peace talks between the Zimbabwean liberation movements and Ian Smith's minority regime. Machel's support for the peace talks earned him Margaret Thatcher's friendship. On the other hand, Mozambique's support for Zimbabwean blacks was costly. Not only did it cost the cash-strapped country much needed transport revenues and trade with Rhodesia, to the tune of an estimated $550 million, but it triggered Rhodesian retaliation.

RENAMO and the Rhodesians

While scholars argue heatedly about the sources of RENAMO support within Mozambique, there is virtual consensus on its origins: RENAMO was a creation of Rhodesia's Central Intelligence Organization (CIO). Indeed, in his 1987 memoirs, CIO chief Ken Flower took the lion's share of credit for creation of the Mozambican resistance movement.[20] The strategy, he said, was based on a simple rationale: to punish Mozambique for its support of Zimbabwean liberation forces. This, it was hoped, would cut Mozambican support and illustrate the painful costs of conducting economic warfare against the minority-ruled country. Not only would RENAMO wreak havoc on Mozambique, but its activities would provide cover for direct Rhodesian aggression, such as the 1979 attack on oil storage facilities in Beira.

Flower was financed in part by Portuguese industrialists and plantation owners who had fled Mozambique for Rhodesia and South Africa at the time of independence. The Portuguese connection meant more than money for the operation. The CIO placed scores of former colonial military men on its payroll and these individuals proved invaluable. They spoke the language, knew the terrain, and had extensive contacts with likely candidates for recruitment. Among the latter were Andre Matsangaissa and Afonso Dhlakama, RENAMO's first and current leaders, respectively.

Both Matsangaissa and Dhlakama were former FRELIMO officers who had had a falling out with the leadership. Both had been arrested for theft (Matsangaissa tried to drive off with a Mercedes-Benz) and had either escaped or been rescued from reeducation centers (known in Mozambique as "camps for mental decolonization") by the CIO. In Hanlon's opinion, Matsangaissa, Dhlakama and other "cashiered FRELIMO petty officials . . . believed that after a decade in the bush, they had an automatic right to take cars, houses and women."[21] In 1976, the CIO set up camps in Rhodesia to train its recruits. The strategy and tactics imparted were clear. "To start off with it was sabotage," a former CIO official recounted,

> to disrupt the population and disrupt the economy which really comes under sabotage, to come back with decent recruits at that stage and hit any

FRELIMO bases they came across. And if they came across ZANLA [Zimbabwe African National Liberation Army] they were to take them on.[22]

This quote brings up two important and rather contentious issues concerning RENAMO during the 1970s. First, its dual mission against Mozambican and Zimbabwean targets illustrates the separate agendas of its Rhodesian and white former Mozambican patrons, though the incidental mention of ZANLA reveals that war against Mozambique was a priority. Second, it alludes to the difference of opinion about whether RENAMO had an ideological agenda. While this critical issue will be examined in chapter 4, a sense of that debate can be had through the following quotes, the first from a Mozambican writer and the second from Dhlakama himself.

From the outset MNR [RENAMO] lacked any genuine nationalist credentials. They were mercenaries—both black and white—working to perpetuate racist domination of southern Africa . . . they no longer had a country to call their own[23]

In Rhodesia there was a concentration of [Mozambican] military men and politicians who were studying how to react to Marxism in Mozambique . . . No, we were not created by Ian Smith. But we had the support of Rhodesia.[24]

Under Rhodesia's tutelage, RENAMO's impact was geographically limited to Zambézia province in central Mozambique, but it was nonetheless devastating. Zambézia had not figured much in the war of liberation against the Portuguese, and thus FRELIMO's legitimacy there had never been firmly established. Furthermore, as residents of a key plantation region under the Portuguese, the peasants were particularly averse to FRELIMO's agricultural reforms, which they saw as a continuation of colonial practices.

At first glance, RENAMO's tactics of "burning villages . . . plundering agricultural cooperatives, shops and clinics, attacks on railway lines . . . [and] destruction of commerce generally" would not appear to be the best method for encouraging anti-FRELIMO sentiment.[25] But that wasn't necessarily RENAMO's intent. Instead, RENAMO attacks were intended to show the peasantry that FRELIMO could not protect them and to make it impossible for the government to provide services. Moreover, FRELIMO was not always effective in combating RENAMO.

Nevertheless, by the end of the 1970s, the Mozambican army had rebounded. Rhodesian efforts to push RENAMO toward the coast, thus cutting Mozambique into thirds, had failed. Then in 1979, Matsangaissa was killed in a battle around RENAMO's in-country headquarters on Gorongosa Mountain in central Mozambique, leading to a bitter succession struggle won by Dhlakama. More importantly, by 1979, the minority regime in Rhodesia was under increasing pressure from Zimbabwean guerrillas to negotiate an end to its own war. The Smith regime, under South African urging, had agreed to British-mediated negotiations, hoping to maintain white influence through the conservative black regime of Bishop Abel Muzorewa. Meanwhile, hard-liners in the military and the CIO were putting out feelers to their South African compatriots about taking the reins over RENAMO. They got a receptive hearing.

REACTION AND CIVIL WAR
(1981–91)

ANGOLA

"[This is] the best news since the beginning of the war of liberation five years ago [against the MPLA]," announced Savimbi in January 1981. "The election of Reagan is our hope . . . for it signifies a telling blow against Soviet expansionism and for Cuban departure."[26] Whatever Savimbi's failings, he proved an able student of both international and American politics. His assessment of Reagan's election was indeed accurate, for it put in place the last piece in Savimbi's strategy for the internationalization of the Angolan conflict.

In 1978, a new hard-line, military-dominated cadre had come to power in Pretoria determined to cast aside Vorster's limited effort at détente with Angola. But the new regime's strategy never seriously included the overthrow of the MPLA regime. Instead, Prime Minister (later State President) P. W. Botha hoped to destabilize Angola and keep the regime in Luanda on the defensive.[27] Whether or not Savimbi had grasped the new thinking in Pretoria, he did understand that South Africa was neither capable or willing to put him in power on its own. But with a new administration in Washington, ideologically akin to Savimbi and sympathetic to South Africa's strategic needs, the balance of power in southern Africa had shifted decidedly in Savimbi's favor. Botha's regional defense of apartheid, Reagan's worldwide strategy of rolling back communism, and Savimbi's ambition were now yoked.

Evidence of the new geopolitical atmosphere quickly emerged. In the winter of 1980–81 issue of *Foreign Affairs*, Chester Crocker, the incoming U.S. undersecretary of state for African affairs, laid out the new thinking.[28] Angola, he said, had not achieved independence in 1975; it had simply exchanged colonial masters and was now "occupied" by Cuban troops and Soviet advisers. Moreover, the presence of these forces represented a genuine threat to South Africa's sovereignty. If the West wanted to encourage antiapartheid reforms, then it must recognize Pretoria's legitimate defense concerns. To that end, Crocker abandoned the Carter administration's policy of isolating South Africa and demanding a unilateral withdrawal from its illegal colony in Namibia. The new idea was "linkage":

Pretoria's withdrawal from Namibia in exchange for Cuban withdrawal from Angola. "This was the most basic rationale for the regionwide pursuit of what I had labeled 'constructive engagement,'" he later wrote in his memoirs.

> Western engagement in southern Africa was not for the purpose of imposing blueprints or timetables for change on the South Africans. We had neither the leverage nor the mandate for such a role. Rather, we had to engage in order to help foster a regional climate conducive to compromise in both southern and South Africa.[29]

Whether Crocker's strategy was simply based on an overly modest assessment of U.S. influence or was openly disingenuous, most scholars agree that constructive engagement had the effect of a green light for South Africa. As even Crocker himself later admitted, "Botha and his colleagues preferred to view Ronald Reagan's 1980 electoral victory as the beginning of an embrace."[30]

The result of this new coordination of interests, if not active cooperation between UNITA, Pretoria and Washington, says Hanlon, "was permanent war in southern Angola" from 1981 on.[31] According to Angolan President José Eduardo dos Santos, who succeeded Neto upon the latter's death in 1979, South African troops conducted over 50 ground operations, 1,000 bombing missions, and 1,600 reconnaissance flights during the first 11 months of 1981. Of these, the largest was Operation Protea, a 5,000-man invasion and occupation of the southern Angolan province of Cunene for several weeks in the summer. While Angolan forces were able to halt the advance about 65 miles from the Namibian border, an estimated 130,000 refugees were driven north. "The idea," says Hanlon, "seemed to be to create a cleared buffer zone" between MPLA-controlled territory and SWAPO guerrillas in Namibia.[32] Further South African offensives, particular in Angola's sparsely populated southeast, followed in 1983, 1985 and 1987–88.

The South African government maintained that its targets were SWAPO bases in Angola, and that it was not supporting UNITA. For his part, Savimbi carefully worded his statements on South African–UNITA relations. He vehemently denied an outright alliance with South Africa. "Black men with flat noses," he argued in 1981, "can hardly agree with a [South African] constitution based on racial discrimination, and we will say it all the time . . . We are absolutely independent, and they don't trust us." But on the more delicate issue of cooperation, he equivocated.

> We cannot fight enemies on two fronts. We don't have any interest at all in having the South Africans come to bomb our areas: as long as they remain in Namibia, we intend trying to maintain good relations with them . . . But countries throughout the region have contacts with South Africa . . . even the MPLA . . . These countries make contact during the day; others do it at

night, but there are contacts. We all feel and hope South Africa will change its internal policies, but meanwhile contacts will continue.[33]

While the American media largely bought the South African and UNITA line, more recent scholarship, even by those sympathetic to Savimbi, is unequivocal: South Africa was, at the very least, a major source of supplies. "UNITA," says Bridgland, "obtained diesel fuel and other non-military items in exchange for diamonds and . . . ivory."[34] Critics of Savimbi go further. "Successive [South African] invasions cleared much of Cunene and Cuando Cubango provinces," writes Minter,

> capturing villages and installing UNITA bases with regular supply links for fuel and ammunition. A stage-set capital was built at Jamba, just north of the Namibian border, and frequent visits arranged for reporters and UNITA supporters overseas. South African troops aided UNITA in capturing Mavinga (1980) and Cangamba (1982). And UNITA acquired a conventional military force, stationed in this protected zone of southeastern Angola.[35]

Nevertheless, to portray UNITA's growth and battlefield victories as merely a byproduct of South Africa's Angola strategy would be to underestimate both UNITA's strength as a military force and Savimbi's capacity as military leader. After being largely abandoned by Washington and Pretoria in the mid-1970s, Savimbi rallied his troops and marched them deep into the Angolan bush; not for nothing had Savimbi received guerrilla warfare training in Mao Tse-tung's Beijing. By the late 1970s, albeit with some South African help, he had created a guerrilla force and a cadre of "fanatically loyal" officers.[36] When South African aggression became bolder in the early 1980s, Savimbi had several thousand guerrillas under his command. By 1983, UNITA forces had penetrated as far as the northeastern provinces of Angola. This advance was especially important for several reasons. It gave Savimbi access to Angola's diamond fields—while denying it to the MPLA—allowing him to raise money through a secret arrangement with the South African diamond conglomerate Anglo-American. In addition, it gave UNITA access to Zaire and another source of military supplies.

UNITA's military successes of the mid-1980s were aided by yet another South African invasion. In December 1983, the SADF launched Operation Askari. As it was later revealed, Askari was not just a mere escalation of South Africa's destabilization strategy, but an outright bid to take Luanda and dispose of the MPLA. Two things forced the South Africans to reconsider. First, the Soviet Union, whose satellites photographed massive South African troop movements in Namibia, put Pretoria on notice. A major invasion would lead to a direct engagement with Cuban troops as well as a flood of Soviet arms. Thus, Pretoria was forced to scale back the number of troops and rethink its strategy. Second, MPLA forces proved more tenacious and skilled in their defense, keeping the SADF and its UNITA allies within 125 miles of the Namibian border. Moreover, even the modified aims of the attack—capturing SWAPO guerrillas, knocking out Angolan missile defenses and forcing Luanda to negotiate with UNITA —were largely a failure.

In short, Askari represented a significant, albeit temporary, setback for both the SADF and UNITA. As in 1975–76, the white South African press, public, business community and political opposition were ambivalent about the invasion, if not outright opposed to it. And unlike Operation Protea in 1981, when the U.S. vetoed a UN resolution condemning South Africa, the response from Washington was less than supportive. The so-called moderates of the State Department, including Crocker and his mentor, George Schultz, increasingly subscribed to the opinion, at least privately, that South African aggression was encouraging Cuba to stay in Angola. There were also domestic politics to consider. 1984 was an election year in the United States. The antiapartheid movement was growing in intensity, with Crocker's constructive engagement policy a major target of its wrath. The Reagan administration was growing desperate for a foreign-policy achievement in southern Africa.

The 1984 Lusaka accords, though hardly ideal, fit the bill. In U.S.-mediated talks that winter, the two sides agreed to disengage their forces. Pretoria agreed to withdraw from Angola while a joint monitoring commission would make sure neither UNITA or SWAPO took advantage of the power vacuum in southern Angola. Though Botha achieved one goal, direct negotiations and hence quasi-recognition by a black African government, he largely caved in on what he had always claimed to be his key security concern in Angola: the continued presence of Cuban troops. South African delays in implementing the withdrawal hint at disagreements within the Botha administration. In fact, however, the hard-liners were still in the ascendant. That is to say, while U.S. pressure and domestic public opinion forced the Botha regime to take the diplomatic plunge, they couldn't force it to keep its promises. As in the contemporaneous Nkomati accords signed with the FRELIMO government, the South African military had little intention of honoring the Lusaka agreement.

Pretoria's true intentions were revealed soon enough. On May 21, 1985, an Angolan military patrol surprised a South African commando as the latter prepared to blow up oil tanks in Cabinda. Under interrogation, the officer in charge of the operation admitted that the plan included scattering "UNITA propaganda at the scene to make it appear Savimbi's group had executed the operation."[37] In public, the Angolan government expressed outrage at this violation of the Lusaka accords, though it said it would continue to honor them. In private, however, the MPLA leadership was frightened at the capacity of the SADF to penetrate anywhere in the country and became even more committed to a Cuban troop presence.

For his part, Savimbi was extremely concerned about the accords and tried to get his right-wing allies in Washington and Pretoria to scuttle them. When that failed, he tried overtures to Luanda, including a first-ever commitment to participate in elections. But the MPLA was in no mood for negotiations. Despite the commando raid, it remained convinced that with South Africa out of the picture, the time was ripe for eliminating UNITA altogether. To that end, it launched a broad and successful offensive in southeastern Angola, which, in turn, drew the SADF back into action. The result was yet another military draw.

1985 marked the tenth year of Angolan independence and the less happy tenth anniversary of post-independence conflict. Not only were both UNITA and the MPLA extremely war-weary, but their tactics were becoming increasingly brutal. While human rights organizations cited the government for its policy of forced villagization of civilians, mistreatment of political and military prisoners, and indiscriminate bombing of civilian populations, they singled out UNITA for their harshest criticism. UNITA, noted UNESCO historian David Birmingham, had made terror and economic disruption its policy.

> The objective of UNITA was to impoverish zones under government control by indiscriminate robbing, killing and burning. Survivors who failed to flee were then marched to the "liberated zones" beyond the reach of government forces. Women were taken as well as men, and children were especially prized as future guerrilla recruits. To further hinder normal economic development plough oxen were stolen and seed corn eaten or destroyed. Worse still, the farm paths were strewn with hidden land mines so that peasants attempting to return to their fields risked being maimed or killed.[38]

To say that the Angolan peasantry was simply caught in the middle of a civil war is to miss the full tragic irony of the situation. On the one hand, UNITA employed its anti-civilian tactics largely against the Ovimbundu people of the central highlands, its supposed ethnic base. This, of course, belied its claims to represent them and have their loyalty. On the other hand, MPLA forces, accepting that ethnic loyalty as a given, mistreated the peasants as well by forcibly herding them into villages and severely punishing young Ovimbundu men who tried to evade the draft. The question of whether unpopular MPLA policies had contributed to UNITA's ranks, as several scholars claim, seems almost incidental in the face of such abuses by both sides. Yet the finale was still to come; the stalemate following the battles of 1985–86 could not last, and it didn't.

1986 represented a year of regrouping and rearming, with each side well aware that the other was preparing for another showdown and lining up support among its allies. Savimbi went on a triumphal tour of Washington and Congress repealed the ban on military aid to UNITA. The Soviet Union was busily replenishing MPLA stocks, and Cuba was vowing to take direct military action against any South African aggression.

The great land battles of 1987 and 1988 at Mavinga and Cuito Cuanavale, the largest ever in sub-Saharan Africa, began paradoxically enough over air defenses. Throughout the early and mid-1980s, the South African air force had routinely launched attacks deep into Angolan territory. By 1987, the MPLA had made great strides in its air defenses but still lacked a key link in the southeast. In the autumn, it launched a major offensive at Mavinga to complete its chain of missile bases. But in so doing, it penetrated deep into UNITA territory. This alarmed the South Africans and Americans, who came to the defense of their UNITA allies, the former with troops and the latter with advanced Stinger ground-to-air missiles, preventing an MPLA victory. But the costs were high. South Africa lost over 200 troops, its highest casualties thus far. More importantly, in the face of ever-tightening international sanctions, it lost a number of its irreplaceable Mirage jets.

Still, SADF generals were determined to roll back MPLA gains and prepared for an assault on the heavily fortified city of Cuito Cuanavale. For a week, South African artillery pounded Cuito in preparation for an invasion force of 6,000 SADF troops and several thousand UNITA guerrillas. MPLA stocks of ammunition and food were running low, and by the end of the year it looked like its forces would be trapped between the SADF to the south and UNITA on the east. In January, however, the Cubans committed as many as 50,000 troops to a ground assault, making a risky but ultimately effective run behind the SADF forces, thereby cutting off their supply lines to Namibia. This gave the Angolan air force, manned by Soviet-trained pilots and equipped with superior MiG jets, time to establish air superiority. To protect their southern flank, the South Africans abandoned their Angolan allies, allowing MPLA forces to overrun UNITA positions. Cuito Cuanavale was held.

While Savimbi and his American and South African supporters tried to make the best of the situation, citing heavy MPLA and Cuban losses, it was clear that South Africa and UNITA had been defeated. "All the objectives of the South African attack failed," concludes Birmingham.

> It did not strengthen UNITA as had been hoped, but on the contrary inflicted heavy losses by an ill-advised switch of tactics . . . The invasion failed to demonstrate the weakness and low morale of the Angolan armed forces, but on the contrary showed they could at last match the almost legendary power of South Africa . . . Above all, the invasion failed to sabotage the peace initiative being opened by the United States.[39]

For the first time since Reagan had come to office, the South Africans found themselves isolated. Their massive military assaults on Mavinga and Cuito had given the lie to any pretense that their sole target was SWAPO. And with another presidential election looming, the Reagan administration was determined to make its increasingly unpopular policy of constructive engagement bear fruit.

Meanwhile, Savimbi, embittered by South Africa's betrayal at Cuito, admitted for the first time that he had both received military aid from South Africa and had coordinated his own strategy with theirs, even if this confession was conditioned by his announcement that any such cooperation was now a thing of the past. Savimbi's declaration of independence, however, was not as bold as he made it out to be. Burned by its losses, South Africa was already committed to the peace process, agreeing to a cease-fire in August 1988 and pulling all its troops from Angola even before it had received a commitment from Cuba to do the same. On December 22, 1988, six months of negotiations between Cuba, the United States, South Africa and Angola (Savimbi was conspicuously not invited, as per request of the MPLA, which refused to accord him diplomatic recognition) led to the linkage agreement long sought by Crocker and the United States. The agreement, signed in New York, entailed a complex series of pullbacks by both Cuban and South African forces. The South Africans were expected to pull out of Namibia before that country's first-ever elections in 1989 (which SWAPO won overwhelmingly). The Cubans were required to withdraw from Angola by May 1991. South Africa met the deadline; Cuba's withdrawal anticipated its own deadline by a month.

But despite the South African withdrawal, which left the nearest major SADF base 700 miles from Angola, Savimbi was not through. He had survived the dabacle of 1975 and was determined to survive what he saw as a betrayal in 1988. Even as the peace talks over Cuban and South African linkage proceeded, Savimbi was making the rounds in Washington, trying to shore up U.S. support. Though the reception he received was not nearly as enthusiastic as that of 1986, it didn't matter. With the election of George Bush, who had headed the CIA during its ill-fated involvement in the Angolan war of independence, Savimbi was assured continued U.S. support and military aid. And with that aid, Angola was fated to endure at least five more years of war.

MOZAMBIQUE

To Nkomati (1980–84)

There are two important differences between the wars in Angola and Mozambique in the 1980s. First, Mozambique's war was less structured. Major land battles were extremely rare and military fronts more fluid. Second, the war in Angola was fought on several levels at once. It involved a Cold War struggle between East and West, a regional conflict between South Africa and black Africa and, to some extent, a confrontation between two broad Angolan ethno-geographic regions. Mozambique's, on the other hand, was largely a regional war, that is, a confrontation between the apartheid regime in Pretoria and the socialist regime in Maputo. The larger Cold War element was absent; RENAMO was never able to find a superpower patron, though extreme right-wing elements in the United States and the United Kingdom offered limited political support and aid.[40]

On the other hand, it is true that RENAMO guerrillas were largely of Mozambican nationality. And, many scholars argue, RENAMO did achieve a certain amount of support among the Mozambican peasantry, largely as a reaction to certain economic, social and political policies of the FRELIMO government. Still, virtually no one in or out of Mozambique believes that RENAMO would have been a serious military or even political threat to the government without Rhodesian and South African aid. Summing up much of the scholarship, Vines writes,

> UNITA has been depicted as a legitimate rebel movement, with its roots in the pre-independence nationalist struggle. RENAMO, in contrast, has been portrayed as a creation of the Rhodesian security forces. It has also been argued that UNITA, unlike RENAMO, has popular support amongst sectors of the Angolan peasantry, and that UNITA is led by a both legitimate and charismatic leader, unlike Dhlakama.[41]

RENAMO, of course, did not exist until Rhodesia's CIO brought it into being, and it never achieved a serious hold over large areas of Mozambique until South Africa, with its substantial resources, offered it arms and logistical support. The transfer of RENAMO from Rhodesian to South African tutelage is perhaps the most important event in the history of the post-independence war in Mozambique.

It began with Pretoria's gradual realization that continued guerrilla warfare in Rhodesia represented a greater threat to the apartheid regime than did a negotiated transfer of power to a conservative black regime. The future Zimbabwe, South Africa hoped, would resemble the pro–South African regime in Malawi. And while Rhodesia had its own internal divisions over majority rule, South Africa's shift in thinking proved critical to the Smith regime's acceptance of a negotiated settlement. In 1979, Rhodesia signed the British-mediated Lancaster House accords, expecting conservative black leader Bishop Abel Muzorewa to win the 1980 elections. Both white Rhodesians and South Africans, however, were shocked when the left-wing Zimbabwe African National Union (ZANU), one of the two main guerrilla organizations, won the elections behind its leader, Robert Mugabe.

FRELIMO leaders, on the other hand, were elated by the events of 1980. Not only had RENAMO's patron been defeated, but its headquarters on Gorongosa Mountain had been overrun, Matsangaissa killed and the organization torn by a succession struggle. "At this stage," writes Newitt, "RENAMO was simply a mercenary unit of a white colonial army," a defeated white colonial army, that is.[42]

Even before the Lancaster accords, however, RENAMO and Rhodesian officials had been in contact with South African officials, but had been turned down by the Vorster administration. The rise to power of pro-military elements under Botha in 1978 changed the equation dramatically, and, by mid-1979, Pretoria's Military Intelligence Department (MID) was supplying arms to RENAMO. It was limited support, perhaps a million dollars worth by 1980, but plans had been made "that, in the case of the collapse of 'white' Rhodesia, the groups that would be 'compromised' by Zimbabwean independence would be integrated into the South African Defense Forces (SADF) and the MID."[43]

Despite these gestures, South Africa's commitment to RENAMO was not total in 1980, with some elements in Pretoria's security establishment advocating direct military intervention in Mozambique. Emboldened by the election of Ronald Reagan, whom many in the SADF saw as an ally, the army conducted a raid on the Maputo suburb of Matola in January 1981. The immediate target was the offices of Nelson Mandela's African National Congress (though casualties were largely confined to Mozambican civilians in a nearby jam factory), but the larger aim was to show Maputo the consequences of supporting the ANC.

The raid, in fact, had the opposite effect. "Nothing will weaken our solidarity with the ANC," Machel pronounced in the wake of the attack. "We and the ANC have always been in solidarity. It is unthinkable that our people and the oppressed South Africans should cease our solidarity toward each other."[44] The raid's failure to convince Mozambique and other frontline states to abandon the ANC, as well as the criticism the raid provoked even from South Africa's international supporters, led to a change in strategy and aims. Rather than engaging in direct military involvement, South Africa would turn RENAMO into a major military force.[45]

To that end, RENAMO's Rhodesian instructors were integrated into the SADF's Special Forces units, RENAMO officials with South African contacts were promoted (the chief contact, Orlando Cristina, became RENAMO's foreign minister), arms shipments increased, military training centers were set up at military bases inside South Africa and a RENAMO radio station was established on South African soil. Within two years of South African involvement, RENAMO had expanded from 1,000 to 8,000 guerrillas. And rather than simply trying to dissuade Mozambique from supporting the ANC, South Africa decided to destabilize the country, thereby killing several birds with one stone: pressuring Maputo to abandon the ANC and neutralizing it militarily, economically and politically. Implicit in the new approach was a message to black Africa: Interference in the internal affairs of South Africa is costly. But there was also a message to the world: Mozambican violence has demonstrated the inability of blacks to govern themselves.

There was indeed violence. RENAMO immediately began new offensives in Manica and Sofala provinces in central Mozambique, and by 1982 had moved south into Inhambane and eastward into Zambézia, the nation's richest agricultural province. RENAMO's strategy was straightforward enough. First, it destabilized the economy through the wholesale destruction of infrastructure. Railroads, a key element of Mozambique's infrastructure and a key source of foreign revenues, were especially hard-hit by RENAMO. To undermine support for FRELIMO, RENAMO destroyed the health and educational facilities established in the early years of independence. According to UNICEF, more than 1,800 schools had been destroyed by 1985, affecting over 300,000 students, as well as 25 percent of the health clinics in the country. Robbery and theft were as endemic as vandalism. RENAMO developed a system for transferring looted property over the border to Malawi, where it was used to purchase luxuries for the officers, necessities for the soldiers and arms for the movement. The victims of these thefts were forcibly recruited as porters to carry their own looted possessions.

RENAMO divided Mozambique into three different zones known as "areas of control," "areas of taxation" and "areas of destruction." Areas of control were the so-called "liberated zones" where RENAMO forcibly resettled peasants around its bases, reestablished a rudimentary peasant economy and set up a few clinics and schools. Life was relatively stable here, though peasants were expected to feed RENAMO troops. Many of these areas were in regions near Zimbabwe where the Ndau people were numerous.[46] Dhlakama was an Ndau, as were many of RENAMO's leaders, and Ndau became the lingua franca of RENAMO. It is important to note, however, that there were many non-Ndau people among the RENAMO leadership and, in contradistinction to UNITA, RENAMO usually did not make appeals based on ethnicity.

The areas of taxation were largely a no-man's-land, with neither RENAMO nor FRELIMO in effective control. Periodically, RENAMO forces would raid these areas in order to "tax" the peasantry, that is, to expropriate what RENAMO officers considered to be surplus food and goods.

Finally, there were the areas of destruction, under FRELIMO control. Here, RENAMO employed its strategy of terror. To undermine the government, RENAMO committed a host of brutal atrocities to demonstrate to Mozambicans FRELIMO's inability to protect them. It also forcibly recruited soldiers, some as young as 12 years old, and then trained them in the most brutal forms of aggression.

While most scholars agree that RENAMO was the creation of outside forces, FRELIMO mistakes contributed, they say, to the rebels' strength. One of these mistakes is conceded even by FRELIMO sympathizers. In the wake of white Rhodesia's fall, FRELIMO took on a too "triumphant" attitude, says Hanlon. It "clearly underestimated the savagery and cunning of white South Africa . . . and also failed to predict that the main Western powers would acquiesce in destabilisation."[47]

But in some scholars' opinions, serious internal errors were committed as well. Long after RENAMO had spread its destructive war to large parts of Mozambique, the government refused to acknowledge the severity of the crisis. By letting RENAMO disrupt the peasants' access to markets, the government allowed a severe economic crisis to engulf the countryside, a crisis the peasants often blamed on the government. According to these scholars, the dilemma FRELIMO was presented with, but failed to resolve, went like this: If it was a case in which peasants were forced to support RENAMO, then the government had failed to defend them adequately or to provide them with the means to defend themselves. And if it was a case of the peasants turning to RENAMO as a reaction to unpopular government programs, then FRELIMO's leaders had failed to adapt quickly enough, maintaining that only they understood what the peasants wanted.

Clearly, FRELIMO embarked on some unpopular policies or, at least, policies that it failed to sell to the Mozambican people. FRELIMO committed some of the classic economic mistakes of the Third World, including an emphasis on capital-draining heavy industry and state farms, a tendency to invest in the capital region, and productivity campaigns that may have been seen by peasants as too much like the forced commercial farming of the Portuguese era.

FRELIMO committed political errors as well. According to some scholars, the government was too hasty and too indiscriminate in replacing local leaders, both spiritual and secular, with centrally appointed administrators. In addition, FRELIMO embarked on a campaign against religious tradition and leadership (both indigenous and Catholic) that further alienated many Mozambicans. While this relationship with the peasantry will be discussed in more detail in chapter 5, one point should be mentioned here. Even those scholars who harshly criticize FRELIMO and believe that its mistakes were the source of much of RENAMO's strength admit that RENAMO rarely redressed the problems. True, it reimposed local leaders deposed by FRELIMO, but these traditional chiefs and spiritual leaders had often been very unpopular to begin with. And if they had been popular, RENAMO authoritarianism made it almost impossible for them to adequately defend and serve their people. In addition, RENAMO failed to redress the agricultural failures of FRELIMO and, in fact, made them worse by further isolating peasants from the market and thus from their access to goods, the main complaint many of them had with the FRELIMO government.

At FRELIMO's Fourth Congress in 1983, the party owned up to some of its mistakes. It decentralized economic decision-making. Major new projects were eschewed and an emphasis was placed on "small-scale projects which have an immediate effect on people's living standards." FRELIMO had never been anti-private sector. At the Third Congress in 1977, for instance, it vowed to support small and medium-scale businesses and farmers, and this policy was extended in 1983. As Hanlon points out, "The Congress recognized many, perhaps most, of FRELIMO's economic errors, and proposed sensible shifts." But, he adds, "it was too late.

> Had the changes been made in 1981, they would have had an effect and perhaps slowed the spread of the MNR [RENAMO]. But by 1983 the growing impact of destabilization made the changes impossible to implement. For example, attacks on the roads meant it was impossible to get newly allocated resources to the peasants or to start small rural projects.[48]

By the mid-1980s, both FRELIMO and Mozambique were in the midst of a multifaceted catastrophe: war, drought and financial collapse.[49] While the drought lifted somewhat by the end of that period, the nation's finances did not. Mozambique was forced to go to the International Monetary Fund (IMF) to reschedule its debt and so was forced to accept economic restructuring, which, in the late 1980s and 1990s, would take a devastating toll both on Mozambique's poor and on the government's ability to act independently of international banking and aid institutions. But it was the war, Machel concluded, that had to be resolved if Mozambique was to recover.

To that end, Machel went on a diplomatic offensive in 1983, hoping to get Western powers to pressure Pretoria to suspend its support for RENAMO. He began in London. Machel's warm relationship with Prime Minister Margaret Thatcher dated back to the time when he had proffered his good offices for the Lancaster House accords of 1979. He used his rapport with Thatcher to get at her good friend and ideological ally Ronald Reagan. Thatcher's letter of introduction to Reagan, as well as Machel's own notorious charm, disarmed Reagan, who, in what may be a unique event of his administration, agreed to fight off right-wing efforts to fund a self-proclaimed anticommunist rebel movement and apply pressure on South Africa. Somehow, in contrast to the contemporaneous policy in Angola, the argument that continued South African aggression would turn Mozambique into a Soviet ally got through. Thus, Mozambique became the sole exception to "constructive engagement" and partner to the other set of accords (along with the 1984 Lusaka agreement in Angola) signed by a black African government and Pretoria in 1984.[50]

In retrospect, it is clear why South Africa agreed to the 1984 Nkomati accords (named after Nkomatiport, the South African/Mozambican border town where they were signed): The Botha government, or at least the military security wing, had no real intention of honoring them. But at the time, observers believed it was due to Western pressure and the triumph of moderates in the South African foreign ministry. In either case, the agreements were straightforward enough: the ANC would be ousted from Mozambique in exchange for a halt in South African support for RENAMO. Because the FRELIMO government had never allowed the

ANC to actually operate within Mozambique (it only permitted transit via Mozambique), it believed it got the better deal. It was wrong. Not only was Maputo hoodwinked by Pretoria, it was humiliated as well. While Machel was trying to convince other frontline states that circumstances had forced him to negotiate with the apartheid administration, the South African security administration was actively subverting the accords.

After Nkomati (1985–89)

Having been excluded from the talks, Dhlakama denounced them as "meaningless."[51] The RENAMO leader was right, but not for the reasons he gave. Dhlakama had always insisted that RENAMO was a home-grown rebel movement, albeit one supported by South Africa, with its own agenda. It is true that Pretoria aimed to destabilize Mozambique and RENAMO fought to have a share of power. But the failure of Nkomati had less to do with RENAMO exclusion than with South African intentions. In the months leading up to the agreement's implementation in March 1984, South Africa delivered six months worth of military aid. This permitted RENAMO to step up attacks throughout the country and bring the war closer to Maputo.

Increased fighting led to a second round of talks between South Africa and FRELIMO. In October, the two sides signed the Pretoria Declaration (sometimes referred to as Nkomati II) in which RENAMO agreed to recognize the FRELIMO government in exchange for a gradual cease-fire under South African auspices. RENAMO's insistence that it be recognized as a legitimate negotiating partner, however, doomed the new agreement. In November, it announced a further escalation of the war, prompting Machel to accuse Pretoria of failing "to destroy the monster it had created." The South African government brushed the charge aside. "Nkomati did not put South Africa under any obligation to stop RENAMO attacks," Foreign Minister Pik Botha said.

> Much as South Africa would want the war to stop, the country does not have the influence over RENAMO to order the guerrilla movement to enter into a cease-fire. A guerrilla movement does not require many weapons to continue with its activities, and wiping out guerrilla forces who operate from the bush is a mere [sic] impossibility, as the Portuguese and Rhodesians found out.[52]

Whether Botha was unaware of the efforts within his own military to sabotage Nkomati or was simply being disingenuous, the truth about South African intentions emerged in September 1985. In a successful raid on RENAMO's headquarters at Casa Banana in central Mozambique, FRELIMO forces came into possession of the diaries of Francisco Vaz, a member of RENAMO's National Council and an aide to Dhlakama. Given widespread publicity by FRELIMO, the diaries could not have been more damning. One entry, covering a meeting between Dhlakama and South

African military officials, records MID head P. W. van der Westhuizen telling the RENAMO leader, "We, the military, will continue to give them [RENAMO] support without the consent of our politicians in a massive way so they can win the war."[53] Other entries have South African military experts urging RENAMO to attack "soft" military targets and especially economic infrastructure as a way to inflict maximum damage with minimum expense.[54]

Predictably, both RENAMO and South Africa rushed to deny the authenticity of the diaries and other documents uncovered at Casa Banana. But, as numerous experts concluded, the sheer quantity of documentation and the details they contained made forgery unlikely. Eventually, even Prime Minister Botha admitted their authenticity, noting that they accurately conveyed what had been said at meetings he had attended, though these were not meetings where secret military aid was discussed.

Internationally, the Nkomati agreement was a mixed blessing for Mozambique. South Africa may have signed the accords in hopes of politically detaching Mozambique from the other frontline states, but the violations produced the opposite effect. Zimbabwe and Tanzania pledged their support, sending several thousand soldiers to guard the transport corridors and the northern part of the country. In addition, Nkomati and Machel's diplomacy helped reduce Mozambican isolation from the West, which dated from the nation's 1977 Friendship Treaty with the Soviet Union. Most importantly, the U.S. agreed to drop its ban on bilateral aid, allowing a rescheduling of the country's debt payments following its default in 1984. But, as many Third World countries discovered during the 1980s, IMF loans came with a price. Mozambique was forced to drastically devalue its currency, cut back on health and education, and abandon its efforts to make consumer goods available in the countryside.

Forgoing this last program was particularly counterproductive, Maputo authorities felt, and they argued their case, unsuccessfully as it turns out, with international bankers. Agricultural production, they said, was the key to Mozambican economic recovery and military success. After shifting from nationalistic and socialistic pleas to get peasants to produce for market in the 1970s, FRELIMO offered more consumer goods in the hopes this would spur production. They also hoped that access to desperately needed goods would lessen peasant discontent and thus RENAMO support. In the short time it was allowed to function, the program produced excellent results, as key agricultural sectors witnessed substantial production gains despite the war.

The war, the renewed drought in the late 1980s and IMF-imposed scarcities had a devastating effect on the country. By 1990, Mozambique was declared both the world's poorest country, with a per capita income of $80 (about half that of Somalia), and the most aid-dependent country as well. Fully two-thirds of its national income by 1990 was provided by aid from other governments and nongovernmental organizations (NGOs). And like IMF funds, aid did not come without strings attached.

In his book-length critique of aid programs in Mozambique, Hanlon points out how well-intentioned and not-so-well-intentioned NGOs and foreign government aid programs damaged the Mozambican economy, reduced FRELIMO sovereignty and exacerbated social tensions.[55] Many aid programs, he says, flooded the country with food and consumer goods, thereby undermining prices paid to farmers and local industry. Convinced that FRELIMO was hopelessly inefficient or corrupt, many NGOs insisted on administering their own programs, which undermined the government's credibility and authority. Moreover, the money NGOs lavished on their staff, many of whom they hired away from the government, helped to dissolve FRELIMO camaraderie and its commitment to sharing the suffering of the people. In what is perhaps the most devastating comment in a scathing report, Hanlon says that destabilization, IMF restructuring and NGO aid combined to "recolonize" Mozambique.[56]

THE PEACE PROCESS (1990–92)

ANGOLA: THE PATH TO BICESSE

The period between the signing of the 1988 New York accords and the final signing of the Bicesse agreement in 1991 was a kind of endgame for the various participants in the Angolan conflict. Negotiations between UNITA and the MPLA were always either ongoing or in the works, but the war continued as well. At the same time, the superpower patrons of the MPLA and UNITA were applying a mix of pressure and incentives to bring their respective allies in Angola to the negotiating table, even as they continued to finance them. In the throes of its own internal collapse, the Soviet Union continued to funnel arms to the MPLA and helped reschedule $2 billion in loans due Moscow, but let it be known that even a reduced flow of arms would depend on MPLA efforts to reach an agreement with UNITA. The U.S., of course, was in a better political and financial position to continue aiding Savimbi, and its policies reflected that. On the one hand, the Bush administration put real pressure on UNITA to negotiate, but, as the MPLA pointed out, "new American aid to UNITA [was to blame] for strengthening UNITA to the point where the rebels [were] not very interested in negotiations."[57] As Harding notes, both sides still had plenty of superpower-supplied weapons during the 1989–91 period. In fact, the CIA had picked up the slack from South Africa since the latter's retreat in 1988, making biweekly arms flight to UNITA's headquarters at Jamba via Zaire.[58]

Meanwhile, the departure of Cuban and South African forces had a paradoxical effect. It simplified the military situation but muddied the political and ideological components of the war. The Cuban departure and easing of Cold War tensions made UNITA's anticommunist argument less compelling. Not surprisingly, Savimbi, ever the ideological chameleon, began to make new accusations against the MPLA government, including charges of human rights violations and an unwillingness to commit to democracy. On the other hand, the MPLA lacked the South African bogey and thus could no longer make claims to being a regime under siege by apartheid. Like UNITA, the MPLA began to evince signs of a commitment or, at least, acquiescence to the idea of negotiations and even multi-party elections.

In June 1989, Zairian president Mobutu Sese Seko invited Savimbi and dos Santos to meet at Gbadolite, a small town in western Zaire. Despite the presence of eighteen African leaders and the famous Savimbi–dos Santos handshake, the Gbadolite agreement was doomed before it was signed. Mobutu was neither a credible mediator, given his less-than-covert support to UNITA, nor a competent one. Inveigling the two parties to come to Gbadolite, he had put forth mutually incompatible promises. He told the MPLA that UNITA would agree to a cease-fire and Savimbi's temporary exile, while he told UNITA the MPLA was willing to integrate UNITA's leaders into preexisting government institutions and rewrite the nation's constitution. As Herman Cohen, Bush's undersecretary of state for African affairs, explained, the problem was not the written agreement, which was sufficiently vague, but the differing interpretations of the oral promises made to both sides.[59]

By the end of the year, the accords were in disarray. The frontline states and Zaire had a falling out over Mobutu's continued support for UNITA, while Savimbi was denouncing the talks and Luanda was stretching the terms of the agreement to the point where they would have meant a complete capitulation by Savimbi. There were also serious disagreements within both Angolan camps. Many in the MPLA were still determined to defeat Savimbi on the battlefield. They had always believed that Savimbi was a South African puppet who would quickly surrender without his master's support. Meanwhile, Savimbi had purged his ranks of pro-negotiating dissidents, a process that included the execution of close confidant Tito Chingunji. In addition, various human rights organizations were accusing both sides of continuing abuses, though again Savimbi's organization received the lion's share of criticism, especially for its kidnapping of foreigners, terrorist bombings of urban targets and, most troubling, the use of famine as a tool of war.

This last accusation had been gradually coming out since 1988, when drought hit the central highlands and, compounding the effects of war, led to the worst famine in modern Angolan history. In fact, the war had a dual impact on food production and famine. Not only did it make farming difficult and dangerous, but it limited access to outside supplies of food. Human rights groups did not blame Savimbi alone for the negative effects of the war, of course. But they did say he was turning the famine to strategic and political ends, using food to reward and punish the peasantry, and exploiting his control over access to the Angolan people as a way of pressuring the international community and the MPLA to meet his terms.

For months, the UN tried to open corridors for food convoys, but Savimbi said that the MPLA would use these roads to bring in troops and arms. The MPLA too had hesitated to open corridors, for fear they would be used by UNITA. But again, human rights observers and the UN singled out UNITA for its obstructionism. "UNITA's use of starvation as a weapon," wrote Human Rights Watch/Africa in 1991, "has had remarkable success. The United Nations estimates that 500,000 children have died in Angola since 1980 as the direct or indirect result of the war." By September 1990, however, the UN and the International Committee of the Red Cross (ICRC) had convinced both sides to open several land corridors, and the first convoy arrived in early November. Unfortunately, a renewal of warfare in December brought the convoys to a halt until the following March.

The renewal of combat in December involved a long-anticipated MPLA offensive against Mavinga, and an unexpected outcome. The reconquest of this city in southeastern Angola gave the government an effective launching point for a full-scale assault on nearby Jamba. But, as it turns out, the victory was a Pyrrhic one. With the Cubans and South Africans gone, the war had taken a new form, and it was Savimbi who first recognized the changing dynamic. Without South African support, he realized it would be impossible to fight conventional battles against superior MPLA forces. Mobility was the key to success. Instead of defending Jamba, Savimbi made a vast flanking movement to the north and east. The geographical shift of forces offered two advantages. First, it gave Savimbi control over revenues from Angola's diamond fields if and when U.S. aid stopped coming. Second, UNITA could now pressure the MPLA by harassing Luanda. A war that had once been confined to the Ovimbundu people of the south now encompassed virtually the whole country.

Despite the renewed tensions and hostilities of 1990, new peace talks under Portuguese auspices, inaugurated in April, continued. The new talks, held at various locations but ultimately signed at the Portuguese resort town of Bicesse, had one crucial advantage over Gbadolite: the presence of the MPLA's and UNITA's superpower patrons. "To say that Angolans can find the path to peace on their own is wishful thinking," a UNITA communiqué noted,

> because the most powerful participants in the Angolan civil war are the Soviets and the Americans. The question of Angola has ceased having regional

characteristics and has become a conflict on an international scale. Only with the involvement of the superpowers, even in the quality of active observers, can a quick, genuine, and just solution for the Angolan conflict be hoped for.[60]

All through late 1990 and early 1991, the parties negotiated in Portugal and fought in Angola. While the negotiations will be examined more thoroughly in chapter 6, the main sticking points are noted here. Early on, they concerned UNITA's demands for recognition as the opposition party and the MPLA's insistence that a cease-fire precede all negotiations. But events off the table were perhaps more important for the lack of progress. In short, both sides were determined to see what they could achieve on the battlefield before they made any concessions.

By spring 1991, the war had once again reached a stalemate. Under pressure from UNITA but in no real threat of collapsing, the MPLA began to bend. This was to Savimbi's liking. He had always displayed an aversion to negotiating from a position of weakness. Now he felt he had the military advantage. Not only did he control large swathes of northern Angola, but he still had a firm commitment of aid from the Bush administration. Furthermore, there were no signs that Congress, having given the president permission to attack Iraq in January, was willing to challenge the administration's prerogatives on foreign affairs.

The final Bicesse accord, signed on May 31, 1991, included the following provisions: a cessation of hostilities within one month; "free and fair" elections within eighteen months; UN monitoring of both the elections and the demobilization of the two forces; and a joint military and political commission, with representatives from the MPLA, UNITA, Portugal, the United States and the Soviet Union, to oversee the creation of a new 50,000-man army made up of equal parts UNITA and MPLA soldiers.

At long last, Angola was at peace again, but the costs of fifteen years of warfare were appalling. Nearly 100,000 Angolans had died in battle, while an estimated 700,000 had died of disease, famine and other indirect consequences of the war. At least 3 million, out of a population of about 10 million, had been displaced from their homes and lands. An estimated 6 million land mines had been laid, leaving Angola with tens of thousands of military and civilian amputees and, in the UN's estimate, the unfortunate distinction of having the highest ratio in the world of such injured people to general population. The economic costs were high as well. During the war, the government had spent approximately half its budget on defense, ringing up a debt of $10 billion, on top of the billions in oil revenues it had earned and spent over the same 15-year period. The Soviet Union had pumped in upwards of $2 billion in arms, South Africa spent another $2 billion on the war, U.S. figures are estimated in the hundreds of millions, and Cuba had sent over 100,000 troops. And still the war would have one (or perhaps more) last chapter to be written.

MOZAMBIQUE: THE PATH TO ROME

As in Angola, negotiations between the government and rebel forces in Mozambique were a long and tortured process, with numerous setbacks and an intensification of fighting as both sides tried to bolster their negotiating position. In both countries, the main obstacles involved timing, recognition, reform and trust. As was the case with the MPLA and UNITA, FRELIMO and RENAMO had to recognize each other's legitimacy and develop a timetable that balanced the rebel's demands for reforms and the government's insistence on a cease-fire.

But negotiations in Mozambique had one additional obstacle: RENAMO itself. Unlike UNITA, RENAMO had been largely isolated from the outside world, with the obvious exception of South Africa, another international pariah. RENAMO's leadership was distrustful of FRELIMO and especially concerned about its own fate in a postwar Mozambique. More importantly, RENAMO had literally had to invent itself. That is to say, it had never elaborated a political ideology in its many years in the bush and so had to develop an agenda of reform as the negotiations proceeded. In fact, RENAMO did not hold its first congress until June 1989, thirteen years after it had started fighting. This necessarily caused delays and frustrating shifts in the substance of and strategy behind its negotiating position.

Adding complexity were the reforms the FRELIMO government instituted independently of the negotiations. Even as RENAMO was formulating its demands for constitutional reform, multiparty democracy and elections, FRELIMO was instituting them. On November 30, 1990, for instance, a new constitution went into effect, legalizing political parties, reinforcing due process of law, enacting freedoms of assembly and speech, and establishing election procedures and schedules. While, on the surface of things, this would seem to have drawn the two parties closer together, it often exacerbated RENAMO's sense of isolation. RENAMO's dilemma was clear to everyone involved in the Rome-based negotiations. It had to formulate a series of political demands to justify its armed opposition, but by preempting those demands, FRELIMO had undermined RENAMO's self-declared raison d'être. At the same time, RENAMO leaders believed that their military capacity was the only thing that protected them from FRELIMO. And yet negotiations were nothing if they were not about replacing the bullet with the ballot. Finally, unlike Savimbi, Dhlakama dreaded facing his country's electorate.

This dilemma helps explain why RENAMO continued its attacks (as did FRELIMO) even as it negotiated. It also explains why so much of the talks were about assuring the safety of RENAMO's leaders and soldiers after they put down their guns. The mediators in Rome, including the United States, Portugal and the Sant'Edigio religious community that hosted the talks, offered RENAMO money to set up its political apparatus, a communications system between Rome and RENAMO's bush headquarters, and appropriately plush and secure offices and residences for RENAMO leaders in Maputo.

While the presence of outside allies was not as acute a problem as it was in Angola, it still had to be addressed. Zimbabwean soldiers continued to guard the transport corridors to Beira. Neutralizing those corridors and making sure Zimbabwean troops stayed within them were issues that required painstaking negotiations of their own. Meanwhile, there was South Africa's role in the war, a factor both simplified and complicated by the tortuous process of reform that began with the inauguration of the F. W. de Klerk administration in 1989, the release of Nelson Mandela and the legalization of the ANC. While both de Klerk and Joaquim Chissano, Mozambique's president since the death of Machel in a 1986 plane crash,[61] denied that South Africa was continuing to support RENAMO, *Africa Report* concluded as late as winter 1992 that elements within South Africa, "a secret element within the South African military as well as right-wing groups [in South Africa and the West]," continued to supply arms to the rebels, "permitting RENAMO to continue spreading violent destabilization throughout Mozambique and . . . slowing the Mozambican peace talks in Rome to a snail's pace."[62]

The peace process evolved gradually. In August 1988, the Mozambican Catholic church broached the subject of talks with both RENAMO and FRELIMO and even hosted some preliminary negotiations. In 1989, the parties agreed on mediation by Mugabe of Zimbabwe and Kenyan president Daniel arap Moi, a nominal RENAMO supporter. When their efforts stalled, largely over FRELIMO's contention that Kenya was training RENAMO guerrillas, the Sant'Edigio community in Rome offered its good offices. In July 1990, the negotiations began; they would eventually involve 10 rounds of talks that lasted through October 1992. The first break came in November 1990 when the two parties reached an agreement on a partial cease-fire in the Zimbabwean-patrolled transport corridors.

But RENAMO's "schizophrenic bargaining behavior" delayed progress in the talks for a year.[63] After having accepted FRELIMO's legitimacy, RENAMO suddenly backtracked and added new untenable demands, including UN control of key ministries and a radical rewriting of the 1990 constitution.[64] Not surprisingly, FRELIMO rejected these unorthodox demands as an infringement on its sovereignty. Most observers of the talks agreed that RENAMO was experiencing internal divisions over how to proceed and was employing delaying tactics because it feared elections. During this period and into the summer of 1992, RENAMO was constantly shifting between demands for a power-sharing agreement and calls for multiparty elections. As political scientists Thomas Ohlson and Stephen John Stedman explain,

Some within RENAMO complained that the organization was not ready for electoral politics because it had not turned itself into a political party. Others, it appeared, never pursued a political role for RENAMO or believed in the possibility of winning an election. For them, the Rome process was a chance to seek a buyout—a guarantee of financial survival for RENAMO leaders and generals in postelection Mozambique—in exchange for ending the war.[65]

Pressure from the United States and Portugal, as well as declining South African support—which severely incapacitated RENAMO—forced the rebels back to the table. In October 1992, the accords were signed by both parties. They included UN-directed demobilization of RENAMO guerrillas and government troops as well as their reintegration into civilian life. A new 30,000-man army, consisting of equal numbers of RENAMO and FRELIMO troops, would be set up. Elections for the presidency and Assembly, held under UN auspices, would take place in one year.

The economic costs of the war had been immense. In 1988, UNICEF calculated direct and indirect losses to Mozambique since 1980 as being in excess of $15 billion. This compared with approximately $3.6 billion in aid over the same period, or roughly ten times Mozambique's GNP in 1992, which itself had fallen between two-thirds and three-quarters since 1980. The government had spent upwards of 40 percent of its budget on defense. By 1989, FRELIMO estimated that 3,000 rural shops and 1,500 trucks had been wrecked, while nearly 1,000 clinics and over 3,000 schools had been looted or destroyed.

The human costs were literally incalculable, with different studies citing widely varying numbers. In 1992, Human Rights Watch/Africa reported that there were at least 10,000 amputees and over 2 million largely unmapped land mines in Mozambique. UNICEF calculated that approximately 500,000 children under five had died as a result of destabilization between 1980 and 1988. Altogether, the UN agency calculated the total number of victims of war and destabilization at just under 1 million, or roughly one out of every sixteen Mozambicans, though a 1992 Human Rights Watch/Africa report put the total at 600,000. The report also pointed out that there were some 200,000 orphans in Mozambique. In addition, between 4 million and 5 million people had been run off their land and forced to seek refuge in cities, transport corridors or neighboring states.

NOTES

[1] McCormick, Shawn, *The Angolan Economy: Prospects for Growth in a Postwar Environment* (Washington: The Center for Strategic and International Studies, 1994), p. 3.

[2] People's Press Angola Book Project, *With Freedom in Their Eyes: A Photo-essay of Angola* (San Francisco: People's Press, 1976), p. 67.

3 Cummings, Nicholas, "Angola: A Case Study in Soviet Neocolonialism" in *Revolution*, Spring 1984, p. 35.

4 Birmingham, David, *Frontline Nationalism in Angola and Mozambique* (Trenton, N.J.: Africa World Press, 1992), pp. 77–79.

5 *Ibid.*; "Angola," pp. 35–37.

6 Bridgland, Fred, *Jonas Savimbi*, p. 290.

7 Birmingham, *Frontline Nationalism*, p. 70.

8 The logic and strategy of the white paper will be explored in more detail in chapter 4.

9 Bridgland, *Jonas Savimbi*, pp. 289–92.

10 Windrich, Elaine, *The Cold War Guerrilla: Jonas Savimbi, the U.S. Media, and the Angolan War* (New York: Greenwood Press, 1992), p. 11.

11 Bridgland, *Jonas Savimbi*, pp. 292–293.

12 Hanlon, Joseph, *Mozambique: Who Calls the Shots?* (Bloomington: Indiana University Press), p. 220.

13 WHO offered more than praise. A year after studying Mozambique's health care system, with its emphasis on preventive rural medicine, WHO adopted a similar program for underdeveloped countries throughout the world.

14 Hanlon, *Who Calls the Shots?*, p. 11.

15 Harding, Jeremy, *The Fate of Africa: Trial by Fire* (New York: Simon and Schuster, 1993), p. 209.

16 Vines, Alex, *Renamo: Terrorism in Mozambique* (Bloomington: Indiana University Press, 1991), p. 9.

17 Hanlon, *Who Calls the Shots?*, p. 12.

18 See Geffray, Christian, *A Causa das Armas*, Oporto, Portugal: Edições Afrontamento, 1991.

19 Africa Watch, *Conspicuous Destruction: War, Famine and the Reform Process in Mozambique* (New York: Human Rights Watch, 1992), pp. 86–88.

20 See Flower, Ken, *Serving Secretly: An Intelligence Chief on Record, Rhodesia into Zimbabwe, 1964–1981* (London: John Murray), 1987.

21 Hanlon, Joseph, *Beggar Your Neighbours: Apartheid Power in Southern Africa* (Bloomington: Indiana University Press, 1986), p. 139.

22 Cited in Martin, D. and Johnson, P. (eds.), *Destructive Engagement: Southern Africa at War* (Harare, Zimbabwe: Zimbabwe Publishing House, 1986), p. 6.

23 Magaia, Lina, *Dumba Nengue: Run for Your Life, Peasant Tales of Tragedy in Mozambique* (Trenton, N.J.: Africa World Press, 1988), p. 7.

24 Cited in Africa Watch, *Conspicuous Destruction*, p. 21.

25 Vines, *Terrorism*, p. 16.

26 Cited in Bridgland, *Jonas Savimbi*, p. 302.

27 See chapter 4 for a fuller discussion of the reasons behind South Africa's destabilization policy in Angola.

[28] Crocker, Chester, "Southern Africa: Eight Years Later" in *Foreign Affairs*, Fall 1989.

[29] Crocker, Chester, *High Noon in Southern Africa: Making Peace in a Rough Neighborhood* (New York: W. W. Norton and Company, 1992), p. 75.

[30] Crocker, "Southern Africa: Eight Years Later," p. 153.

[31] Hanlon, *Beggar Your Neighbours*, p. 159.

[32] *Ibid.*

[33] Bridgland, *Jonas Savimbi*, p. 330.

[34] *Ibid.*

[35] Minter, William (ed.), *Operation Timber: Pages from the Savimbi Dossier* (Trenton, N.J.: Africa World Press, 1988), p. 26.

[36] Minter, William, *Apartheid's Contras: An Inquiry into the Roots of War in Angola and Mozambique* (London: Zed Books, 1994), p. 219.

[37] Gunn, Gillian, "Cuba and Angola" in Fauriol, Georges and Loser, Eva, *Cuba: The International Dimension* (New Brunswick, N.J.: Transaction Publishers, 1990), p. 173.

[38] Birmingham, *Frontline Nationalism*, p. 42.

[39] *Ibid.*, p. 107.

[40] This largely consisted of far-right Republicans in the United States, and evangelical Christian and extreme anticommunist groups and individuals in both Britain and America. See chapter 4 for a more thorough discussion of RENAMO's western supporters.

[41] Vines, *Terrorism*, p. 73.

[42] Newitt, Malyn, *A History of Mozambique* (Bloomington: Indiana University Press, 1995), p. 564.

[43] Vines, *Terrorism*, p. 18.

[44] Cited in Khadiagala, Gilbert, *Allies in Adversity: The Frontline States in Southern African Security, 1975–1993* (Athens: Ohio University Press, 1994), p. 181. A coda to this statement came in an interview with Steve Grundlingh, the Mandela administration's Consulate General in New York. Discussing the problem of illegal Mozambican immigrants in South Africa, Grundlingh, an Afrikaner, explained that the Mandela administration's leniency was due to the fact that during "our struggle, they [Mozambique] sheltered our people. How can we turn them out?" Interview with author, November 28, 1995.

[45] The frontline states, that is, the front line with South Africa, included Angola, Botswana, Lesotho, Malawi, Mozambique, Namibia (after 1989), Tanzania, Zambia and Zimbabwe.

[46] The Ndau are a subgroup of the larger Shona people.

[47] Hanlon, *Beggar Your Neighbours*, p. 259.

[48] Hanlon, *Who Calls the Shots?*, p. 26

[49] Unfortunately, the drought was broken only by a January 1984 cyclone, which displaced a half million Mozambicans from their homes, and flood-

ing, which destroyed 10,000 farms, 5,000 head of cattle and Maputo's water supply.

50 Another anomaly in U.S.-Mozambican relations emerged in 1985 when the Reagan administration presented a bill to Congress providing $15 million in economic aid to FRELIMO. At the same time, conservative Congressional Republicans presented a bill offering $5 million to RENAMO. It may have been the only time in congressional history when bills supporting two sides in a civil war were debated at the same time. Congress resolved the contradiction by voting down both measures.

51 Khadaglia, *Allies in Adversity*, p. 191.

52 *Ibid.*

53 Cited in Vines, *Terrorism*, p. 24.

54 Revealing the contradictions within the South African establishment, the military men specifically instructed RENAMO to attack both the Cabora Bassa dam and pylons that delivered its electricity to South Africa. This at a time when South African industrial leaders were expressing concern about a likely energy shortage in the wake of international oil sanctions against the apartheid regime.

55 Hanlon, Joseph, *Who Calls the Shots?*, p. 3.

56 *Ibid.*

57 Meldrum, Andrew, "The American Connection" in *Africa Report*, September–October 1990, p. 57.

58 Harding, *Fate of Africa*, p. 60.

59 Cited in Khadaglia, *Allies in Adversity*, pp. 161–162.

60 Cited, *ibid.*, p. 165.

61 The controversy over Machel's death in an October 1986 plane crash has never been resolved. One school of thought argues that he was assassinated by South Africa, which, they say, had sent out decoy beacons to his Soviet-piloted aircraft, causing it to hit a mountain in northern South Africa. Pretoria, of course, denied any involvement in the crash. The evidence both for and against the assassination theory is laid out in Chan, Stephen, *Exporting Apartheid: Foreign Policies in Southern Africa, 1978–1988* (New York: St. Martin's Press, 1990), pp. 52–54 and Magaia, *Dumba Nengue*, pp. 112–113.

62 Ayisi, Ruth Ansah, "The Path to Privatization" in *Africa Report*, January–February 1992, pp. 30–31.

63 Hume, Cameron, *Ending Mozambique's War: The Role of Mediation and Good Offices* (Washington: United States Institute of Peace Press, 1994), p. 74.

64 Ohlson, Thomas and Stedman, Stephen John, *The New Is Not Yet Born: Conflict Resolution in Southern Africa* (Washington: Brookings Institution, 1994), p. 114.

65 *Ibid.*, p. 115.

....

4

REBEL FORCES

In my language, we have a saying: A guest is like a cloud, it passes on, but I am not a guest and I am here to stay.
      —UNITA President Jonas Savimbi

What greed, what promises, what drugs could transform children of the same womb into destroyers, "brain-smashers," people who could set fire to their own brothers and sisters?
      —FRELIMO organizer Lina Magaia

ANGOLA

UNITA

Origins and development

Conceived in 1964 at a hotel in the Swiss Alps, the Union for the Total Independence of Angola (UNITA) was the product of founder Jonas Savimbi's frustration and ambition. The acronym was chosen with care. "It symbolised the unity we believed was necessary among all Angola's peoples," Savimbi later explained, "if we were to have any hope of defeating the Portuguese."[1] Indeed, among Savimbi's disappointments with Holden Roberto's National Front for the Liberation of Angola (FNLA), which he had joined in 1961 and served as foreign minister, was its parochialism. "Roberto," notes historian William Minter,

> had little inclination towards power-sharing, and little understanding of Angola beyond the Kikongo-speaking area of the north. Angolans from other parts of the country in the UPA [later FNLA] leadership found themselves sidelined, and unity efforts with other groups repeatedly capsized on Roberto's intransigence.[2]

Savimbi was also irritated by the organization's unwillingness to commit itself to a permanent presence in Angola and establish closer ties with the peasantry.

Nor was the Popular Movement for the Liberation of Angola (MPLA) to Savimbi's liking. If anything, he felt it was less effective than the FNLA. "The MPLA had only thirty men there," said Savimbi of the organization's Congo-Brazzaville base near Cabinda, and between five and ten of them might go into Cabinda at a time. They might ambush a Portuguese car and then run back immediately to Doilise [the base]: they never stayed to mobilise the people. Though the FNLA was disorganised and Roberto was politically inarticulate, it was clear to me that the FNLA was doing more than the MPLA.[3]

While conceived in 1964, UNITA was officially born in 1966 at a congress of 67 local chieftains and other delegates held in the southeastern Angolan town of Muangai. A central committee was chosen, and a constitution, largely written by Savimbi, was ratified. Its preamble announced UNITA's mission to educate "all Angolans living outside the country to the idea that real independence for Angola will only be achieved through armed struggle waged against the Portuguese colonial power inside the country."[4] At the end of the year, UNITA launched its first attack, a Savimbi-led raid on a timber camp and Portuguese garrison at nearby Cassamba. "It was a disaster," Savimbi said later, admitting better training was needed.[5] In 1968, UNITA established its headquarters and several training camps in the Lungue Bungu River valley east of the central highlands.

In the late 1960s, the MPLA also moved into southeastern Angola. While both organizations engaged Portuguese forces, minor clashes between the two erupted along the eastern reaches of UNITA territory close to the Zambian border. "It seems that as early as 1967–68," writes Minter,

UNITA clashes with the MPLA were at least as common as its confrontations with Portuguese troops. None of the published sources gives much detail on these clashes, but it is clear that each movement regarded the east as its rightful zone of operations.[6]

Eastern Angola was dominated by none of the colony's three major ethnic groups and was therefore an important region for each organization to demonstrate its cross-ethnic strength. Both organizations remained hostile to each other through much of the colonial war period. The MPLA was angry at Savimbi for turning down its offer to join it in 1964. As for Savimbi, one American diplomat noted, he "showed much more hostility toward other rebel groups in Angola than he did against the Portuguese."[7]

By early 1969, Savimbi decided his newly trained guerrillas were ready to engage the Portuguese again and sent a battalion to attack a Portuguese military convoy north of the Benguela railway. While this cohort was away from camp, one of UNITA's generals, Samuel Chivala, and 150 of his men deserted to the FNLA after a surprise attack on its camp by MPLA guerrillas. Other bad news filtered in to Savimbi that winter and spring. Outgunned and outmanned, numerous guerrillas at small bases throughout UNITA territory were taking up Portuguese offers of amnesty. Savimbi then made arms capture the priority of every mission and, by the end of the year, had stopped the hemorrhaging of troops.

The early 1970s were a pivotal time for UNITA. First, Savimbi felt confident enough to transform some of his guerrilla units into larger 300-man battalions armed for conventional warfare and led by the so-called "black Chinese," the dozen or so guerrillas who, with Savimbi, had received military and political training in the People's Republic of China in the mid-1960s. Throughout 1970, UNITA began engaging Portuguese forces on a larger scale. In 1972, Portugal counterattacked. Its last major offensive of the colonial war, code-named Operation Attila, devastated MPLA and, to a lesser extent, UNITA forces in eastern Angola, using defoliants, napalm and other "scorched earth" tactics.[8] The attacks finished the MPLA in eastern Angola and led to unity talks between the MPLA and the FNLA. While these negotiations came to nothing, they increased the sense of isolation of UNITA, now alone in southern and eastern Angola.

It was around this time that the so-called Operation Timber, or secret truce between UNITA and Portuguese forces, was put into effect. Documents later released by the French magazine *AfriqueAsie* reveal contacts between UNITA and Portugal's secret police, via colonial timber merchants in southern Angola. In one of the documents, a Portuguese agent comments that UNITA is ripe for a deal since its "strategy is directly [sic] solely for survival."[9] Operation Timber's intent was to maintain the status quo in southern Angola, leaving UNITA in control of isolated areas in return for its stopping attacks on the Portuguese. According to Minter,

> The Operation Timber connection gave Savimbi a head start on the political maneuvering following the Portuguese coup [in April 1974]. For the next four months, UNITA, unlike the FNLA or MPLA, would be permitted to operate openly in Angola.[10]

The independence war, covered extensively in chapter 2, need not be reexamined here, except as it pertains to the all-important relationship UNITA established with South Africa and the United States during this period. Without a superpower or regional patron of his own, Savimbi worried he would be left out of any military or negotiated settlement of Angola's future. In desperation, he approached any party that would hear him out. He got an offer from Zaire's Mobutu Sese Seko and Zambia's Kenneth Kaunda. Both Zaire and Zambia were concerned about the MPLA's Marxist rhetoric and its control of the crucial Benguela railway, both countries' main outlet to the Atlantic. If Savimbi could gain control of the 700-mile railway by independence day (November 11, 1975), they would support him and might even recognize him as the legitimate authority in Angola.

To accomplish this end, both presidents put Savimbi in touch with American and South African officials, though both Mobutu and Kaunda denied having contacts with Pretoria. While these black African intermediaries facilitated "deniability" of U.S.–South Africa–UNITA contacts by allowing arms transshipments through their countries, "cooperation was extensive."[11] CIA agents were in regular contact with their counterparts in South Africa and Zaire. And as soon as South African Defense Forces invaded Angola in late 1975, they began training some 2,000 UNITA guerrillas in the use of American-supplied arms.

The MPLA/Cuban victory over South Africa, and Pretoria's subsequent withdrawal from Angola, led to renewed isolation for Savimbi. Embittered by what he saw as an American betrayal, that is, Congress' decision to cut off all funding, Savimbi vowed to fight on. He led several hundred guerrillas and their families on the so-called "long march," a circuitous 2,000-mile retreat into the southern Angolan bush, where they began to retrain and regroup.[12] Hard-liner P. W. Botha's 1978 ascension to power in South Africa, however, allowed for a renewed relationship between Pretoria and UNITA.

All through the 1980s, South Africa offered massive aid to UNITA, and the two forces frequently coordinated their attacks. As historian Joseph Hanlon noted in 1986, "It is obvious that the chaos in Angola, and UNITA's position today, is due largely to South African and other foreign involvement [largely right-wing groups in Europe and the United States]." Nevertheless, he adds, "that is not the entire story."[13] Though armed by South Africa, UNITA was a formidable military force of its own. It had also established such a solid base of support among the peasantry in its "liberated areas" in Ovimbunduland that even Angolan President José Eduardo dos Santos was forced to admit it. "There are those who are misled into staying in the bush," he complained in 1984, "either because they believe in certain family or tribal ties with some UNITA elements, or because they do not yet understand the presence in our country of the Cuban internationalists."[14]

Despite the major battles between UNITA/South African and MPLA/Cuban forces in the late 1980s, the stalemate in Angola remained largely unchanged except for two things. Following assaults by the MPLA in 1989 and 1990, UNITA returned to its earlier more mobile strategy, shifting large numbers of forces to the north, thereby flanking the government and putting direct pressure on Luanda. Equally important, UNITA found a powerful new patron in the United States.

In 1986, the Clark amendment banning aid to Angola was repealed by Congress, opening up a new source of aid to UNITA. The following year, Reagan invited Savimbi to the White House where "he was received like a head of state" and lionized by conservatives as a "freedom fighter."[15] While liberal members of Congress complained that the Reagan administration was emphasizing military solutions over negotiations in Angola, they were unable to stop the first of many aid packages to UNITA, averaging in the tens of millions of dollars each year. This aid would prove crucial after South Africa agreed to back out of Angola and Namibia in 1988–89 and especially after the reform movement in South Africa of the early 1990s began to hem in the military/security establishment's ability to finance and manage covert operations abroad.[16]

Membership

Savimbi UNITA, as most students of the movement agree, is largely a manifestation of Savimbi—his personality, his character and his ideas. But who is Savimbi? His biographer Fred Bridgland once lionized him as a masterful tactician and speaker, an Angolan patriot of deep convictions, and, as the subtitle of his biography notes, "a key to Africa."[17] Others see a different Savimbi. "The image of Jonas Savimbi as a 'freedom fighter' deserving of U.S. support," writes media analyst Elaine Windrich, "was largely a product of the publicity efforts of the Pretoria regime and American right-wing pressure groups that had unique access to the Reagan/Bush White House."[18]

At one time or another in his 35-year career as a guerrilla leader, Savimbi has received praise from Mao Tse-tung and Ronald Reagan, Che Guevara and Jesse Helms. *Washington Post* reporter Leon Dash, who spent a good deal of time with Savimbi in the 1970s and 1980s, described him as "an enigma,

> a man on whom many labels can stick—brilliant, charismatic, affable, unyielding, forgiving, temporizing, Machiavellian, opportunistic, lying, nationalistic, Marxist, Maoist, pro-Western and socialist.[19]

It is not that the truth lies somewhere in the middle of all these opinions, but that it lies everywhere. Whatever he appeared to be, Savimbi is an ideological chameleon, a masterful manipulator of public relations, and above all else a political survivor.

He was born in 1934 to an Ovimbundu *assimilado* father and an African-American missionary mother. The two had met at a Protestant school, and evangelical Christianity would help shape their son's character, outlook and career. Savimbi's family nurtured in him a strong sense of personal ambition and Angolan nationalism; his grandfather had fought in one of the last nineteenth-century rebellions against the Portuguese. Hoping to earn a doctorate in political science, Savimbi was one of the few Angolans to obtain an education in Europe, though his growing involvement in anticolonial politics stopped him short of his degree.[20] Upon returning to Angola in the late 1950s, Savimbi joined the UPA (later the FNLA), but had a falling out with them in 1964.

That break offers a key to both the limits and expansiveness of Savimbi's thinking. First, he was deeply disappointed with the ethnic politics of the FNLA. He rightfully saw its parochialism as a major impediment to uniting Angolans against the Portuguese and as a force for promoting an Angolan nationalism that would hold the country together after independence. Yet, at the same time, Savimbi believed that the Ovimbundus needed an organization of their own and, as the largest ethnic group, deserved to lead the revolution and be a senior partner in any governing coalition that followed.

In addition, Savimbi was deeply disappointed by the FNLA's failure to establish bases inside Angola. As a disciple of the guerrilla warfare ideas of Mao, Savimbi believed that a successful anticolonial movement must coexist with the peasantry. "Jonas Savimbi," writes historian John Marcum,

> was the first Angolan leader to return from exile to lead his movement from inside, in conformity with UNITA doctrine which criticised over-reliance on outside help and stressed the need to mobilise for a people's war inside Angola.[21]

While Savimbi would never be accused of distancing himself physically from the struggle in Angola, either before or after independence, his willingness to accept aid from and cooperate with dictators like Mobutu, superpowers like the U.S. and China, and even the pariah regime in Pretoria was a source of notoriety. Savimbi, of course, always justified these alliances as a reaction to his opponent's relations with the Soviet bloc, but many scholars have questioned whether UNITA could have even survived without foreign support.

Savimbi's ideas about the necessity of close guerrilla-peasant relations were meant to convey more than merely a strategy for winning the war against Portugal and the MPLA. It was also about developing a relationship of mutual trust and respect that would serve the movement if and when it took power. Savimbi required that all of his field commanders receive political as well as military training. According to Bridgland, Savimbi believed that "an undisciplined army was a threat to the peasantry." Bridgland quotes Savimbi to the effect that without a sense of responsibility,

> [the guerrillas] would not be working for the people, but rather the people would be working for them. If the man who has the gun in his hand does not understand why he has the gun, he is going to abuse the power of the gun against the people.[22]

Yet all during the fierce warfare of the 1980s, human rights organizations, as well as the UN, continually singled out UNITA for the most egregious human rights violations, including massacres of peasants, forced labor, indiscriminate laying of antipersonnel mines, forced recruitment of soldiers and, perhaps most disturbingly, the use of famine (that is, denying relief aid) as a weapon of war.

The discrepancies in Savimbi's history extend to his relationships with foreign leaders. As a young man, Savimbi appeared deeply moved by the radical rhetoric and ideals of both the Cuban and Chinese revolutions.[23] Yet Savimbi began espousing a virulent anticommunist message during the war of independence. Of course, he did find himself fighting Cuban forces, and ideological change can be as much a sign of political growth (or reaction) as opportunism. Anticommunism was a message that he knew would appeal to his stridently anticommunist patrons in South Africa and, later, the Reagan White House. Finally, the consistency with which Savimbi has been inconsistent is revealing in and of itself. During the ebbing of the Cold War and under U.S. pressure to commit to negotiations in the late 1980s and early 1990s, Savimbi metamorphosed, this time from anticommunist fighter to pro-democracy advocate. More recently, he has changed his tune again, from support of elections and multiparty democracy to the need for a one-party government of national unity.

According to virtually everyone who has seen Savimbi in action, he is a masterful stump speaker, at least when it comes to inspiring his own troops. Well versed in classical Ovimbundu rhetoric, a tradition rich in proverb and allegory, Savimbi could apparently hold his guerrillas captivated for hours with speeches that mixed dashes of anticommunism, Angolan nationalism, appeals to Ovimbundu pride, and claims to his own gifts as a leader and his destiny as the future president of Angola. Savimbi dressed and played the part as well. Ovimbundu tradition dictates that a leader conduct himself with a mix of imperiousness and concern, that he display camaraderie with his men and yet hold himself above them, that he share their suffering during hard times but that he also receive the best of everything when times are good.

Savimbi, says Bridgland, was a true "charismatic" leader, both in the modern demagogic and traditional tribal chieftain senses.[24] That is to say, he sustained his followers' loyalty with both a political and personal appeal. He spoke about improving their standard of living and getting them the power, respect and wealth they deserved. He also emphasized that they would get these things if they believed strongly enough in him as their leader. In short, Savimbi has always displayed to his men and to outsiders an almost messianic determination. Long before he had even formed UNITA, he appeared to know his destiny. On a visit to the U.S. embassy in Switzerland in the late 1950s, he presented himself as the "future president of Angola." He was, to borrow political scientist Anthony Pereira's term, an "ethno-populist."[25]

Guerrillas Despite a number of desertions in the 1960s, usually due to a lack of weapons or training, UNITA has been largely free of divisions and dissidence in its 30-year history, or, at least, that has been the image presented to the outside world. The organization's unity has always been based on a mix of "fanatical" loyalty—especially among the upper echelon officers, who have been with the organization since its early days and stuck with it through the troubled times of the South African retreat and "long march" of the mid-1970s—and fear.[26]

Savimbi, notes Minter, has displayed an "intense personal hostility to those he saw as his chief rivals."[27] Both supporters and observers of UNITA justice in action report numerous cases of public executions of officers and aides, including that of Tito Chingunji, one of Savimbi's most trusted confidants, in the early 1990s for supposedly challenging Savimbi's commitment to the negotiation process. Chingunji's murder became a cause célèbre among those in Washington trying to cut off aid to UNITA. But, as Minter says, Savimbi's relationship with his officers is better reflected in the case of UNITA vice president Jermias Chitunda, killed by MPLA followers in Luanda in the post-election violence of November 1992.

> Chitunda, a loyal follower of Jonas Savimbi to the end, nevertheless feared for his life when rebuked by *O Mais Velho* (the "Oldest One"). Returning to Jamba [UNITA headquarters] in May, 1989, he recorded [in his diary] abject apologies for being deceived by Chingunji and rejoiced in a presidential pardon. The mix of genuine loyalty to a movement many identified with, together with fear of the consequences should they show doubt or disloyalty is an apt paradigm for the relationship between UNITA and the constituency it claimed among rank-and-file soldiers and civilians alike.[28]

This history of tight UNITA discipline should be kept in mind for the period after the 1992 elections, when Savimbi blamed out-of-control local commanders for outbreaks of violence. True, these men may have acted on their own, but they may very well have chosen to respond violently only because they believed Savimbi would approve.[29]

As for regular recruits, the record is equally mixed. Writing about UNITA in the early 1980s, Bridgland says the organization's strength came from the loyalty of its troops. "UNITA's was an unpaid volunteer army," he writes, "offering only food, comradeship and a chance to die for a particular vision of Angola."[30] Minter disagrees. After interviewing a number of former UNITA soldiers who joined between 1982 and 1989, he reported that "most . . . were taken by UNITA in attacks on government zones or abducted, and two spoke of being conscripted while living in UNITA-controlled areas."[31] Minter admits, however, that the exact proportion of volunteer to forced conscripts will probably never be determined. And, of course, a portrait of UNITA recruitment based on the eyewitness accounts of deserters is suspect to begin with. Nevertheless, Minter's findings are corroborated by numerous human rights organization studies. Among the recommendations to UNITA in Human Rights Watch's 1991 report on Angola was a request that the organization "put an end to inducting persons captured from MPLA-controlled areas."[32]

FOREIGN INVOLVEMENT

Africa

South Africa   South Africa's involvement in Angola goes back to the late colonial era. Because guerrillas of the South-West Africa People's Organization (SWAPO) crossed the Portuguese colony from their bases in Zambia, South Africa had conducted reconnaissance patrols over southern Angola since the late 1960s. In 1968, Lisbon and Pretoria signed a secret agreement allowing for the establishment of a South African command center at Cuito Cuanavale, in southwest Angola, as well as arms shipments to the Portuguese military.

Nevertheless, Pretoria's involvement was minimal and largely concerned with defending its illegal occupation of Namibia.[33] This noninterventionist policy was based on two factors. First, South Africa was confident of its position in the 1960s. Like much of the West, it did not consider the liberation movements in Angola, Mozambique or Rhodesia as serious threats. This confidence was reflected in the foreign policy of Prime Minister John Vorster's administration (1966–78). Known as the "dialogue initiative," Vorster's efforts to win over conservative black African regimes had some limited success in the late 1960s and early 1970s, but suffered a setback when the Organization of African Unity (OAU) passed a resolution in 1971 condemning the initiative as a "maneuver" intended to "divide African states and confuse public opinion in order to end the isolation of South Africa, and thus to maintain the status quo in South Africa."[34]

A bigger setback, of course, came with the collapse of the colonial regimes in Mozambique and Angola (and, in 1979–80, the end of white rule in Rhodesia) and the crumbling of the "impregnable perimeter of white redoubt" around South Africa.[35] According to John Stockwell, the CIA's Angola operations point man in 1975–76, this produced a sense of crisis in the apartheid republic and helped galvanize the military-security establishment wing of the government.[36] A hostile regime in Angola clearly represented a threat, if not to South Africa directly, then to its colony of Namibia. According to many South Africa watchers, Vorster's decision to invade Angola was less a matter of his own personal convictions and more the result of a propaganda campaign in the South African media and pressure from the military. "Despite Vorster's determination to keep his hand securely on the throttle," writes historian Daniel Spikes, "to the South African Defense Forces this war was very much their own."[37] The prime minister tried to put the best face on things. He claimed his government was simply responding to the presence of socialist bloc forces but, as Bridgland argues, most observers remain convinced that South Africa committed to the battle in southern Angola first, thus drawing in the Cubans.[38] After several months of heavy fighting, Pretoria withdrew.

Though the Angolan debacle was arguably the SADF's doing, Vorster became its political victim, especially after the 1976 Soweto uprisings, which many on the right blamed on Vorster liberalism. Following a scandal that exposed massive fraud and incompetence in Pretoria, called "Muldergate" by the South African press (after the minister involved), the Vorster wing of the ruling National Party was turned out in elections in 1978 and replaced by the hard-liners behind Defense Minister P. W. Botha.[39] The elections of 1978 did not simply lead to a rightward political shift, but to a major revamping of the South African government, eventually leading to the establishment of a powerful presidency and the creation of the State Security Council (SSC) a potent secretive agency in charge of domestic and foreign intelligence as well as covert operations.

Even before the 1978 elections, however, the military-security estab-lishment in South Africa was formulating a new approach to southern Africa. Labeled "total strategy" in a 1977 defense white paper, "it argued," say historians Thomas Ohlson and Stephen Stedman,

> for the fundamental reorganization and buildup of the white state's capacity to intervene militarily in the region. It also held that the mobilization of all available resources—economic, political, social, psychological, and mili-tary—was essential to defend South Africa at home and in the region.[40]

Officially, Pretoria justified the policy by raising the specter of com-munism, thereby linking its own defense to that of the West. But, many observers claim, the real aims and methods of "total strategy" were more invidious. Rather than heavily committing its own forces, which risked more international obloquy and increasing white protest at home, Pretoria opted for the use of surrogate armies. These were not necessarily meant to take power. Indeed, many of South Africa's business and political elites feared that a defeated MPLA (or FRELIMO) might represent a greater threat as a guerrilla movement than it did as a government. According to political scientist Stephen Chan, South Africa hoped to use UNITA (and RENAMO) to increase the economic dependency of the region on South Africa, hence the emphasis on infrastructure ruination.[41] This, the Botha administration believed, would blunt the use of international sanctions against South Africa since, it would be argued, they hurt all of southern Africa. Thus, whatever Savimbi (or Dhlakama) may have wanted for their movements, their patrons tried to steer them in a direction that served South Africa's overall strategy of economic, political and social destabilization.

There was also a racist component to destabilization. Rendering Angola and Mozambique ungovernable substantiated Pretoria's main ra-tionale for apartheid rule: that blacks cannot govern themselves or effectively run their economies. The destabilization of Angola, says Hanlon, was particularly important to Pretoria's strategy. "Just as gold paid for the industrialisation of South Africa," he wrote in 1986, so oil can for Angolan development—on a Marxist rather than a capitalist model . . . But such development requires peace, so a primary South African goal must be simple destabilisation—preventing the peace needed for development.[42]

The flurry of negotiations in the mid-1980s, including the 1984 Lusaka accords involving simultaneous pullbacks of Cuban and, South African troops, indicated a brief ascendance of the so-called "settlement" wing of the ruling government, but it was a deceptive shift. Indeed, it has been argued that simply getting Angola to negotiate with the apartheid regime was the goal of the Botha administration, while fulfilling the terms of the agreement was incidental. Either way, further destabilization efforts in the wake of Lusaka, as well as increasing township violence, led to a further consolidation of the South African right's approach, culminating in the great land battles of Mavinga and Cuito in 1987–88.

South Africa's defeat in those battles was the primary reason, say most scholars, that led Pretoria to negotiate and sign the New York accords calling for Cuban withdrawal from Angola and South African decolonization of Namibia. In a larger sense, it can be argued that the Angola defeat helped usher in the reforms of the F. W. de Klerk administration after 1989. The defeat in Angola was both a blow to white South Africa's confidence and to the hegemony of the SSC in determining foreign policy.

Since its final withdrawal from Namibia in 1990, South Africa's role in Angola has been minimized for several reasons. First, Savimbi's ability to finance his own operations with smuggled diamonds (traded with South Africa's Anglo-American conglomerate) lessened the need for South African aid. Second, whatever radical economic agenda the MPLA had for Angola was being effectively undermined by IMF restrictions. Finally, of course, the ANC was able to effectively pressure the de Klerk administration to rein in the military by the early 1990s, though Luanda complained of arms shipments to Savimbi as late as 1993. Needless to say, the Mandela administration has not aided UNITA.[43]

Zaire and Zambia   As noted in chapter 2, the Congo (now Zaire) underwent a bloody civil war after Belgium's sudden retreat from its former colony in 1960. With CIA help, Joseph Mobutu (now Mobutu Sese Seko), a right-wing officer, murdered the radical Patrice Lumumba and took power in Leopoldville (now Kinshasa) in 1961. These events helped precipitate Angola's own war of liberation against the Portuguese, which Mobutu aided through his support of Holden Roberto's FNLA, which was headquartered in the Zairian capital.

Mobutu had several reasons for aiding the FNLA against the MPLA. First, Roberto's politics were more akin to Mobutu's and the two shared longstanding personal and family relations. Second, Mobutu had designs on the coffee and diamond districts of northern Angola and felt Zairian involvement in their exploitation could be better facilitated with Roberto in power. And finally there was the Katangese issue. In the 1960s, the left-wing Moise Tshombe led several thousand guerrillas in an armed struggle to establish an independent republic of the Katangese people in the copper-rich Zairian province of Shaba. With French and Belgian help, Mobutu crushed the rebellion, and the guerrillas filtered into Angola. When the MPLA began recruiting Katangese to fight against FNLA/Zairian forces, Mobutu was outraged.

Mobutu did more than simply send his troops into Angola to support the FNLA. He also allowed the CIA to use the Kinshasa airport as its main transport link to Roberto, and he solicited South African help for the FNLA and UNITA. By supporting the FNLA, of course, Mobutu had gambled on a loser and was eventually forced, grudgingly, to recognize the MPLA government in Angola, especially since it controlled his railroad access to the Atlantic. Those relations were seriously strained when the Katangese invaded Shaba in the late 1970s and were again driven out by French and Zairian forces. Though maintaining cool but official relations with Luanda, Mobutu supported UNITA throughout the 1980s. According to Bridgland, Zaire permitted French advisers to train UNITA guerrillas on its territory since at least 1983.[44]

After the U.S. Congress's repeal of the ban on aid to UNITA in 1986, Zairian support came into the open. Joint U.S./Zairian military exercises in the late 1980s, says journalist Victoria Brittain, were partially conducted to supply UNITA with arms.[45] And during his offensives in the post–South African phase of the war, Savimbi made it a point to secure territory in northern Angola in order to assure a steady supply of U.S. arms from Zaire. It is unclear if there has been any Zairian support for UNITA since the return to war following the 1992 elections. However, Zairian support was largely confined to serving as a conduit for U.S. arms from the 1975–76 war of independence on. With the U.S. having cut off military shipments to UNITA and recognized the MPLA government, it is probable that Zairian aid to UNITA has been minimal in recent years.

Unlike Mobutu, who is largely a U.S. creation, former Zambian President Kenneth Kaunda (from 1964 to 1991) was a legitimate black African nationalist, albeit an ideologically conservative one. Thus, Zambia's relationship with the opposition in Angola has been far more ambivalent than Zaire's.[46] Bordering Angola to its east, Zambia became a launching point for raids by both the MPLA and UNITA during the colonial war. After Portugal's offensive in eastern Angola in 1972, the Zambian wing of the MPLA descended into internecine fighting on Zambian soil. This exasperated Kaunda and led to a falling-out between him and MPLA head Agostinho Neto.

Since Portugal's retreat from Angola, Zambia's main concern has been the trans-Angolan railway, which connects Zambia to the Atlantic.

With the railway traversing UNITA's home territory, Kaunda naturally leaned towards Savimbi, who had the additional advantage of sharing Kaunda's conservative peasant-based politics. Thus, during the war of independence, Kaunda hinted to Savimbi that if he could control the Benguela railway from one end to the other, Zambia might officially recognize his organization as the legitimate government in Angola. Kaunda even urged the South Africans to drive all the way to Luanda and install a UNITA government. In turn, the Vorster administration made Zambia the linchpin of its African détente initiative, but Kaunda maintained his distance.

While Zambia was one of the last African countries to recognize the MPLA government, and even fought against the idea at the Organization of African Unity's 1976 emergency session, it has enjoyed relatively warm relations with Luanda since. In 1984, it sponsored talks that led to the Lusaka accords calling for the mutual pullback of South African and Cuban forces. A decade later, it played host to a new round of talks aimed at ending the postelection civil war in Angola.

International

The United States The foreign policies of the U.S. and South Africa in the post–World War II era bear some revealing parallels. First, both countries subscribed to their own domino theories: Washington nervously eyed the spread of communism while Pretoria anxiously watched the tide of black rule. During the 1960s and early 1970s, both countries applied a mix of force and détente to further their foreign policy goals, only to watch that approach succumb to spectacular failures during the mid-1970s: South Africa in Angola and the U.S. in Southeast Asia. Both then took a sharp turn to the right, funding surrogate forces to roll back enemy gains but applying overwhelming forces of their own when necessary.

With the end of the Cold War, the makers of foreign policy in both countries suddenly found themselves without an appropriately threatening ideological enemy against which they could identify themselves and justify the extraordinary commitment of resources and national will needed to fight. And as far as Angola was concerned, both Washington and Pretoria arguably got what they wanted: a country so devastated by war that it could not challenge the status quo in southern Africa. The main difference between the United States and apartheid South Africa, however, is that one survived to enjoy the fruits of its success and the other didn't.

Pretoria's and Washington's policies toward Angola, of course, influenced each other, though scholars continue to debate the degree of that influence as well as the direction in which it tended to flow. Some say that South Africa cleverly drew Washington along, by presenting itself as a bulwark of Western interests in southern Africa and forcing the U.S. to side with a regime whose domestic policies it officially deplored. "It appears that the United States has fallen into a trap dug by South Africa," Hanlon wrote in 1986. "[The war in Angola] is part of Pretoria's wider defence of apartheid, and seems designed particularly to embroil the United States."[47]

Others argue that U.S. and South African interests coincided so neatly in southern Africa that cajoling by one side or the other was unnecessary. According to political scientist Ann Seidman, constructive engagement, the Reagan administration's policy of including South Africa's security requirements in its overall approach to southern Africa, "involved stabilizing the region to give South Africa time to accommodate the forces pressing for change within a framework consistent with U.S. interests."[48]

Still others, such as Donald McHenry, Jimmy Carter's ambassador to the UN and John Stockwell, the CIA's point man in Angola during the independence war, say the U.S. actually pushed the situation further than its allies in Pretoria and clients in Angola wanted to go. McHenry argued that South Africa was prepared to unilaterally retreat from Namibia in 1981, when the U.S. convinced it to stay on in order to further the "linkage" component of constructive engagement, wherein a quid pro quo involving South Africa's withdrawal from Namibia would be tied to a Cuban pullout from Angola, Washington's main priority in Angola.[49] And according to Stockwell, the CIA dissuaded Savimbi from seeking a negotiated settlement with the MPLA in 1975, telling him, "We wanted no 'soft' allies in our war against the MPLA."[50]

Not surprisingly, those involved in U.S. policy toward southern Africa during the Reagan administration advance a more nuanced but somewhat self-serving portrayal of U.S.–South African–Angolan relations. Chester Crocker, undersecretary of state for African affairs and author of the constructive engagement policy, depicts a State Department torn between right-wingers in South Africa and the U.S., trying to force American support for some of the most egregious acts of aggression by Pretoria, and the American antiapartheid left, who argued that "the way to deal with a sick society and a rattled and divided regime [i.e., South Africa] was to strike a virile pose and increase their economic and political isolation."[51]

There is a general consensus, however, about two aspects of the U.S. position concerning southern Africa. First, there were its many contradictions. The U.S. was indeed in a strange position vis-à-vis South Africa and Angola during the 1980s. On the one hand, the U.S. funded UNITA to the tune of tens of millions of dollars annually and offered a green—or, at least, amber—light to South Africa's foreign policymakers. On the other, Gulf Oil, through its operations in Cabinda, indirectly funded the MPLA military with several hundred millions in revenue each year. Thus, at one point in the 1980s, a politically surrealistic tableau emerged wherein Cuban troops were protecting an American oil company's investments against U.S.-funded rebel attacks.

Second, there was the anticommunist ideology that smoothed over these contradictions. For all the talk of Soviet access to the vital sea lanes around the Cape of Good Hope, specific strategic interests have never really been the engine of U.S. policy toward Angola. The fact that Angola became a battleground in the Cold War was incidental to the country itself. That is to say, Angola was a convenient place to apply America's containment doctrine of the 1960s and 1970s. Secretary of State Henry Kissinger, who never considered Angola part of America's strategic perimeter, explained what was at stake. "America's *modest* direct strategic and economic interests in Angola are not the central issue," he testified to Congress in opposition to the ban on military aid to UNITA in early 1976. "The question is whether America still maintains the resolve to act responsibly as a great power."[52] To which State Department consultant Michael Clough adds, "If the Soviet factor had not been present, Kissinger and the rest of the foreign policy establishment would not have cared which party came to power in Luanda."[53]

During the height of U.S. involvement in the late 1980s, a new rule applied: communist rollback. Savimbi understood this and, accordingly, reinvented himself successfully as an anticommunist guerrilla leader and "freedom fighter." Naturally, there was infighting in the Reagan administration about the appropriate balance of pressure the U.S. should apply. Far-right ideologues in the administration, such as National Security Council staffer Constantine Menges, advocated an all-stick approach to force Gulf (and later Chevron) out of Angola and increase the level of aid to UNITA.[54] Meanwhile, the self-proclaimed moderates like Crocker tried to find a negotiated way of putting Savimbi in power, or at least getting him a share of power, in Luanda. But as Hanlon points out, their argument, that more aid to UNITA would both force Luanda to the negotiating table and help put Savimbi in a powerful enough position that he would be encouraged to talk, proved mistaken. "Events . . . indicated that aid to UNITA," he noted, "led to an escalation of war."[55]

As noted above, the extent to which U.S. and South African interests and goals in Angola coincided is a subject of much debate. Whether it is true, as some observers note, that both countries sought the destabilization of Angola, it is also clear that the two had different priorities. South Africa, of course, sought the political and military neutralization of the country. The Reagan administration wanted the Cubans out. On one occasion, Crocker expressed his frustration with the South Africans, telling them that their aggression only made Luanda more likely to cling to Castro. But generally, it was a case of an enemy's enemy being a friend. As long as South Africa was fighting Cuban troops and their Angolan allies, Washington and Pretoria saw eye to eye.

The denouement of the Cold War, however, changed everything, if only gradually. Since its inception, the Reagan administration had argued for a South African–Namibian/Cuban-Angolan linkage agreement, and by 1988 that goal was in sight. According to Brittain, the New York accords met the Reagan administration's expectations and "the South Africans found themselves isolated from the U.S. delegation for the first time."[56] With the Cuban threat gone, the Reagan/Bush administration had no need to maintain its unofficial and very unpopular alliance with South Africa.[57] South Africa's new isolation from the U.S. was a major factor, say most experts, leading to its decision to pull out of both Angola and Namibia.

And yet, with Cuban troops gone and the Soviet Union in increasing disarray, the Bush administration maintained both a substantial flow of arms to UNITA and a policy of nonrecognition toward the MPLA government. At the same time, the U.S. participated in the Bicesse talks, calling for a negotiated settlement of the MPLA/UNITA conflict and national elections, and served as a guarantor of their implementation. Whether continuing aid to UNITA under Bush was simply a case of Cold War inertia or a product of Bush's long-standing relationship with Savimbi is hard to know. Officially, the Bush administration argued that continuing military pressure on Luanda was the only way to make sure it negotiated in good faith.

The September 1992 elections in Angola and the November ones in the U.S. changed everything once again. Savimbi, of course, lost and then led his forces back to war. According to the *Economist*, he did so in expectation of renewed U.S. funding.[58] But the incoming Clinton administration expressed outrage over Savimbi's postelection behavior and responded to it with an official recognition of the MPLA government in Luanda, almost 17 years after it had come into power. Yet the Clinton White House was not so much interested in cultivating a new relationship with Angola as it was in putting the whole episode behind it. With the Cold War officially over and South Africa firmly on the road to reform, southern Africa (and Africa generally) returned to its 1960s-era place on the list of U.S. foreign policy priorities—that is, near the bottom.

Portugal and Western Europe Since its departure at the end of 1975, Portugal has had limited involvement with its former colony. Nevertheless, while Lisbon turned its attention to integrating into the European community (Portugal achieved full membership in 1982), there remained talk of establishing an international Lusophone community akin to the British Commonwealth. To that end, Portugal has provided some aid to the MPLA government but has more often lent itself to peace efforts, notably the Bicesse accords of 1991, as well as assisting in their implementation.

Much of the rest of Western Europe has followed the U.S. lead in Angola. In the late 1970s, the so-called Contact Group, consisting of England, France, Germany and the United States, was formed to coordinate aid and peace initiatives in southern Africa. While Germany and England continued to work with the U.S. through much of the 1980s, France withdrew from the group in 1983, largely over Paris' contention that the U.S. was placing too much emphasis on a military solution.

People's Republic of China   If politics make strange bedfellows, then Angolan politics have made for positively bizarre ones. Still, the alliance between the FNLA (and/or UNITA), the U.S., South Africa, Zaire and China did have a common thread, anti-Sovietism, which helps to explain why Chinese arms were being shipped on U.S. planes to Angola via South Africa in the mid-1970s.

China's involvement in Angola goes back to the late colonial period, when it brought Savimbi and several UNITA leaders to Beijing for training. But during the war of independence, China's main ally in Africa, Tanzania's Julius Nyerere, convinced Beijing to back Roberto's FNLA as the most likely candidate to stop the installation of the pro-Soviet MPLA. There were, nonetheless, positive reasons for Beijing's support of UNITA and the FNLA as well. Both claimed to be peasant-based organizations and were highly critical of the urban intellectualism of the MPLA. This appealed to a Chinese government that had come to power as the result of a peasant-based revolution. But as historian Steven Jackson points out, China's leaders, having led a revolution where race was not a significant factor, were largely ignorant of the racism that underlay the FNLA's and UNITA's anti-elitist, anti-MPLA, anti-mestizo appeal.[59]

After the FNLA collapsed in late 1975, China briefly backed UNITA and then an anti-Soviet faction of the MPLA. Eventually, the sheer scale of the war in Angola worried Beijing and it pulled out in the late 1970s, never to return as an arms supplier. Gradually, as Chinese-Soviet relations improved in the 1980s, so did those between Beijing and Luanda.

MOZAMBIQUE

RENAMO[60]

Membership

Leaders   RENAMO has had two leaders in its 20-year history, and neither has been of the stature of a Jonas Savimbi. Andre Matsangaissa, RENAMO's head from 1976 until his murder by government forces in 1979, was a former FRELIMO commander who either escaped or was rescued from one of FRELIMO's "camps for mental decolonization," where he had been imprisoned for theft. Not much is known about Matsangaissa's role as head of RENAMO, and it is arguable that he served largely as a figurehead, with the real power in the organization belonging to a former Portuguese agent named Orlando Cristina, who served as RENAMO's first general secretary. Indeed, it was Cristina who served as liaison between Rhodesian security officials and RENAMO forces in the field. "It is the Rhodesians who pay my wages and my upkeep here [Rhodesia] as well as costs for those taken inside Mozambique," he wrote to a FRELIMO defector in the late 1970s. "Without this support we would all be sitting in cafes in Lisbon, dreaming of unrealistic battles."[61]

After South Africa took control of RENAMO in 1980, Cristina moved his offices from Salisbury (Rhodesia's capital, now Harare) to Pretoria. The South Africans wanted to create a political leadership for RENAMO in order to lend the organization some legitimacy. To that end, they sent Cristina to Europe and black Africa to recruit black Mozambicans who had fled FRELIMO rule at independence or defected since. There were many such disgruntled Mozambicans, but few wanted to ally themselves with the apartheid regime. Mostly, Cristina ended up recruiting former Portuguese agents like himself who, in political scientist John Saul's words, represented "the dregs of Portugal's former colonial security apparatus."[62] In 1983, Cristina was murdered at a South African air base under mysterious circumstances. It is rumored he was shot by FRELIMO agents posing as defectors.

As for Matsangaissa, though he may have largely been a figurehead in life, he became something more in death. RENAMO propaganda often included the so-called "Matsangaissa myth," which says that his spirit lives on and protects RENAMO guerrillas, whom Mozambican peasants usually refer to as *matsangas*. His death also triggered a major power struggle in RENAMO. Though Dhlakama was Matsangaissa's handpicked successor, he was unpopular with the Rhodesians. After the "mysterious disappearance" of several challengers, Rhodesia tried to divide RENAMO into two commands, but the idea failed after Dhlakama's forces emerged victorious from a gunfight at RENAMO's main base in Rhodesia.[63] Despite several challenges, the most serious following the signing of the South African–Mozambican Nkomati accords in 1984, Dhlakama has ruled ever since.

Unlike FRELIMO leaders Samora Machel and Joaquim Chissano, or, for that matter, UNITA's Savimbi, Dhlakama is poorly educated and had never traveled outside southern Africa before he became head of RENAMO. According to U.S. diplomat Cameron Hume, who mediated at the Rome talks between RENAMO and FRELIMO, "[Dhlakama] lacked the political polish that marked FRELIMO's leadership." And, he adds, "other RENAMO leaders . . . [also] came from a rural background and lacked the education advantages of the government's leaders."[64] This fact helps explain both RENAMO's inability to establish effective public relations abroad and its hesitancy in negotiations. According to Hume, Dhlakama and other RENAMO negotiators lived in constant fear that they were at a disadvantage in talks where the cosmopolitan FRELIMO negotiators could converse with the mediators and the press in European languages.[65]

Guerrillas On paper, Dhlakama headed an organization with a well-established political structure, including a national council that determined policy and strategy. In reality, however, RENAMO was a strictly military operation, though it rarely engaged in major confrontations with FRE-LIMO's army, preferring instead to operate in battalions of about 250 men. While, at first glance, this would imply a loose structure with a large degree of initiative given to commanders and guerrillas in the field, RENAMO was, in fact, a rather tightly run organization. Every unit was outfitted with sophisticated radio equipment, provided by South Africa and private right-wing supporters in the West, which allowed them to keep in touch with the main RENAMO base at Gorongosa (Casa Banana) in central Mozambique.

According to most observers, including Human Rights Watch/Africa, RENAMO has largely recruited its guerrillas by force. Hanlon describes the process.

> Armed bands would simply kidnap hundreds of young men (and women); many escaped, but those caught escaping were killed. Those who stayed were given rudimentary training, and often forced at gunpoint to kill someone, and thus made part of the band.[66]

In addition, illegal immigrants rounded up by South African police were often given the choice of jail or joining RENAMO. There were, of course, some voluntary recruits, largely young men who out of a sense of adventure or despair preferred a life of pillage and violence to one of grinding poverty. According to one study, Mozambique's poorest and least educated peasants were the ones most likely to stay with RENAMO the longest.[67] As conditions worsened due to the war, and as FRELIMO sometimes overreacted by forcing peasants into garrisoned villages and conducting recruiting dragnets, the number of RENAMO's voluntary recruits grew. Sometimes, voluntary recruits were the results of local politics. Disputes over land or with a local chief or political administrator led some peasants to join RENAMO. Nevertheless, after conducting numerous interviews with demobilized RENAMO soldiers in 1992, Human Rights Watch/Africa concluded that "forced conscription appears to be the primary form of recruitment by RENAMO . . . [with] a significant number of recruits [being] taken by RENAMO units when they [come] across them by chance in the countryside while working in their fields, fetching food, or tending animals."[68]

FOREIGN INVOLVEMENT

Africa

Rhodesia   Following the decolonization of Northern Rhodesia (now Zambia) in 1964, Southern Rhodesia's minority white population issued its Unilateral Declaration of Independence (UDI) from Britain, emerging as the second white regime on the continent. Like the South Africans, they were ejected from the British Commonwealth and the UN and became an international pariah state. Several years before the UDI, Robert Mugabe, independent Zimbabwe's first and only president, and Joshua Nkomo helped found two independent guerrilla organizations, the Zimbabwe African National Union (ZANU) and Zimbabwe African People's Union (ZAPU) respectively. Both organizations were nationalist, though ZANU was more akin to Mozambique's FRELIMO in that it advocated socialist economics and one-party politics.

With Mozambique's independence in 1975, Pretoria turned up the pressure on the white Rhodesian regime of Ian Smith. Prime Minister Vorster felt that a conservative black regime would have a more stabilizing effect on the region than a besieged white one. Pretoria even enlisted Henry Kissinger to make its case to Smith. But the white Rhodesians were unwilling to negotiate. As Chan notes, "The main obstacle was that white Rhodesia's interest was not in political stability as such, but a position from which it could exploit African nationalist divisions to increase its own leverage to defend white privileges."[69] Destabilizing neighboring Mozambique, which both allowed ZANU and ZAPU to operate bases in its territory and rigorously enforced international sanctions against Rhodesia by cutting its rail links to the sea, was also in Smith's interest.

At first, the white regime's strategy paid off. By refusing to negotiate with the guerrilla movements in Rhodesia, it paved the way for a transfer of power to the conservative black leader Bishop Abel Murozewa. Though this meant black majority rule, it also allowed the white regime to muddle the racial aspect of the conflict and put it in Cold War terms, as a confrontation between a pro-Western regime and Soviet-backed guerrillas. The strategy, of course, failed when Mugabe's ZANU won the 1980 elections. But in the year-long interim between the Lancaster House agreement that ended the Rhodesian war and the election of Mugabe, Rhodesian security personnel helped convince the South African regime, if indeed any convincing was needed, that furthering Mozambican destabilization was in its interest as well.

South Africa [70]Although South Africa has never actually invaded Mozambique, its destabilization policies have arguably had a much greater impact there than in Angola. And being geographically adjacent (they are separated by a 300-mile border), the two countries have shared a longer and more intimate history. Economically, South Africa has long dominated its neighbor. Millions of Mozambicans over the past century have worked in South African mines, and several hundred thousand continue to live there today, largely as illegal aliens. South Africa helped finance the building of southern Mozambique's railroads and, until disrupted by war and economic boycott, used them to ship about one-fifth of its exports. In colonial times, South African whites flocked to Mozambican resorts and, after independence, tens of thousands of white Mozambicans fled to South Africa.

The pre-independence relationship between Mozambique and South Africa was about more than just money. The Portuguese colony represented the eastern bastion of Pretoria's *cordon sanitaire* of white regimes that stood between it and black Africa. As the FRELIMO war of liberation in the late 1960s and early 1970s escalated, the South African military supplied Portugal with arms and advisers. In turn, Portugal tried to secure its hold over Mozambique by linking its economic fate to South Africa's. In the 1970s, Portuguese, South African and European capital financed the construction in central Mozambique of what was then the world's fifth largest dam, the Cabora Bassa, which transmitted most of its output southward, supplying the apartheid republic with about 10 percent of its electricity.

At first, South Africa responded tentatively to the new Mozambican government. On the one hand, the Vorster administration believed that it could foster a businesslike relationship with FRELIMO. In fact, Pretoria became the first government in the world to extend diplomatic relations. On the other hand, in anticipation of self-rule in Maputo, South Africa began shifting its railroad traffic away from Mozambique in 1973. By the end of the decade, total traffic was about half of what it had been at the beginning. In 1976, Pretoria also cut sharply the number of Mozambicans permitted to work in South African mines. Still, Pretoria's larger goal of creating a southern African economy at once interdependent and subservient to Pretoria's own needs was not necessarily obviated by Mozambican independence. Until the fall of the Vorster government in 1978 and the collapse of white rule in Rhodesia in 1979–80, Mozambique and South Africa enjoyed amicable, if cool, relations.

In 1980, Mozambique and eight other southern African nations established the Southern African Development Coordination Conference (known after 1992 as the South African Development Community, or SADC).[71] The general purpose of the organization was simple: to enhance regional security by lessening economic dependence on South Africa. To that end, each country took on the planning and coordination of a specific economic activity. With its critical transport system, Mozambique was assigned that sector. To Pretoria's rulers, the establishment of SADC represented a direct challenge to their own economic plans for the region. They responded with their own organization, known as the Constellation of Southern African States (CONSAS), which included the pseudo-sovereign *bantustans* of South Africa. But not even South Africa's most economically dependent neighbors, the Customs Union group of Botswana, Lesotho and Swaziland, opted to join. While scholars disagree over how seriously Pretoria took the SADC threat, given that the region's economic dependence on South Africa was not likely to diminish soon, South Africa's directives to RENAMO to specifically target railroads indicates that Pretoria understood the potential of Mozambican transport to the region's economic independence.

Still, in the early 1980s, South Africa was not sure how best to destabilize the Mozambican economy. A number of firms, including the Anglo-American-owned cashew plantations (cashews being one of Mozambique's leading exports), were ordered to divest. There was also a certain amount of petty economic sabotage whereby South African firms would delay repairs on South African-made machinery or the shipping of spare parts to Mozambique. And, of course, there were the direct raids against targets in Mozambique in January 1981 and May and October 1983. While these were largely aimed at ANC facilities in Mozambique, the sheer destructiveness of the attacks and the aerial bombings, as well as the loss of civilian lives, was meant to convey the message that support for the ANC came with a high price. The 1983 attacks, coming as they did during South African–Mozambican negotiations over noninterference in each other's internal politics, led Foreign Minister Joaquim Chissano to declare that "every time we explain our position to the South Africans, they bring us a reply we do not understand."[72]

The Nkomati accords of 1984, the final product of those negotiations, were seen by the Botha administration as a triumph for its policy of defending apartheid through aggression abroad. "Military force, economic muscle, and diplomatic pressure," wrote the pro-government *Sunday Times* (Johannesburg),

> were part of a long-term strategy worked out in a rational assessment of the best way to defend South African interests. That being so, military "destabilisation" of neighbouring states becomes something not antithetical to South Africa's foreign policy but complementary.[73]

While, as noted in chapter 3, South Africa's powerful State Security Council was working out ways to get around and even sink the Nkomati accords, the foreign policy wing of the government and the business community hoped it was the first step in a resuscitation of CONSAS and a blow to SADC. But when it became clear that the South African military had no intention of honoring the agreement, SADC solidarity was enhanced, with a new commitment by Zimbabwe and Tanzania to defend the FRELIMO regime.

Despite this help, the balance of power remained in South Africa's favor as its policy of destabilization created a vicious circle from which Mozambique was unable to escape. First, aid to RENAMO destabilized the nation's economy, which made it more dependent on international relief. Donor governments and organizations, with their emphasis on neutrality and through their use of South African facilities to deliver the aid, lent both RENAMO and Pretoria credibility and legitimacy. In addition, efforts to prevent mass starvation and epidemics allowed the international community to believe it was doing something about the problem. But by not addressing the South African source of the problem, it allowed the war to go on and maintained a situation in which Mozambique became ever more dependent on donors and their agenda.

As Mozambique slid into economic dependency and FRELIMO was forced to surrender political power, it was forced to go hat in hand to the IMF and other lenders to rescue its finances. Their demands for economic restructuring, including substantial cutbacks in social services, led to more discontent among the Mozambican people, which, in turn, led many to join forces with RENAMO, thereby furthering South African aims and completing the circle. "It is what might be called a 'conspiracy of interests' or 'collective self-interest,'" concludes Hanlon, "in which a wide range of participants develop a common interest and then exert pressure in different ways, while encouraging and facilitating the actions of other participants."[74]

Nevertheless, there were disagreements between South Africa and the West over Mozambique. Even more than in Angola, the Reagan administration feared that continued South African aggression might push Mozambique into the Soviet camp. By the late 1980s, the United States was actively urging Pretoria to disengage itself from RENAMO. Under the F. W. de Klerk administration (1989–94), that began to happen, though some in FRELIMO accused South Africa of aiding RENAMO as late as 1992. In addition, South Africa provided much needed diplomatic support to RENAMO during the Rome negotiations. But, says Hanlon, that was because RENAMO was no longer seen as crucial in defeating FRELIMO.

> The failure to turn RENAMO into a credible alternative, combined with the weakness and poverty of Mozambique itself, led to a different strategy of coopting the FRELIMO government. The scale of destruction meant that Mozambique could be rebuilt in a different way. The IMF, the World Bank, and the donors then became the agents of its restructuring.[75]

Mozambique, he adds, had been effectively "recolonized" and returned to its pre-independence economic place as a subservient partner to South Africa.[76]

A coda to the story of South Africa's destabilization policy of the 1980s illustrates the point. In 1995, the Mozambican government agreed to sell or lease some of the country's most valuable farmland. Most of the takers were either South Africans or former Portuguese landowners who intended to use the land, and the cheap labor that comes with it, to supply fruits and vegetables for the South African market or tropical products for international export.[77]

Malawi and Kenya During the late 1970s and early 1980s, Malawi served as RENAMO's main foreign staging point for attacks against Mozambique. In fact, the earliest attacks against Zambézia province were made possible by the complicity of Malawi's President Hastings Banda. As Malawi is a landlocked country almost entirely dependent on Mozambican access to the sea, this policy appeared self-defeating. But Banda was rumored to have annexation designs on northern Mozambique. RENAMO attacks from Malawian territory became so numerous by the mid-1980s that Mozambican president Samora Machel threatened to place missiles on the border. These allegations were denied by Banda, but FRELIMO presented extensive documentation and Banda was forced to admit he had allowed RENAMO to operate from his territory.

At a southern African conference in 1986, Banda was pressured by FRELIMO and other black African states to eject RENAMO from Malawi, an agreement formalized in the Lilongwe accords in December. The immediate result of RENAMO's ejection, however, proved disastrous for Mozambique, as rebels, forced back into the country, increased their destabilization campaign in nearby provinces. In the years since, Malawi's unique geographical position between two parts of Mozambique has meant that RENAMO can use the country as a safe transit corridor for moving troops. FRELIMO alleges this is done with the complicity of Malawi's armed forces. On the other hand, Malawi has served as a home for refugees from Mozambique's war. In 1990, it was estimated that approximately 1.5 million Mozambicans were living in Malawi.

Although separated by 700 miles of Tanzanian territory from Mozambique, Kenya has supported RENAMO in a variety of ways. During the early 1980s, it offered asylum to RENAMO leaders and let them travel on Kenyan passports. By the late 1980s, it was rumored that Kenya had taken the place of South Africa as RENAMO's main training and logistical base. According to FRELIMO, Kenyan-trained rebels were flown to secret airstrips in Malawi before penetrating Mozambique itself. On the other hand, Kenyan president Daniel arap Moi was an active intermediary between RENAMO and FRELIMO in the months leading up to the Rome talks, though his direct participation in the negotiations was refused by FRELIMO because of Kenyan support for RENAMO.

International

Individuals and Organizations   No government outside Africa has directly supported RENAMO, but a number of evangelical and anticommunist organizations and individuals in the United States and Western Europe have. In response to Machel's visit to Washington in 1985 and the Reagan administration's tilt toward FRELIMO, the Conservative Caucus sponsored a trip by RENAMO's secretary for foreign affairs. It also lobbied Congress to defeat Reagan's aid bill to Mozambique and pass its own proposed measure to fund RENAMO. Both bills were defeated.

Nevertheless, meetings between RENAMO and Reagan administration officials, including White House communications director Patrick

Buchanan and CIA chief William Casey, continued until 1987. But news-paper stories of RENAMO massacres of civilians began to have an impact. In 1988, the State Department published a report by staffer Robert Gersony. Based on interviews with Mozambican refugees, the Gersony report was a scathing indictment of RENAMO tactics and strategy. It effectively ended all attempts at lobbying the U.S. government to aid RENAMO.

Private funding efforts, however, continued, though the amounts were relatively small. Anticommunist Louisiana businessman James Blanchard III told the *New York Times* in 1988 that he had donated about $75,000 to RENAMO since 1986, largely for radio equipment.[78] The extreme anticommunist organization Free the Eagle allowed RENAMO to use its Washington offices in the 1980s. In addition, Thomas Schaaf, an evangelical Christian and former Rhodesian agriculture official, has success-fully lobbied several evangelical organizations for aid to RENAMO.

RENAMO also maintained offices and was active in Portugal during the 1980s. In Lisbon, its office was run by Evo Fernandes, a lawyer from the former Portuguese colony of Goa (now part of India). Fernandes successfully solicited funds and other support among the so-called *retornados* (colonists who had returned to Portugal) and Portuguese colonial émigrés in South Africa. He also served as a liaison between RENAMO and the Portuguese government, the latter being concerned about attacks on the Cabora Bassa dam, which it partly owns. Fernandes died in a 1988 car accident in Portugal, though it is rumored the accident was staged by Mozambican government agents.

In West Germany, RENAMO operated out of offices in Heidelberg, where it solicited funds from Portuguese guest workers, some of whom were *retornados*. RENAMO's German office also maintained cordial rela-tions with conservative Franz-Josef Strauss and his Bavarian-based Christian Social Union, which was part of Chancellor Helmut Kohl's ruling coalition during most of the 1980s. RENAMO's main connection in the United Kingdom came via its relations with Lonhro Corporation CEO Tiny Rowlands. Lonhro has extensive investments in Mozambican agriculture, mining and transport, and Rowlands has often contacted FRELIMO on RENAMO's behalf. During negotiations in Rome, Rowlands made his private jet available to Dhlakama.

NOTES

[1] Bridgland, Fred, *Jonas Savimbi: A Key to Africa* (Edinburgh: Mainstream Publishing Company), 1986, p. 66.
[2] Minter, William (ed.), *Operation Timber: Pages from the Savimbi Dossier* (Trenton, N.J.: Africa World Press, 1988), p. 7.
[3] Bridgland, *Jonas Savimbi*, p. 65.
[4] *Ibid.*, p. 69.

5 *Ibid.*, p. 71.

6 Minter, *Operation Timber*, p. 13.

7 Cited in Bender, Gerald, "Angola: Left, Right & Wrong" in *Foreign Affairs*, Summer 1981, p. 59.

8 Bridgland, *Jonas Savimbi*, p. 96.

9 Minter, *Operation Timber*, p. 19.

10 *Ibid.*, p. 21.

11 Spikes, Daniel, *Angola and the Politics of Intervention* (Jefferson, N.C.: McFarland and Company, 1993), p. 222.

12 According to journalist and historian Joseph Hanlon, there have been "repeated suggestions that the CIA was aiding UNITA despite the Clark amendment" (the ban on aid in effect from February 1976 to July 1985), but no documented proof. Hanlon, Joseph, *Beggar Your Neighbours: Apartheid Power in Southern Africa* (Bloomington: Indiana University Press, 1986), p. 165.

13 *Ibid.*, p. 166.

14 *Ibid.*

15 Windrich, Elaine, *The Cold War Guerrilla: Jonas Savimbi, the U.S. Media, and the Angolan War* (New York: Greenwood Press, 1992), p. 50.

16 UNITA's involvement in the negotiations leading to the Bicesse accords is discussed more extensively in chapter 6. The 1992 elections and Savimbi's return to war are covered in chapter 7.

17 See Bridgland, *Jonas Savimbi*.

18 Windrich, *Cold War Guerrilla*, p. 1.

19 Cited in Minter, William, *Apartheid's Contras: An Inquiry into the Roots of War in Angola and Mozambique* (London: Zed Books, 1994), p. 221.

20 Journalists and his own followers often refer to him as Dr. Savimbi, though this is inaccurate. The degree Savimbi earned at the University of Lausanne, Switzerland, is roughly equivalent to a master's degree in the U.S.

21 Marcum, John, *The Angolan Revolution: Volume 2: Exile Politics and Guerrilla Warfare* (Cambridge, Mass.: MIT Press, 1978), pp. 182–183.

22 Cited in Bridgland, *Jonas Savimbi*, p. 80.

23 Savimbi even tried to teach Che Guevara a thing or two about the need for mobility in guerrilla warfare when the Cuban revolutionary was working in the Congo in the early 1960s.

24 Bridgland, *Jonas Savimbi*, p. 19.

25 Pereira, Anthony, "The Neglected Tragedy: the Return to War in Angola, 1992–3" in *The Journal of African Studies*, Winter 1994, p. 8.

26 Minter, William, "Behind the UNITA Curtain" in *Africa Report*, May-June, 1990, p. 46.

27 Minter, *Apartheid's Contras*, p. 221.

28 *Ibid.*, p. 225.

29 See chapter 7.

[30] Bridgland, *Jonas Savimbi*, p. 311.

[31] Minter, "UNITA Curtain," p. 47.

[32] Human Rights Watch/Africa, *Angola: Civilians Devastated by 15 Year War* (New York: Human Rights Watch, 1991), p. 5.

[33] In 1966, the UN General Assembly terminated South Africa's trustee-ship over Namibia and in 1971 the International Court of Justice declared Pretoria's occupation illegal. The UN granted SWAPO, which had been at war with South Africa since the mid-1960s, official recognition in 1973 and endorsed its armed struggle for self-determination in 1976.

[34] Cited in Davies, Robert and O'Meara, Dan, "Total Strategy in Southern Africa—An Analysis of South African Regional Policy since 1978" in Chan, Stephen (ed.), *Exporting Apartheid: Foreign Policies in Southern Africa, 1978–1988*, (New York: St. Martin's Press, 1990), pp. 184–185. The biggest success was the establishment of formal diplomatic relations with Malawi. In addition to that, Malawi, Gabon, Mauritania, the Malagasy Republic and Lesotho voted against the 1971 resolution, and Dahomey (now Benin), Niger, Swaziland, Upper Volta (now Burkina Faso) and Togo abstained.

[35] Khadiagala, Gilbert, *Allies in Adversity: The Frontline States in Southern African Security, 1975–1993* (Athens: Ohio University Press, 1994), p. 19.

[36] Stockwell, John, *In Search of Enemies: A CIA Story* (New York: W.W. Norton and Company, 1978), pp. 185–7.

[37] Spikes, *Angola and Intervention*, p. 221.

[38] Bridgland, *Jonas Savimbi*, p. 153.

[39] "Muldergate" refers to Information Minister Connie Mulder who, among other violations of South African law, illegally funneled money to the opponent of U.S. senator Dick Clark, a harsh critic of UNITA funding.

[40] Ohlson, Thomas and Stedman, Stephen John, *The New Is Not Yet Born: Conflict Resolution in Southern Africa* (Washington: Brookings Institution, 1994), pp. 61–62.

[41] Guelke, Adrian, "Southern Africa and the Superpowers" in Chan (ed.), *Exporting Apartheid*, pp. 241–242.

[42] Hanlon, *Beggar Your Neighbours*, p. 154.

[43] There has been an ironic coda to South Africa's involvement in Angola. Along with government support, a private South African firm with the apt name of Executive Outcomes supplied mercenaries to UNITA until early 1993, when it switched sides and hired out several hundred mercenaries to the MPLA to protect oil installations.

[44] Bridgland, *Jonas Savimbi*, p. 401.

[45] Brittain, Victoria, "Cuba and Southern Africa" in *New Left Review*, November–December 1988, p. 122.

[46] Technically, since this book puts pro-rebel foreign involvement in this chapter and pro-government foreign involvement in the next, ambivalent Zambia should have a chapter of its own.

47 Hanlon, *Beggar Your Neighbours*, p. 171.

48 Seidman, Ann, *The Roots of Crisis in Southern Africa* (Trenton, N.J.: Africa World Press, 1985), p. 115.

49 Seidman, *Roots of Crisis*, p. 125.

50 Stockwell, *Search of Enemies*, p. 193.

51 Crocker, Chester, *High Noon in Southern Africa: Making Peace in a Rough Neighborhood* (New York: W.W. Norton and Company, 1992), p. 266.

52 Cited in Clough, Michael, *Free at Last? U.S. Policy Toward Africa and the End of the Cold War* (New York: Council on Foreign Relations, 1992), pp. 9–10.

53 Clough, *Free at Last*, p. 10.

54 Chevron is still operating its offshore rigs in Cabinda and was engaged in further exploration in 1995.

55 Hanlon, *Beggar Your Neighbours*, pp. 170–171.

56 Brittain, "Cuba and Africa", p. 117.

57 For the reasons Cuba agreed to the withdrawal, see chapter 5.

58 *The Economist*, October 17, 1992, p. 51.

59 Jackson, Steven, "China's Third World Foreign Policy: The Case of Angola and Mozambique, 1961–93" in *The China Quarterly*, June 1995, pp. 392–395.

60 As RENAMO was and is largely a creation of Rhodesia and South Africa, its origins are covered in chapter 3 and the Rhodesia and South Africa sections of this chapter. Its development is examined in chapter 3 and its recent past in chapter 7.

61 Cited in Abrahamsson, Hans and Nilsson, Anders, *Mozambique, The Troubled Transition: From Socialist Construction to Free Market Capitalism* (London: Zed Books, 1995), p. 62.

62 Saul, John, *Recolonization and Resistance in Southern Africa in the 1990s* (Trenton, N.J.: Africa World Press, 1993), p. 9.

63 Vines, Alex, *Renamo: Terrorism in Mozambique* (Bloomington: Indiana University Press), 1991, p. 16.

64 Hume, Cameron, *Ending Mozambique's War: The Role of Mediation and Good Offices* (Washington: United States Institute of Peace Press), 1994, p. 13.

65 Hume, *Ending Mozambique's War*, pp. 117–139.

66 Hanlon, *Beggar Your Neighbours*, p. 141.

67 Cited in Abrahamsson, *Troubled Transition*, p. 90.

68 Africa Watch, *Conspicuous Destruction: War, Famine and the Reform Process in Mozambique* (New York: Human Rights Watch, 1992), pp. 87–88.

69 Guelke, "Superpowers," p. 233.

[70] For South Africa's general approach to southern Africa, see the Angola section of this chapter. Much of it applies to Mozambique as well and thus won't be repeated here.

[71] The original members were Angola, Botswana, Lesotho, Malawi, Mozambique, Swaziland, Tanzania, Zambia and Zimbabwe. South Africa joined after Mandela became president in 1994. For simplicity, the new acronym will be used throughout the text. For a more detailed discussion of SADCC, see chapter 5.

[72] Khadiagala, *Allies in Adversity*, p. 183.

[73] Cited in Hanlon, *Beggar Your Neighbours*, p. 39.

[74] Hanlon, *Who Calls the Shots?*, p. 3.

[75] *Ibid.*

[76] *Ibid.*

[77] Another story is illustrative here. After a 1995 trip to Mozambique, Prexi Nesbitt, a former consultant to FRELIMO from the United States, described the scene at one of Mozambique's resorts that was recently opened again to tourists. "These South African soldiers were treating the staff at the hotel like shit. I saw this waiter just humiliated and grimacing . . . I suppose that's what it was like before [during colonial days]." Interview with author, December 13, 1995.

[78] Minter, *Apartheid's Contras*, pp. 156–159.

5

GOVERNMENTS

*[The MPLA] were plunged into the East-West conflict and now we
don't know who we are. Every aspect of our lives is imbued with
alienation and contradiction . . . proletarian ideology in a rural
society . . . pro-Soviet rhetoric while doing business with the West.
Only peace will allow us finally to realize who we are.*
> —Angolan Education Minister Artur Lestana Pepetela

FRELIMO-itis is a local sickness. Many, many *people here,
including me, have been seriously affected by it. It's the inability to
analyze . . . what goes on in Mozambique.*
> —Janet Mondlane, widow of FRELIMO founder Eduardo
> Mondlane

ANGOLA

ORIGINS AND DEVELOPMENT

Ever since its founding in 1956, the Popular Movement for the Liberation
of Angola (MPLA) has been dogged by charges that it has essentially been
a communist party in nationalist garb. The truth, however, is a bit more
complicated than that. A few of its early organizers were indeed members
of the Stalinist-era Portuguese Communist Party, or its Angola affiliate, but
most were noncommunist progressives and nationalists of various political
stripes. Influenced by the rhetoric of decolonization propounded by the
pro-Soviet communist parties of Western Europe and nationalist movements in black Africa, the MPLA's founders were united largely in their
"opposition to Portuguese domination."[1]

As important as its political roots, and perhaps more so, are its racial
and ethnic origins. The MPLA has always been a party of racial, if not
necessarily ethnic, inclusiveness, a tendency that has been clear from the
beginning. Among its early organizers were whites, mestizos and *assimilados*, the latter largely of Kimbundu origin. While this multiracial tag is
proudly worn by the MPLA and the communist one downplayed, it has
also been a source of contention within Angolan politics. Both Holden
Roberto of the National Front for the Liberation of Angola (FNLA) and
the Union for the Total Independence of Angola (UNITA) head, Jonas
Savimbi—the MPLA's two organizational competitors at independence—

123

have tried to stir up popular feelings against an organization led by people they claim are elitists and out of touch with the concerns of ordinary Angolan peasants.

During the MPLA's first five years of existence, these charges had a valid basis. While spontaneous revolts against Portuguese rule rocked the rural areas of northern Angola, the tiny organization failed to leave the capital, except to meet with the leaders of other African liberation movements. As tensions increased, the MPLA leaders continued to meet clandestinely in Luanda and in their various places of exile, debating how best to carry out the liberation of the colony and what socialist policies would be most appropriate for post-independence Angola. "The MPLA," says Africanist Basil Davidson, "were certainly in favor of revolt [in the late 1950s], but they believed the time was premature."[2]

As turmoil engulfed the neighboring Belgian Congo (now Zaire) in 1960, the destinies of the rural Kimbundu people and the MPLA began to intersect. As a part of a general crackdown in the wake of Congolese independence, Portuguese authorities arrested Neto, touching off protests and violent repression in the town of Catete, the birthplace of Neto (60 miles east of Luanda). The following February, a spontaneous protest, which the MPLA later took credit for, led to an assault on a Luanda prison and violent repression by Portuguese police and citizens. The MPLA's history has since been officially rewritten. Despite the organization's hesitancy, it made February 4 the Angolan national holiday marking the beginning of the armed struggle against Lisbon.

As far as establishing a base of support inside Angola, the MPLA stood somewhere between Savimbi's total commitment to a strictly Angola-based liberation struggle and Roberto's chumminess with his sponsor and host, Zaire's Joseph Mobutu (later Mobutu Sese Seko). According to Portuguese documents released after the war, the vast majority of military engagements involved the MPLA. Yet the organization's infrastructure was always based in other countries: first in Congo-Brazzaville—until its president was overthrown in a coup in 1963—then Zaire, Tanzania, Algeria and, lastly and most importantly, Zambia. Since only Zambia shared a frontier with Angola (Congo-Brazzaville bordered only the Angolan enclave of Cabinda), MPLA guerrillas were forced to work with Zairian authorities who were, at best, lukewarm to them. Worse still, the MPLA had to contend with an even more hostile FNLA. As early as October 1961, Roberto's forces had launched attacks against MPLA guerrillas as they tried to penetrate Angola from Congo-Brazzaville. The FNLA, however, did not confine its internecine attacks to combatants. During the FNLA-sponsored revolt among the Kikongo of northern Angola, its ethnic base, educated *assimilados*, whether affiliated with the MPLA or not, were targeted for attacks as well.

The expulsion from Congo-Brazzaville, FNLA attacks, Zairian hostility and beefed-up Portuguese counterinsurgency measures were some of the reasons the MPLA decided to move much of its military operations to Zambia in 1966. But so was the MPLA leadership's desire to prove that their base of support was not confined to the Kimbundu heartland around Luanda. While Zambia offered a more conducive environment for organizing and a frontier with Angola proper, it had major drawbacks. Zambia bordered the least developed part of Angola, hundreds of virtually roadless miles from the Portuguese centers of settlement in the central highlands and on the coast. Moreover, operating in eastern Angola put the MPLA into direct conflict with Savimbi's UNITA. Skirmishes between the two forces, usually instigated by the latter, according to most scholars, increased throughout the late 1960s and early 1970s. In 1972, a Portuguese offensive broke the back of the MPLA, leading to a falling-out between Neto and the MPLA's eastern commander, Daniel Chipenda, and a retreat from the east.

The 1974 Portuguese coup caught all three liberation groups unawares, as it did the intelligence agencies of the U.S. and South Africa.[3] In some ways, the MPLA was at a disadvantage as the events of the independence era unfolded. While it had the largest number of guerrillas, an estimated 5,000, it was arguably in the least tenable position militarily, isolated in two areas and facing a foreign-supported FNLA in the north and a well-entrenched, South African–supported UNITA in the south and east.

Nevertheless, the MPLA had several less obvious advantages. First, its inclusiveness helped to expand its ethnic and racial base. Second, the MPLA refused to compromise with the Portuguese, who, under the conservative general Antonio de Spinola, were trying to arrange a "neocolonial settlement" and signing secret agreements with the FNLA and UNITA to achieve it. The MPLA's hard line benefited the organization in two ways: Its political position was more in tune with the vast majority of Angolans, who wanted nothing to do with the Portuguese; and its more radical nationalism was more in sync with the leftward drift of Portuguese politics following the resignation of Spinola. A third advantage the MPLA possessed was its leadership. According to John Stockwell, the point man for the CIA's covert operation in Angola, the MPLA's leaders were both better educated and better strategists. "Marxism," he writes, "gave them organizational skills to develop a revolutionary movement."[4]

Finally, of course, the MPLA had the backing of the Soviet Union and Cuba. But as journalist Joseph Hanlon points out, "South African and U.S. pressure forced Angola into a much closer relationship with the eastern bloc than had been intended."[5] Moreover, South Africa's 1975–76 invasion and the United States' reputation as weapons supplier to the Portuguese undercut the legitimacy of their respective clients, the FNLA and UNITA, and alienated many Angolans. Nothing more effectively rallied other African regimes and the Organization of African Unity (OAU) to the MPLA's side than the knowledge that it was fighting against the hated apartheid regime.

At the time, the MPLA's victory seemed complete. The FNLA had been utterly defeated and UNITA driven deep into the southern Angolan bush. In fact, serious threats to its governance quickly emerged. The first involved factions within the organization itself. In the final years of the colonial struggle, the MPLA had been riven by internal conflicts. The main faction, led by Neto, was challenged by Daniel Chipenda's Active Revolt group. A temporary truce united the factions in time for the war of independence but did little to reconcile the underlying grievances amongst them. Convinced that his eastern forces had won Angolan independence and angered by his exclusion from the Alvor peace talks, Chipenda marched on Luanda but was attacked and defeated by the main wing of the MPLA. Chipenda then joined forces with the FNLA and went down to defeat with Roberto. After many years in exile, he was eventually reconciled to the MPLA and became its ambassador to Egypt in the late 1980s.

While the Chipenda revolt was largely a personal power struggle, the factional split that reemerged after independence was more ideologically based. In order to preempt any challenges to its authority, the MPLA immediately cracked down on moderate dissenters to one-party rule. These included former leaders of Active Revolt as well as more radical groups pushing for decentralized administration, worker and peasant democratic councils and an economic development plan calling for the total nationalization of foreign- owned oil concessions and plantations.

Another source of dissent emerged out of the *poder popular* (people's power) committees organized by the MPLA in its defense against white settlers and the FNLA. While these were ruthlessly suppressed shortly before independence, many of the committees retained their arms and their militancy. Anger between these working class cadres and the MPLA government grew steadily. Many of Luanda's poorest citizens, who had fought in the streets and countryside against the FNLA and UNITA, did not approve of the lifestyles of the new MPLA elite, who had commandeered the residences of the Portuguese. They also began to chafe at the production quotas established by the new government, which increased output rather than pay. Many soldiers and officers, too, were angry. They felt that they had carried the brunt of the war but that the Cuban troops received the praise, as well as the best accommodations and assignments in peacetime Angola. Added to all this was a resentment against the dominance of mestizos and *assimilados* among the MPLA leadership.

By 1977, conditions were ripe for violent protest, lacking only a leader with military experience to organize the dissent in an assault on the MPLA government. In 1977, such a leader emerged. Nito Alves, the MPLA's minister of internal administration, had had a long and complex relationship with the popular committees of Luanda. He had both organized them in the struggle against reactionary white colonists and the FNLA, and been responsible for neutralizing them shortly before independence. But by 1976, the poorly educated and military-oriented Alves was angry with what he perceived as the elitism of the MPLA and their unwillingness to effectively empower worker committees in the factories and neighborhoods. Thus, he began to woo the popular committees by lacing his speeches with racial attacks on the mestizo leadership of the MPLA. Alves also had the tacit backing of the Soviet Union, which was growing increasingly frustrated with the MPLA's inability to put Angola's political and economic affairs in order.

The coup of May 27, 1977, in which the armed committees of Luanda's *musseques*, or slums, appeared to be a spontaneous affair but was in fact the final act in a comedy of errors. Originally, Alves, as interior minister, had cultivated relations with provincial leaders in the hopes of a nationwide uprising. When that failed, he decided to kidnap Neto at the next central committee meeting, but the venue of the session was changed more than ten times and Neto could not put this plan into effect. Finally, he decided on an uprising in the capital itself, but this too failed when a force of Cuban and loyal Angolan soldiers came to Neto's rescue. Alves was arrested, tried and, though this was never confirmed by the MPLA, executed.

The response to the Alves coup was swift and thorough. A political crackdown against all dissenting groups was conducted in Luanda and the provinces. At its next party congress in December, the MPLA was officially renamed the MPLA–Parthido de Trabalho (Workers' Party) and modeled directly on that of the Communist Party of Cuba and the Soviet Union. Much of the army's officer corps received training in the Soviet Union. Cuban and Eastern European technicians were brought to Angola to organize agricultural and industrial production on bureaucratic, centrally planned lines. East Germans trained the Angolan national police in maintaining social order and rooting out deviant political groups and individuals. Women, student, peasant and worker organizations were harnessed to the party. Leaders who were suspected of deviance from the official party line were replaced by ones appointed by the MPLA's central committee. These popular organizations became top-down forums and tools for the Luanda government to publicize its goals and rally the people. Rather than being democratic organs to express the will of their members, the organizations were yoked to the rule of a one-party state.

In 1979, Agostinho Neto died in a Moscow hospital, and dos Santos, party secretary for planning and economic development, succeeded him in a smooth transition of power. Dos Santos did little to change the structure of the MPLA or its mission as the vanguard revolutionary party of the Angolan people through the war-torn 1980s. If anything, the war increased the MPLA's commitment to a command economy and repression of political dissent. The MPLA argued that these measures were necessary to defend the state, the party and the revolution, which, in the leadership's thinking, were all synonymous. The war also served to deflect criticism of government policies. Only after a dozen or so years of war with UNITA and South Africa, immense international pressure, and the collapse of its patron, the Soviet Union, did the MPLA finally agree to multiparty elections and an end to the one-party state.

MEMBERSHIP

Political leadership

The national leaders of the MPLA are far from typical Angolans. Most, for one thing, are well-educated. The two longest-serving presidents, Neto and dos Santos, hold advanced degrees in medicine and petroleum engineering, respectively. While it is true that UNITA head Jonas Savimbi received a master's degree in political science, higher education among the UNITA leadership largely ends with him, whereas MPLA cadres are filled with men and women possessing college degrees and fluency in European languages.

The national leadership does not reflect the racial and class composition of Angola either. Its cadres include a much higher percentage of people of mestizo and *assimilado* backgrounds, and members of the Kimbundu ethnic group predominate. Many of the MPLA leaders were also raised in Christian households, even if they are currently nonpracticing. But perhaps most importantly, the MPLA leadership has been shaped by its Luanda-based origins. The strategies employed by the MPLA in its war against the Portuguese and in its running of post-independence Angola reflect these urban origins. "Independence movements in Africa," notes historian David Birmingham,

> had almost without exception begun by capturing the colonial capital of the territory which they aspired to govern. Such a strategy came naturally to a nationalist movement like the MPLA whose cultural roots were in Luanda; it was doubly attractive after the bloody feuds and physical hardships of the guerrilla war.[6]

The MPLA leadership's preference for an urban-based liberation movement and politics undermined its effectiveness as a guerrilla movement and as the government of a nation where 85 percent of the people at independence lived in the countryside. Eventually, adjustments were made. But, says journalist Jeremy Harding, they were ineffectual. "Great stress was placed on the idea of the 'worker-peasant alliance,'" he writes.

> The MPLA even put a hoe, a machete, one corncob and a sprig of cotton in the national emblem, but it might as well have been two clods of dung and a chicken's head for all that peasant life meant to people in Luanda. To many intellectuals in the MPLA, the countryside was a disagreeable place, steeped in rural idiocy.[7]

Neto himself, says historian Daniel Spikes, was especially frustrated by the MPLA's experience in the east during the liberation war. While the organization tried to establish friendly ties with local peoples, including efforts to learn their language, they were stymied by the deep cultural rift between them. "Confronted with a worldview so alien to one that life in Luanda, Lisbon, and Brazzaville had conditioned," writes Spikes of the MPLA president, "the intellectual Neto would in time lose patience with these peoples." And they would lose patience with him. As Birmingham notes, during wartime the MPLA often found itself militarily isolated in the capital. "Even Malange, the Kimbundu twin to Luanda [200 miles east]," he says, "ceased to be accessible by road and the state president had to put his Mercedes on a military transport plane when visiting his closest provincial capital."[8]

Yet despite their common roots in urban culture and politics, the MPLA was plagued with factionalism, as the history of internal struggles and coups recounted above indicates. While some of these struggles had an ideological veneer, they were often the result of competition among the leaders. Chipenda's challenge, for instance, was motivated in large part by ambition and his sense that he were being left out of the MPLA's decision-making process. This was true even of the Alves coup, though as far as the old *poder* committees were concerned, it was a confrontation between the elite MPLA cadres ruling Angola and the masses of slum dwellers who felt they had carried the brunt of fighting the Portuguese and the FNLA and then been abandoned and even attacked by MPLA forces. According to historian Nicholas Cummings, Alves' challenge to Neto, though

cloaked . . . in the garb of nationalism and opposition to Neto's leniency towards Western imperialist economic activity in Angola, started out as a contradiction within the ranks of the MPLA over just what role and how big a share of the spoils the MPLA would get in "liberated Angola."[9]

The organizational structure and history of the MPLA aggravated the factionalism within it. Specifically, by advocating an inclusive popular-front approach to decolonization, the MPLA gathered into its ranks a disparate collection of political opinions under a nationalist umbrella. Once the common Portuguese enemy was driven from Angola, the inevitable political divisions emerged, intensified by the isolated geographic regions where the organization operated, the personalities who led these varied factions, and the machinations of the Cubans and Soviets who backed them.[10]

Yet the main MPLA faction, led by Neto and dos Santos, was never defeated politically or militarily. Its resilience was due to both internal and external factors. Angola's leaders were never reticent to use the power of the state to crush their political opposition and purge their ranks of dissidents. In fact, the MPLA's efforts to impose a centralized political administration, a vast security apparatus and command economics were motivated in part by the leadership's fear of factionalism and dissent, both from elements within its own cadres and from the rank and file of Luanda.

This fear had a legitimate basis, in that from the late 1970s on, the MPLA was fighting a life-and-death struggle against a formidable enemy backed by South Africa and the U.S. The war justified both administrative centralization and political crackdown, even as it accelerated them. As the MPLA became more dependent on the Soviet Union and Cuba, it increasingly began to adopt the political and economic model they advocated.

On the other hand, the war produced its own divisions within the MPLA leadership. As the possibility of a negotiated solution to the war increased in the late 1980s and early 1990s, MPLA military leaders began to dissent from the dos Santos faction that ruled Angola. Believing Savimbi was little more than a lackey of Pretoria and that UNITA was incapable of defending itself without its South African patrons, Angola's generals advocated a hard-line military approach. With UNITA on the defensive in 1990–91, they devised a plan for a final push to smash UNITA forces. They were vetoed by dos Santos, who was trying to establish better relations with the United States and the West. With the decline of the Soviet Union and its retreat from Angola, the hard-liners found themselves without the patronage of the country's major arms supplier and international supporter.

Savimbi's decision to plunge the nation into civil war after the 1992 elections, of course, confirmed the military's position, leading to a massive arms-buying spree in 1993 and offensive in 1994. While the military successfully destroyed UNITA as a conventional armed force, dos Santos has kept a rein on the military as talks proceed in Lusaka for a government of national reconciliation. Not unreasonably, the MPLA leader dreads a scenario in which Savimbi and UNITA might return to the bush and carry on guerrilla warfare from there.

The MPLA's firm and long-standing grip on state power, in an economy dominated by the state and the multinational oil firms that subsidized it, encouraged corrupt and incompetent leadership. While the war against UNITA was the most important factor behind Angola's economic woes, the secret defense budget swallowed an estimated 70 percent of oil and other government revenues, and mismanagement played a part as well. "As far back as 1985, the ruling MPLA admitted some harsh truths to itself," notes journalist Anita Coulson. "Overstaffing, impenetrable bureaucracy, mal-administration, and incompetence had all but destroyed productivity."[11]

The impact on the citizens of Angola, particularly its urban residents, was acute. As journalist Xan Smiley wrote in the 1980s,

> The biggest grumble of Luandans, as of all Angolans, is lack of food. Queues are everywhere. The black market in practically every essential and edible commodity flourishes, while the unofficial currency exchange rate . . . stands at about fifteen times the official one . . . The price of cabbage or a couple of eggs sometimes exceeds the daily wage.[12]

The perquisites enjoyed by MPLA leaders added insult to injury. "Full-time MPLA party workers can buy essential goods in special shops," says Smiley, "adding to the resentment that Marxist egalitarianism does not extend to the new ruling class which preaches it most fiercely."[13]

Thus, a vicious political cycle ensued. As worker absenteeism increased because people had to search for food, and as hunger took its toll on productivity, the MPLA-controlled press and worker organizations began to hint of "sabotage" and lash out at "laziness," which only increased popular discontent. The drop in oil prices in the 1980s didn't help either. And with the largest army in black Africa to maintain, the MPLA found it difficult to continue the health and education services that had been a hallmark of its early years.

The partial restructuring imposed on Angola by international banking institutions has, if anything, aggravated the situation.[14] The removal of certain subsidies for foodstuffs and health has increased the suffering of Angola's urban poor, even as mid-level MPLA members maintain their perquisites and the leaders take advantage of privatization to line their pockets. The city of Luanda has reflected the changes. In 1983, Smiley found the "squalor acute" with broken windows in every building, "rubbish . . . everywhere . . . and excrement . . . stinking on staircases, even in fairly modern offices."[15] But journalists visiting the city in the 1990s report new European sedans on the streets, and new restaurants and pricey boutiques in the refurbished high-rise blocks. "Officials are selling buildings, laboratories and vehicles," noted an *Economist* reporter in late 1992, "and presumably stuffing the proceeds into their own pockets."[16]

Armed forces

The armed forces of Angola, according to its critics, have frequently acted like an army of occupation rather than a force defending the citizens of the country. During the war of liberation against the Portuguese, many of the officers were recruited from the ranks of educated Luandans, while much of the soldiering was performed by guerrillas recruited from Luanda or the Kimbundu homeland along the northern and central coast. As with the leadership of the MPLA, the officers in the field frequently found it difficult to relate to the concerns of the peasantry, while Kimbundu-speaking soldiers were unable to communicate with local civilians, especially along the front opened by the MPLA in eastern Angola and among the Ovimbundu of the central highlands. The hostility between FNLA and MPLA forces in the north prevented much contact with the peasant population in that part of the colony. This disconnectedness was exacerbated by Portuguese counterinsurgency methods that effectively prevented the establishment of a liberated zone where guerrillas might have established and defended social services and trade independent of the colonial administration.

In the defense of Luanda during the war of independence, the MPLA recruited heavily among the *musseques* of the capital, creating both local militias to defend city neighborhoods and regular units to protect the city itself against the FNLA and Zairians. South Africa's 1975 invasion of southern Angola in support of its UNITA and FNLA allies forced the MPLA to augment its 10,000- to 12,000-man force (including several thousand Katangese rebels from Zaire) with several thousand Cuban regulars.[17] While Cuban soldiers largely stayed in the rear during the early 1980s, serving as trainers, medics and technicians, resentment between the two forces grew, though it never appeared to hamper military operations and Cubans seemed to mix well with the local population. Nevertheless, the Cubans complained of the ineffectiveness of the MPLA, and MPLA soldiers grumbled about favored treatment given to Castro's troops, who maintained an independent command structure.

Like civilian leadership in Luanda, the military quickly adopted the bureaucratic, top-down command structure of its Soviet and Cuban patrons. Any thought of a people's army, based on a democratic command structure and guerrilla action coordinated with the peasantry, was abandoned by the time of independence. "Beginning right away in 1976, top-level Soviet military delegations worked hand in hand with the MPLA to set up Angola's military establishment and tie it as closely as possible to the Soviets," says historian Nicholas Cummings, adding that the extensive training of high-level officers in Cuba and the USSR, as well as instruction given to mid- and low-ranking officers on training bases run by the Soviets, Cubans and East Germans in Angola itself, were the key components of this strategy.[18] In a speech to the first graduating class of an Angola-based school, and long before the war with UNITA heated up, Neto said that the MPLA's strategy was to build an army "capable of waging a *modern* war by mastering military techniques and tactics [emphasis added]."[19]

As part of the MPLA's strategy of protecting peasants and denying support to UNITA troops, the army began to create garrison villages in areas of conflict. While the villagization will be explored more thoroughly in chapter 6, one aspect of the policy needs mention here. In the early 1980s, the MPLA established the People's Defense Organization (ODP), which recruited villagers, mostly older men who were not in the army, to serve in local militias. Whether the ODP was voluntary or forced—the MPLA insists it was the former, while Human Rights Watch asserts the contrary—UNITA forces made the village militias, many of which were poorly armed and trained, a special target of their attacks.[20]

Not surprisingly, as the war ground on and casualties mounted during the 1980s, the Angolan armed forces suffered from a serious desertion problem, though this had more to do with conditions in the camps than with political dissent. As one noncommissioned officer explained in 1983, "There have been three desertions in my platoon, and maybe 120 altogether. They are leaving because of hunger."[21] To fill the ranks, the MPLA turned to forced recruitment and sweeps of urban neighborhoods and villages under its control. "Criticism of the way army recruiters conduct draft sweeps is widespread," HRW reported in 1991.

> They shoot at young draft evaders, injuring and killing many, including bystanders. Young men try to escape conscription because there is no limit on the number of years they must serve in the army . . . Also, they fear mutilation or death by UNITA land mines.[22]

A 1994 Human Rights Watch observer reported seeing teenagers rounded up by recruiters in Luanda. "Many families," the reporter added, "try to keep their teenage sons off the streets in an attempt to keep them from being grabbed."[23] A lack of discipline has also plagued the Angolan armed forces, though like the desertions, it has more to do with hunger than ethnic or political hatred. "So pathetic is the food situation in Angola," says Human Rights Watch, "that when food convoys for the military are ambushed or do not arrive, the press-ganged troops resort to stealing food from the homes and fields of the peasants they are supposedly protecting against UNITA cruelties."[24] In general, however, most journalists and human rights organizations say that the MPLA soldiers have been far less guilty of looting, executing civilians or forcing them into porterage than has UNITA, though upon recapturing Huambo in early 1994, "their drunken behavior and wild shooting into the air after dark left civilians frightened."[25]

Like the armed forces, the MPLA's security police were largely trained by Eastern Bloc advisers, usually East Germans. The security forces acted as a law unto themselves, with the power to detain suspected UNITA collaborators up to four years in the agency's own jails as an "administrative penalty." Suspects never saw judge or counsel or the inside of a courtroom. In addition, the military conducted special tribunals where long sentences and even executions were handed down. By the late 1980s, human rights organizations estimated there were over 5,000 UNITA collaborators in Angola's largest prison alone.

Under the constitutional reforms of 1990, the power of the security forces was reined in. However, to evade demobilization as required by the 1991 Bicesse accords, the MPLA established a new national police force, popularly known as "ninjas" for the black uniforms they wear. The ninjas had new weapons and equipment lavished upon them, including matériel such as mortars that were obviously not intended for routine police activities. It seems clear that besides patrolling the streets against UNITA saboteurs, the ninjas did double duty as an elite antiterrorist force and personal security guard for the MPLA leadership.

FOREIGN

Africa

Nations and Organizations Angola has not enjoyed friendly relations with its neighbors. As discussed in chapter 4, Zaire has been openly hostile,

Zambia wavering and Namibia noncommittal. Only Congo-Brazzaville supported the MPLA, and that was largely before and immediately after independence when it allowed its bases to be used as transit points for Soviet and Cuban shipments to the MPLA.

As for multilateral African organizations, the record has been a bit more mixed. The OAU recognized the MPLA in 1970, but only reluctantly and only because it had become disenchanted with the FNLA's ineffectiveness as a guerrilla movement. After Portugal's decision to pull out, the OAU backed away from its recognition of the MPLA and refused to accept its single-party declaration of independence in November 1975. Only with the collapse of the FNLA in 1975 and revelations of South African support for UNITA did the OAU decide to recognize the MPLA. Nevertheless, the MPLA government has remained a full-fledged member of the organization ever since. Like other African and international organizations, the OAU harshly condemned Savimbi's decision to renew the civil war after he was defeated in the 1992 elections.

In the Southern African Development Community (SADC), the MPLA government has found a more hospitable home. One of the founding members of the organization, Angola is responsible, under the SADC's decentralized administrative system, for energy. Since the SADC was largely founded to break Pretoria's hold on the economy of southern Africa, apartheid South Africa tried to destroy the organization by diplomatic, economic and military means. Along with Mozambique, Angola has suffered the brunt of such military attacks. Hanlon explained why in 1986:

> With peace and the present [MPLA] government, Angola could become a major supplier of fuel to the [SADC]; with a South African surrogate government, it could ensure a permanent oil supply for apartheid in spite of the embargo. Second, the oil income means that Angola cannot be economically squeezed . . . With no diplomatic or economic leverage, armed force is South Africa's only weapon.[26]

International

Soviet Union Whether Soviet involvement in Angola was part of a grand strategy for world domination or simply an act of solidarity with a fellow socialist regime, the country and, in fact, the entirety of Africa have largely been peripheral to Moscow's interests, according to most scholars. But if that is true, how can the Soviets' massive financial commitment to the MPLA, amounting in some estimates to $8 billion by the early 1980s, be explained? Part of the answer lies in the Soviet expansionist policies of the 1970s.

By the early part of that decade, the USSR had reached an approximate arms parity with the U.S. and was looking to establish bases throughout the world to project that power. The long-standing relationship with the MPLA and then the sudden collapse of the Portuguese colonial regimes in Africa provided the Soviets with an opportunity that couldn't be passed up. "With reliable access to basing facilities in southern Africa," notes political scientist R. Craig Nation, "the Soviets could importantly reduce the transit time required to project a naval presence in the Indian Ocean."[27] But strategy, international relations expert Stephen Chan points out, is not simply a military matter. "Soviet intervention," he writes, "was explicable as an element in the Soviet quest to achieve the status of a global power with a stake in the settlement of all major international conflicts, including the racial confrontation in southern Africa."[28]

Related to this was the Soviet fear of Chinese involvement. Beijing had begun backing both UNITA and the FNLA in the 1960s and, as independence approached, was working with both the United States and South Africa to funnel even more arms to its favored groups. This odd collection of political bedfellows was, in turn, driven by the fear of Soviet hegemony shared by Pretoria, Beijing and Washington. Chan writes, "It can be argued that the displacement of China as the principal supporter of armed struggle against white rule was the most important motivation of Soviet involvement in Angola."[29]

Soviet involvement was nothing new. It is estimated that Moscow was annually funneling as much as $100 million to the MPLA in the final years of the war against Portugal. But Soviet-MPLA relations had never been as solid as many Western observers thought. The Brezhnevian doctrine held that most of the Third World was not ripe for the kind of revolution the Soviets wanted to see and felt that many of the so-called liberation groups were led by "petit-bourgeois nationalists."[30] MPLA factionalism and Neto's reticence to make post-independence promises of Soviet bases didn't help either. In 1973, relations between the Neto wing of the MPLA and Moscow deteriorated to the point where the Soviets actively courted party dissidents like Chipenda. And, as noted above, during the coup of 1977, they passively supported Alves by denying intelligence to Neto.

Massive support during the war of independence, as much as $1 billion worth, would seem to belie the existence of any deep rifts between Moscow and the MPLA. But that support was partly based on a misreading of U.S. intentions. Believing that Washington was fully distracted by the collapse of South Vietnam, the Soviets moved into Angola believing that they would face no serious challenge from the U.S. In addition, the commitment to the MPLA had a lot to do with the Soviets' fear that abandoning it, in the face of limited U.S. support for the FNLA and South African support for UNITA, would cause Moscow to lose face and credibility in Africa and, indeed, much of the Third World.

Clearly, as the Soviet Union became more deeply involved with the MPLA, its need to continue supporting it grew. As Bridgland points out, by early 1976, Moscow had signed an agreement with the MPLA "that virtually guaranteed Soviet responsibility for the security of Angola."[31] Still, it is impossible to understand Soviet decision making on Angola without exploring the complicated relationship between Moscow and Havana. The conventional wisdom of the Cold War maintains that Cuba acted as a proxy for Soviet interests in the Third World generally and Angola specifically, with "Castro . . . motivated by economic self-interest [that is, Soviet subsidies] and slavish devotion to the Soviet cause."[32] In this scenario, the Soviets displayed unusual discretion and acumen in using a fellow Third World country to promote its interests and avoid offending African sensibilities about European involvement on the continent.

In fact, it was more complicated than that. Castro, most scholars agree, was always a far more enthusiastic supporter of the MPLA and the cause of Third World revolution generally than the Soviet Union ever was. But the Soviet commitment to the victory and security of the MPLA was not a simple case of the Russians being blindly led by an overenthusiastic Castro. Rather, the Soviet Union's decision making on Angola was based on a combination of a conservative assessment of Soviet-Angolan relations, cool strategic thinking and a desire to promote its image as a defender of the Third World. Cuba, though motivated by reasons of its own (see below), was thus viewed as a useful means to a desired end. As historian Daniel Spikes writes,

> The cost of intervening in Angola had been reduced to a palatable level when Moscow realized that Castro was serious about paying for the delivery of Angola into the socialist camp with Cuban blood. This was probably the single greatest factor in the Soviet Union's decision.[33]

With the MPLA firmly ensconced in power by 1976, the Soviet Union became its major source of arms, aid and international diplomatic support. True, the Soviets may not have considered the regime a genuine revolutionary one, but their consistent support of Luanda helped make sure that a reactionary, South African-imposed government would never come to power. As noted above, Soviet patronage came at a price, including a misplaced emphasis by the Soviet-trained and -influenced MPLA on industrialization, inefficient state economic planning and stifling bureaucracy. And as Cummings points out, the Soviets reaped significant benefits from Angola, including oil revenues in exchange for arms and a presence in the South Atlantic at a time when their military strategists were seriously considering the possibility that Moscow and Washington were heading for a global military showdown.[34]

The rise of Gorbachev and the increasingly weakened state of the Soviet economy after 1985 changed the equation entirely. Virtually from the time he came to power, Gorbachev began approaching the U.S. about a negotiated resolution to the Angola conflict that would allow the Soviet Union to reduce its commitments there without losing diplomatic face. According to political scientist Gillian Gunn, it was the Reagan/Bush administration's firm commitment to a UNITA victory that prevented the

Soviets from withdrawing their support of the MPLA in the late 1980s.[35] At the same time, Moscow clearly put pressure on Castro to accept the 1988 New York accords and pull out of Angola. The Soviet Union also acted as one of the guarantors, along with Portugal and the United States, of the 1991 Bicesse accords and multiparty elections. As one political analyst explained, "For the former Soviet Union and Cuba, the Angolan elections provided a face-saving exit from a conflict that had bogged down their economies for years without producing any discernible benefits."[36]

Cuba Havana's involvement in African politics dates back to the early 1960s and Che Guevara's failed efforts to organize revolution in the Congo (now Zaire). But these early efforts, says former Cuban diplomat Juan Benemelis, were motivated by a "romantic" commitment to exporting revolution that died by the end of the decade as Cuba began to take a more "serious" and sober assessment of its foreign policy aims, though these continued to be marked by attempts to spread revolution in the Third World.[37] And, unlike Moscow, Havana never wavered in its support for the MPLA after it began sending advisers in the mid-1960s.

The beginning of Cuba's massive airlift of troops and advisers to Angola, known as Operation Carlota, dates from the period just before independence, at a time when the MPLA found itself besieged by Zaire and the FNLA. While Western observers at the time were convinced that Castro was simply acting on instructions from Moscow, later revelations from Washington, Moscow and Havana point to another scenario. According to political scientist William LeoGrande, the Ford administration and Henry Kissinger himself believed that Castro acted on his own initiative.[38] Arkady Shevchenko, a high-ranking Soviet diplomat who defected to the United States, confirms that Moscow assessed the situation similarly. He reports a 1976 conversation between himself and Soviet deputy foreign minister Vasily Kuznetsov in which he asked the minister, "How did we persuade the Cubans to provide their contingent?" and was told, "The idea for the large-scale military operation had originated in Havana, not Moscow."[39]

While Western observers at the time were also convinced that it was the sudden escalation of Castro's involvement in Angola that drew South Africa and the United States into the fray, the chronology of events speaks otherwise. According to Gunn,

> South African, U.S., and Cuban officials were making parallel but fairly independent decisions, responding to their allies' appeals. The results of each secret decision were then seen in the field, in the form of new military equipment and free spending by the aid recipients. Though each side generally could not prove its opponent was making secret decisions, each speculated that the other was preparing to intervene directly and acted accordingly. Thus, nobody really "moved first" and nobody really "responded" . . . Who started the chain reaction? The chronology . . . suggests everybody.[40]

Nevertheless, Castro believed that the MPLA had to control Luanda at independence, and Havana was determined to make sure that happened. Nor was Castro reticent about admitting his country's involvement in establishing the MPLA as the undisputed government of Angola. Indeed, former CIA operative John Stockwell says it was Havana's willingness to operate openly and the U.S.' need to keep its support of the FNLA a secret that led to the MPLA's victory.[41] At the Cuban Communist Party's 1976 Congress, Lucio Lara, an MPLA political theoretician, told an appreciative audience that it was Havana's "concrete acts of assistance" that enabled the MPLA "to face French and American tanks and cannon used by South African expansionists to invade Angola."[42] Castro responded with a commitment to continue granting all military equipment the MPLA needed.

Cuba maintained its presence in Angola for several interrelated reasons. First, and most importantly, Havana had committed itself to the MPLA's security, and this could never be certain as long as Pretoria continued to invade Angola. While Cuba did not have the same worldwide strategic concerns of the Soviet Union, it felt its prestige as the leader of Third World revolution would be jeopardized by cutting and running from Angola when the going got tough, as it certainly did during the late 1980s. Havana was also motivated by its complex relationship with Moscow. Dependent on the Soviets for its economic survival, the Cuban government believed that its willingness to support a pro-Soviet regime maintained its leverage over Moscow. Not only did this oblige the Soviet Union, but Havana's presence in southern Africa served as a point of contention between the USSR and the U.S., thus helping to stymie a rapprochement between the two superpowers, which would leave Cuba out in the cold, a fear that grew as Gorbachev's intentions to strike Third World deals with Reagan became more obvious.

Havana's relations with Washington were another factor. Cuba felt that American hostility justified countermoves, including providing the MPLA with an effective defense against one of Washington's most favored Third World clients. The Reagan administration recognized this, and tried to break apart the MPLA-Havana alliance with its linkage policy of removing Cuban troops from Angola in return for a South African withdrawal from Namibia. The policy was partially effective. The MPLA feared Cuba might abandon it, and Havana became disconcerted, perhaps unfairly, that a desperate Luanda government was willing to trade peace for a tacit recognition of the apartheid regime. But according to Gunn, Havana's policies began to adjust to the possibility of a linkage agreement by the mid-1980s. It began to maneuver itself into a position where it was ready for any contingency. "If the MPLA wanted more troops, and if Cuban prestige would suffer should the troops not arrive, the soldiers would be provided," Gunn writes. "On the other hand, if the MPLA wanted to negotiate withdrawal, Cuba was prepared to uneasily go along."[43]

Despite this uneasiness, Havana lived up to the letter of the New York accords and pulled its troops out on or ahead of schedule. In assessing Cuban involvement in Angola, two final points needed to be addressed. First, without Havana's help, it is very likely UNITA and South Africa would have triumphed, leading either to Savimbi's succession as president of Angola or to the permanent division of the country. In that sense, Cuba clearly lived up to its commitment to the MPLA, and served South Africa what many commentators argue was a body blow to its prestige, a blow that may very well have hastened the political defeat of the hard-line P. W. Botha administration and the legalization of Nelson Mandela's African National Congress. On the other hand, say critics of the MPLA-Havana alliance, the Cubans profited by their involvement in Angola. While they provided large numbers of both troops and civilian aid workers, particularly in health care and education, they were paid handsomely for it. The MPLA always insisted that the Cubans were compensated for the costs of their assistance only, but Cummings disagrees. "It should also be pointed out," he wrote in 1983, "that none of this Cuban 'humanitarian' comes without reciprocity in the form of hard currency."[44]

MOZAMBIQUE

ORIGINS AND DEVELOPMENT

Unlike the MPLA, FRELIMO was formed in exile, a direct result of the effectiveness of the Portuguese authorities in snuffing out indigenous nationalist movements. Largely composed of students and intellectuals living and working abroad, either in Africa or Europe, FRELIMO organized its first congress in June 1962 in Dar es Salaam, Tanzania. Despite their educational backgrounds and lives in exile, the first organizers were deeply affected by events in Mozambique in the 1950s and early 1960s, including the wildcat strikes by urban workers (only government-approved unions were legal) and the peasant protests of 1960 near the northern town and Portuguese army base of Mueda. The latter event, ending in a massacre of unarmed protesters, was especially galvanizing. "This experience," writes historian Malyn Newitt, "showed that the Portuguese were committed to using troops in civil disturbances and proved the futility of pitting unarmed peasants in demonstrations against a ruthless regime."[45] It also had a deep impact on the Makonde people of the north, who were politicized by the event and became a solid base of support for FRELIMO in the early years of the war against Portugal.

For its first several years of existence, the party was a fact but not a presence in Mozambican politics. As FRELIMO's founder and first president Eduardo Mondlane wrote, "During the time of secret underground work . . . there is little to be seen of the party except a name, an office and a group of exiles who claim to be national leaders but whose integrity is always open to question."[46] Mondlane had put his finger on the problem. From the very beginning, FRELIMO emphasized ethnic, political and even racial inclusiveness, seeing unity as the key to creating a Mozambican nationalism that could both defeat the Portuguese and establish a meaningful polity after independence. But in opening its ranks to all comers of good will, FRELIMO's founder sowed the seeds of dissent, division and factionalism.

The divisions reflected questions of both substance and means. Was FRELIMO a black or multiracial party? Was its political agenda restricted to national liberation, or did it also include social revolution? And should it pursue its ends through peaceful agitation or armed insurrection? Finally, if it did choose the latter course—and the party was deeply divided on this question in the early years—should it pursue an urban or rural strategy? In the end, circumstances dictated the course FRELIMO would take. The early 1960s in Mozambique were marked by a series of sporadic outbursts of peasant and worker violence against the colonial regime, and the Portuguese authorities had responded with a repressive state of emergency. Fearing spontaneous mass uprisings, such as those that had struck Angola in 1960 and 1961, FRELIMO decided to move first. With only 250 combatants in its ranks, the organization launched its first offensive against the Portuguese on September 25, 1964, attacking a military base at Chai in northern Mozambique.

This tactical decision, however, did not preempt other possible strategies. Until its cells in the capital were broken up by Portuguese police in December, FRELIMO had intended to move its struggle to the south, hoping to create an urban uprising that would overwhelm the Portuguese in one blow. Military failures split the party further, causing defections to other small and transient parties or out of the movement altogether, effectively ending FRELIMO's plans to spread the struggle to the heavily populated central provinces. Nevertheless, by the mid-1960s, FRELIMO had consolidated its hold over the Makonde homeland in the north.

Despite their animus toward the Portuguese, the Makonde leaders who supported FRELIMO were traditionalist in outlook. While they wholeheartedly supported FRELIMO guerrillas, they were reticent to allow political and social agitation in their homeland. This resistance led FRELIMO to undertake a restructuring of its organization and its political agenda. It consolidated its military and political wings into one organizational unit and embarked on the cultivation of independent local authorities, more amenable to its social and political agenda. This decision, in turn, caused local resistance and hence military disaster for FRELIMO. These setbacks galvanized the radicals within the movement, that is, those who called for a political "softening up" of the peasantry in preparation for military campaigning, and led to a profound decision that would affect the subsequent history of the organization, the war, and Mozambique's post-independence government.[47]

Unfortunately for FRELIMO, the decision led to neither military success nor a quelling of the divisions within the organization and between FRELIMO and local Makonde leaders. In 1968, responding to Makonde complaints that they were taking the brunt of the conflict, FRELIMO once again attempted to open a front in central Mozambique, but was thwarted by neighboring Malawi's cooperation with the Portuguese military. The continuing military setbacks led to further Makonde discontent and to a decision by Mondlane. Worried that its Second Congress would be dominated by Makonde leaders if it was held in next-door Tanzania (Makonde members had also killed a southern leader in Dar es Salaam in early 1968), FRELIMO decided to hold the session inside Mozambique. There was more than internal politics behind this decision, however. It would represent a propaganda victory against the Portuguese and avoid charges that the leadership remained detached from the people. As Mondlane wrote in the wake of the congress,

> in the liberated areas of Mozambique, FRELIMO is in fact the government, a government operating within its national territory and not a government in exile. . . . this in itself should give us greater authority in international circles [as well].[48]

The congress turned out to be a total vindication of the radicals' agenda, which included social transformation, a long-term peasant-based revolution, political education and the establishment of rural cooperatives. The emphasis on class solidarity over race was also reaffirmed. The shift toward a more radical definition of the national liberation struggle, however, failed to turn the failing military campaign around. FRELIMO was never able to establish a fully liberated zone anywhere in Mozambique in which to put its theories into practice. Continued efforts to make inroads in the central provinces met with failure, though a campaign in the early 1970s to destroy Portuguese infrastructure stretched the colonial army to its limits and bred dissatisfaction among the regular soldiers and in the ranks of the officer corps. Finally, the decisions made at the congress alienated the Makonde chieftains, some of whom, it has been alleged, were involved in the mail-bomb assassination of Mondlane in 1969.

Unlike the MPLA, FRELIMO faced no serious organizational challenges when it took power from the Portuguese in 1975. As the undisputed leaders of the Mozambican revolution, FRELIMO wielded power in the immediate post-independence era with a mix of heavy-handed political repression and an openness to all sectors of the Mozambican nation, transforming itself from a liberation movement to a vanguard revolutionary party. On the one hand, FRELIMO refused to hold nationwide elections because, as Minter says, it "was not their conception of how to build democracy."[49] On the other, says Birmingham, "the nationalist movement became wondrously pragmatic in facing up to its inheritance," making great efforts not to alienate any of Mozambique's racial or ethnic groups.[50] There were, of course, serious ethnic divisions within FRELIMO, largely between the socialist southerners and black nationalist central Mozambicans, and potential conflict between the elite leadership and the masses of impoverished peasants and workers, but all of these were "effectively concealed behind the rejoicing over independence."[51]

While FRELIMO's political and economic philosophy will be examined in chapter 6, some of the general trends and shifts in its ideology are brought up here to show its development as the ruling party in a one-party state. FRELIMO, of course, was confronted with an agricultural and industrial economy largely abandoned by its Portuguese owners, managers and technicians. Thus, by necessity and choice, the party established a state planning board to map out Mozambique's economic future. In order to do this, and to see its plans carried out, FRELIMO created a large bureaucratic structure whose tentacles quickly spread throughout the country as traditional and colonial-era local leaders were replaced by inexperienced and often ideologically rigid administrators. The policy of forced communalization and state farms, on the ruins of the old Portuguese plantation system, was pursued both for reasons of productivity and to better provide social services.

Whether or not these policies were part of the reason for RENAMO's success in the 1970s and 1980s, the war forced FRELIMO to change its policies and its methods of operation in the early 1980s, changes that were formalized at the party's Fourth Congress in 1983. Previously, FRELIMO had been able to avoid the kinds of factional infighting that plagued the MPLA by seeking consensus and avoiding unilateral decision making by the president and the central committee. But the early paralysis in the face of South African–supported RENAMO offensives gave way to a new authoritarianism emanating from the office of President Samora Machel. At the same time, FRELIMO moved toward a more populist position on economic issues. It discontinued forced communalization, permitted land ownership (technically, long-term leases) among the peasantry, and moved to make consumer goods more available in the countryside to stimulate production and introduce a market economy. While these reforms were popular with much of the peasantry, the war made it extremely difficult to implement them.

The escalation of the RENAMO war and South African efforts at destabilization through the late 1980s brought the party and the nation to its knees. In order to shore up its support in the West, FRELIMO abandoned "Marxism-Leninism as the dominant ideology" and dropped the words "People's Republic" from the official name of the country at its Fifth Congress in 1989. Like the tendency toward authoritarianism in the early 1980s and the changes in governance voted on at the 1983 congress, the economic reforms of the 1989 meeting merely formalized trends in FRELIMO policy that had been emerging gradually in the preceding years. In 1984, FRELIMO had found itself unable to meet its obligations to its international creditors. Facing an economic restructuring imposed from outside, FRELIMO moved first, inaugurating its Economic Rehabilitation Program (PRE) in 1986, which included the familiar IMF-imposed devaluation of currency, lowered subsidies, and legislation liberalizing foreign investment and privatization, but also increased wages and higher prices paid to farmers.

While FRELIMO eventually agreed to multiparty elections as the price to be paid for peace, it has been extremely jealous of surrendering power to RENAMO. During the talks in Rome, FRELIMO refused to entertain RENAMO demands that a transition government, run by the UN, be placed in power until elections could be held, seeing in this both a threat to Mozambican sovereignty and its own right to rule. In the wake of the elections, which FRELIMO won by a substantial margin, the party has been unwilling to offer governorships or any important cabinet posts to the opposition. Moreover, through the president's office, it has established a variety of commissions to consider political, economic and constitutional reforms, but has largely excluded opposition parties from participation, leaving the back benches of the national assembly as the only forum for RENAMO and other opposition leaders.

MEMBERSHIP

Political leadership

Despite the emphasis on unity, the FRELIMO leadership has suffered from its share of factionalism, though nothing approaching that which has afflicted the MPLA in Angola. As mentioned above, there was the division between northern chieftains who supported FRELIMO early on and the exiled intellectuals who formed the leadership cadres of the organization. As FRELIMO tried to expand its leadership to include other ethnic groups, including those in the key central provinces, the factionalism increased. Having borne the brunt of Portugal's exploitative plantation system, central Mozambican leaders were far more hostile to racial inclusiveness, and wanted FRELIMO to be an essentially black nationalist movement like that of the Pan-African Congress of South Africa, rather than the multiracial African National Congress.

Eduardo Mondlane, a FRELIMO founder and its president until 1969, was both an important source of the factionalism, and perhaps the single most important figure in making sure the divisions he helped create did not pull FRELIMO apart. Holding a Ph.D. in sociology, Mondlane had spent many years working at the UN headquarters in New York as a research officer on Africa. In fact, he never permanently moved to Africa until the late 1960s. After the First Congress, he placed his imprimatur on a shadowy African American named Leo Milas (aka Leo Aldridge) and returned to his job in New York. Mondlane refused to acknowledge that placing Americans and Mozambican mestizos at the head of the organization might be resented by black Africans in the movement, who even accused Milas and, by implication, Mondlane of being CIA agents.[52] While much of the early factional fighting within FRELIMO can be traced to these choices in personnel, Mondlane commanded broad respect within the organization and the colony as a whole. He rarely shied away from addressing the most divisive issues facing the future of the organization and the course of its armed struggle, and was adept at placing himself above the internal political fray and forging an identity as a kind of father figure to the movement.

Mondlane's assassination was widely blamed on conservative Makonde factions within FRELIMO, allegedly with the help of the Portuguese secret police. These allegations helped assure that Mondlane's ideological protégé, Samora Machel, would succeed him as president, which he did in 1970 after a year-long internal power struggle within FRELIMO. Machel was more authentically Mozambican than Mondlane. The son of an impoverished peasant family from southern Mozambique, Machel had attended local Catholic schools, though his family was Presbyterian. He was trained and registered as a nurse at Lourenço Marques' (now Maputo) main hospital and became one of the founding members of FRELIMO in 1962. Like Mondlane, Machel emphasized decision making by consensus and eschewed a high profile for himself. But whereas Mondlane commanded respect, Machel maintained party unity through his noted charm.[53] Joaquim Chissano, who replaced Machel after the latter's death in a suspicious airplane crash in 1986, was more in the Mondlane mold, an exiled intellectual who completed several years of medical school in Lisbon before returning to Africa to help found FRELIMO.

During the war against the Portuguese, FRELIMO had rigorously condemned traditional chieftains, even though these leaders had neither been appointed by the Portuguese nor worked in the colonialists' interests. In his 1969 manifesto/history, Mondlane applauded one example of local villagers, supported by FRELIMO guerrillas, forming a people's tribunal to impeach an unpopular chief. A predictable enough position for a revolutionary, Mondlane's modernist colors come out in the remarks that followed this example.

> In other instances, where the chiefs have remained neutral or even come out positively on the side of the struggle, the progress of revolutionary power has the effect that traditional power gradually fades away. Certainly, where the

traditional power does not actively uphold the colonial structure or oppose the revolution, the change has to come through positive developments, the emergence of new forms of power, of new political ideas.[54]

Upon attaining power in 1975, FRELIMO attempted to speed the process up. As political scientist John Saul writes, "It seems fair to say that FRELIMO's earlier errors had been primarily those of a genuinely left leadership become too triumphalist and too self-confident of its ability to force the pace of advance."[55] First, FRELIMO immediately placed all schools under its control and adjusted the curriculum accordingly. More controversially, it placed FRELIMO-appointed administrators at the head of village councils throughout the country and established the so-called "dynamizing groups," committees of local FRELIMO supporters who acted as ideological guides (as FRELIMO saw them) or police (as the opposition characterized them) making sure government dictates were carried out.

While many of the FRELIMO administrators offered sensitive and thoughtful leadership, others were heavy-handed in their approach to local politics. Several factors were responsible. First, many of the administrators were inexperienced in dealing with rural folk, having trained in the Portuguese colonial bureaucratic tradition of seeing human beings as obstacles to efficient administration. Second, most were urban and educated, at least to the high school level, with all the prejudices toward illiterate peasants that implies, prejudices that were exacerbated by their belief in themselves as a revolutionary vanguard with a historical mission to politicize the peasants whether the latter wanted it or not.

At the national leadership level, FRELIMO officials were equally guilty of heavy-handedness, though it took some time for this to emerge. According to Hanlon, FRELIMO believed in the "traditional view that 'chiefs should eat first.'

> President Samora Machel used this as part of his nation-building project. He argued that people expected their leaders to be well dressed, and live properly . . . This was true at all levels; students stood when the teacher entered the room, and journalists stood when a minister entered a press conference.[56]

There were practical considerations as well.

> [H]igh state officials could not be expected to work 12-hour days if they also had to queue for bread and buses. Initially, no one objected, because FRELIMO maintained an attitude of common sacrifice; privilege was paired with puritanism. Ministers and high officials lived modestly and were manifestly honest. They did not abuse their privileges; they were not getting rich and building grand houses.[57]

But as Hanlon points out, this gradually changed during the middle and late 1980s. Again, several interrelated factors played a role in this. First, the cart began to be put before the horse; rather than being seen as a necessary side effect of nation-building, privilege began to be seen as an important ingredient to it. More important, however, was the role of the war, the resulting economic collapse of the Mozambican economy, and intrusion of international lenders and aid agencies into the internal politics of the country. The lavish money thrown about by the Maputo offices of many large NGOs had a corrupting effect, leading to bribes and moonlighting by officials.

More insidious, however, was the impact of restructuring. By dismantling the limited but all-encompassing health and welfare safety net established by FRELIMO in its first years of governing, restructuring forced officials to begin to think of private, individualist solutions to their own and their family's economic situation, especially as they feared they might be forced out of government through restructural downsizing. In addition, FRELIMO adjusted to the enforced regimen of privatization and free market expansion by encouraging party members and officials to open up farms and businesses. Both practical and political considerations were part of this decision. As Mozambique's most experienced and educated citizens, government officials were probably best suited to run private enterprise. But the party also hoped that by placing like-minded people in positions of power in the private sector, it could hold on to its authority and maintain a modicum of its initial revolutionary agenda for Mozambican peasants and workers.

Armed forces

Since the mid-1960s, FRELIMO's armed forces have had a dual role as traditional defenders of the nation's sovereignty and as agents of revolutionary transformation. That, at least, has been the official party position. Given the viciousness of the two wars it has had to fight, first against the Portuguese and then against RENAMO, the reality has been something different.

During the first years of the liberation war, the army had no central command; regional commanders managed military affairs in their districts. In 1966, however, the FRELIMO central committee decided that the growing size of the guerrilla forces under its command needed overall leadership, and a fixed headquarters was established in the northern Mozambican bush. Worried that in a wartime situation the army might assume hegemony over the party, the central committee established a command structure that required civilians and military leaders to reach decisions collectively. FRELIMO also established a "people's militia" of "militant members of their civilian population, who carry on with their normal occupations and, at the same time, though not incorporated in the guerrilla army, undertake certain duties." Specifically, this meant defending its home regions and communities and providing logistical support and information to guerrillas.[58]

FRELIMO's decision to politically radicalize the peasantry as part of its guerrilla war had a deeper and more long-lasting impact on the civilian organizations than it did on the military, however. As Saul writes, "The FRELIMO-inspired political structures were still cast [after independence] in a discernibly military mould, with, critics would argue, a degree of centralization of authority that could translate all too readily into a danger-ous kind of 'vanguardism' in the post-liberation phase—especially when the model had to be generalized to that considerable proportion of the country which had not been directly touched by the experience of the liberated areas."[59]

During the transition period, FRELIMO forces were remarkably disciplined, integrating themselves easily into a joint force with the Portu-guese soldiers to maintain order in the country until power was transferred from the colonialists to FRELIMO. Ironically, this display of discipline would portend serious problems for the Mozambican armed forces when they first confronted RENAMO insurgents. The army was not only down-sized after independence but was turned into a more or less conventional force. The FRELIMO leadership refused to believe that it did not have the support of the peasantry, thus there was no need for an army geared to counter-insurgency. If anything, FRELIMO expected that a military threat would come from South Africa. But since there was no chance a Mozam-bican army could possibly defend the country against Pretoria, the FRELIMO leadership decided that appeals to the international community, and especially the socialist bloc, represented the only feasible defense.

Thus, the army was ill-prepared to confront the RENAMO menace in the early years, both during its Rhodesian tutelage and during the first years of South Africa's patronage. By the time the FRELIMO leadership had adjusted to the new order of things, with re-recruitment of officers and soldiers from the war of liberation days, it did not have the resources to effectively train, arm, pay and feed its soldiers. Observing the situation in the mid-1980s, journalist William Finnegan wrote,

> troops in the field often did not receive pay, uniforms, ammunition, or rations. Morale suffered, and when soldiers were forced to find any food they could, the army's reputation suffered.[60]

While human rights groups are careful to single out RENAMO forces for their brutal atrocities against civilians, which include murder, forced labor, the use of civilians as defense shields, forced prostitution and the recruitment of child soldiers as young as 10 years old, they do not completely acquit FRELIMO forces. Killing of civilians by FRELIMO soldiers, while rather rare, does occur and looting is common, says Human Rights Watch in a 1992 report, though it notes that internal discipline has improved and some soldiers have been punished by military tribunals for crimes against civilians and property.[61] Human Rights Watch also accuses FRELIMO forces of widespread illegal conscription of youths, "with soldiers picking up young men as they emerge from schools, cinemas and discotheques."[62]

As part of the 1992 Rome accords, both FRELIMO and RENAMO forces were expected to demobilize at cantonments established by UN observers in various parts of the country. This went smoothly enough, though fears by each side that the other was holding back troops in reserve slowed the process down. After full demobilization, a joint army of roughly 30,000 was formed out of equal numbers of FRELIMO and RENAMO soldiers, though this has been beset with problems as well. Many soldiers on both sides "self-demobilized" or, having experienced the poverty-stricken conditions in which they had to serve, refused to stay in the armed forces. While the sheer size of FRELIMO forces assured that there would be enough of them to fill the quota, RENAMO found it difficult to meet its quota.

Since the creation of a joint armed force, the Mozambican military has been plagued by discipline problems arising out of the same shortage of food and money that plagued it during the war. As *MozambiqueFile*, the official international newsletter of the Mozambican government, has pointed out, the military is failing to maintain civil peace and fight rural crime. Part of the problem is that the soldiers themselves are participating in the hijackings and are running lucrative roadblocks throughout the country. Adding to the chaos have been several strikes by soldiers since 1992. Demanding that they be paid and fed, they have blocked railways and roads in an effort to get a bigger share of the government's shrinking budget.

FOREIGN

Africa

Zimbabwe and Tanzania   Relations between the leaders of Zimbabwe and FRELIMO go back to the days when both were fighting the white minority or colonial regime of their respective countries. Though there was little contact between the Zimbabwean liberation forces and those of Mozambique, and hence little opportunity to cooperate, cordial relations were established. Mozambique's participation in the Lancaster House accords ending white rule in Rhodesia and, more importantly, its commitment to the Zimbabwean struggle and its support of international sanctions against the regime in Salisbury (now Harare) built up a deep well of friendship and obligation on the part of Zimbabwe's new leadership. FRELIMO's moral, economic and political support for Zimbabweans in their struggle would be fully reciprocated during FRELIMO's struggle with South Africa and RENAMO.

Aside from a moral obligation and a sense of solidarity with a like-minded regime, Zimbabwe has had practical reasons to aid FRELIMO. First, much of landlocked Zimbabwe's exports must pass through Mozambican territory and ports to reach the sea. These transport corridors are critical to Zimbabwe's economic well-being, especially since Pretoria began to impose restrictions on the black regime's use of the South African railroad system. Like all of Mozambique's infrastructure, the railroad that connects Zimbabwe's heartland and capital with the Indian Ocean port of Beira has been particularly vulnerable to RENAMO attacks and sabotage. In 1982, Zimbabwean President Robert Mugabe pledged 1,200 troops to protect the Beira corridor.

The Nkomati accords were signed by South Africa partly in the hopes that they would divide the frontline states and establish closer ties between Harare and Pretoria. But the accords failed to have the desired effects. After South Africa violated the agreement, Zimbabwe added another 1,800 soldiers to defend the Beira corridor, which included an oil pipeline and highway as well as the railroad. In June 1985, the leaders of Mozambique, Zimbabwe and Tanzania signed an agreement to triple the number of Zimbabwean and Tanzanian forces in Mozambique and give them a more active role in fighting RENAMO. Zimbabwean troops helped establish peaceful corridors within Mozambique where hundreds of thousands of peasants could find refuge from RENAMO and the war. In addition, several hundred thousand Mozambicans fled to Zimbabwe proper during the war, making it, after Malawi, the country with the largest population of Mozambican refugees.

Zimbabwe's aid to Mozambique came at a price. RENAMO escalated its attack on Zimbabwean towns and villages along the border with Mozambique. Largely conducted to obtain food and other commodities, the raids had a political motivation as well. "Important for RENAMO's operational economy," writes Vines, "[the raids] are also used as a tactical reminder of the rebels' potential for further destabilization in the whole region."[63] In other words, to extract greater negotiating concessions from FRELIMO, RENAMO hoped to put pressure indirectly on the leadership in Maputo through its allies in Harare. In addition, RENAMO hoped to demonstrate to the international community that ignoring the organization would create a risk of regional war in southern Africa. As late as May 1992, just five months before the Rome accords were signed, RENAMO launched a major raid on the Chisumbanje district in eastern Zimbabwe.

Thus, Zimbabwe's commitment to the peace process in Mozambique was motivated by a desire both to achieve peace in an allied state and to prevent RENAMO raids on Zimbabwe, which might, Harare feared, feed into the small but potentially dangerous rebel uprising within the country, the so-called "Super-ZANU" (Zimbabwean Army of National Unity) movement. While RENAMO refused to accept Mugabe as a mediator at the Rome talks, due to Zimbabwean offensives against its guerrillas, Harare committed itself to cooperating with whatever deal would bring its troops home. In fact, says U.S. diplomat Cameron Hume, who participated in the talks, Zimbabwe was "desperate" for a cease-fire.[64] And while there was much wrangling over where and when Zimbabwean troops could conduct operations during the negotiations period, once a settlement was reached, Mugabe pulled his troops out on schedule.

Tanzania's commitments to FRELIMO began during the war against the Portuguese, when the organization was based in Dar es Salaam. While President Julius Nyerere agreed to train FRELIMO troops in the 1970s, he admitted Tanzania's aid to Mozambique would be limited by its own impoverished circumstances. Tanzania, of course, was not dependent on Mozambique for access to the sea, a fact that contributed to its decision to limit its involvement to 3,000 troops. RENAMO's cross-border raids provided another impetus to defend FRELIMO. To end such raids and bring peace to Mozambique, Tanzania strongly supported the Rome negotiations in African and international forums.

International

The Soviet Union and China   Compared with the war in Angola, Mozambique's conflict was largely a sideshow of the Cold War. Neither the Soviet Union nor the United States considered the country strategically important (Mozambique lacked major reserves of oil or minerals) and the absence of existing alternatives to FRELIMO limited foreign policy interference. While Portugal tried to rouse the West to the possibilities of Soviet bases in a FRELIMO-controlled Mozambique during the war of liberation, most Western leaders did not take the threat seriously. At the same time, FRELIMO received most of its superpower arms and support from China, and thus the Soviets never looked on Mozambique as a reliable ally. Soviet concern with Chinese hegemony, however, persuaded Moscow to sign a friendship treaty with Maputo in 1977 and supply FRELIMO forces with air defenses in the early 1980s.

Scholars have long debated the strategic importance of southern Africa to the Soviet Union. Those who focus on Moscow's rhetoric have tended to support the theory that Soviet intervention in the region reflects a grand strategy for domination of the Third World. But the history of the Soviet Union and Mozambique suggests a more reactive pattern: friendship treaties to block Chinese influence, and a small supply of weapons to keep up the pretense of socialist solidarity. In general, Soviet theoreticians considered economic and political conditions in Africa unsuitable for Soviet-style revolution, and its nationalist leadership lacking in the appropriate ideological rigor.

Nevertheless, Mozambique's relationship with the Soviet Union remained closer than that with the U.S., at least up to 1982, when Moscow did little to promote the African nation's membership in Comecon, the Eastern Bloc economic alliance. Thus, a gradual cooling of Soviet-Mozambican relations, and FRELIMO's subsequent overtures to the West, preceded perestroika and the Soviet retreat from the continent.

Like its initial involvement with Mozambique in the 1970s, the Soviet Union's retreat was determined by geopolitics rather than ideological commitment. FRELIMO, recognizing that the Soviet Union was not going to commit itself to combating South African aggression nor able or willing to provide the economic links and aid necessary to develop Mozambique, began to move toward the West, both for funds and to help put pressure on Pretoria. In turn, the Soviets surrendered the diplomatic initiative to the U.S., which was the only superpower involved in the Rome accords. Still, as Saul points out, the retreat of the Soviet Union from southern Africa, and the end of Cold War tensions generally, has diminished Mozambique's maneuvering room in an increasingly Western-dominated world economy and political climate.

During China's Cultural Revolution, radicalism prevailed in the country's foreign policy. Thus, in Mozambique, Beijing supported marginal Maoist-influenced organizations. Beginning in the early 1970s, however, the Chinese moved closer to FRELIMO and became its major foreign supplier of weapons, largely as a result of Beijing's cozy relations with FRELIMO ally Nyerere. Given the hostility between the Soviet Union and China during this period, the fact that both communist superpowers were supporting the organization speaks to both Nyerere's influence on Chinese policy toward Africa and FRELIMO's own diplomatic agility.

The Soviet-Mozambican Friendship Treaty of 1977 was the immediate reason for Beijing's withdrawal of support for FRELIMO, but the move was part of a larger Chinese withdrawal from military and diplomatic entanglements in Africa after the mid-1970s and China's rapprochement with Washington. Describing the nation in the 1980s and 1990s, historian Steven Jackson writes, "China was no longer a revolutionary country, had reduced its once-ambitious economic aid programme in Africa, and paid far less attention to the continent than it once had."[65] Still, Mozambique's relationship with China remains cordial, and Chissano paid a state visit to Beijing in 1988, where he signed a series of agreements on cultural exchanges, political solidarity and economic cooperation.

The United States and the West Assessing U.S. policy toward Mozambique, and whether in sum it was more pro-FRELIMO or pro-RENAMO, requires a set of scales with delicate calibration. The U.S. government was hardly pro-FRELIMO, but neither was it enthusiastic or supportive of RENAMO. Compared with Angola, Washington maintained a studied indifference to the war in Mozambique and certainly didn't react to FRELIMO in the same visceral way it did to the MPLA, which is rather ironic given that most scholars consider FRELIMO the more radical of the two governing parties. In sum, it might be said that the U.S. supported FRELIMO in theory but not in practice. That is to say, it supported FRELIMO's right to govern, but not how it governed; its right to power, but not what it did with it.[66] As Hanlon writes, "in . . . Angola, the goal became putting the opposition in power.

> In Mozambique, however, the failure to turn RENAMO into a credible alternative, combined with the weakness and poverty of Mozambique itself, led to a different strategy of coopting the FRELIMO government.[67]

In and of itself, Mozambique was marginal to U.S. foreign policy. Therefore, the only way to understand U.S.-Mozambican relations is to set them in the context of the U.S. policy towards South Africa on the one hand and the SADC countries on the other. Under the Carter administration, the U.S. extended recognition to the FRELIMO government, in contrast to its stance on the MPLA, and offered nominal support. With the election of Reagan, everything changed, though not as dramatically as with Angola and not necessarily as a direct result of policy changes.

The first effect of Reagan's election on Mozambique was a new aggressiveness on the part of South Africa, including the raids on Maputo just days after the inauguration ceremonies in Washington. According to Hanlon, with Reagan in the White House, the Botha administration believed it had an implicit green light to further destabilize FRELIMO, a phenomenon, some scholars argue, that was repeated after Reagan's reelection in 1984 with South Africa's decision to abrogate the recently signed Nkomati accords.

During the first two years of the Reagan administration, the U.S. did almost nothing to condemn South Africa's policy against FRELIMO. But, according to Chan, by 1983 the so-called State Department moderates had come to the conclusion that South African policies toward Mozambique ran counter to U.S. interests. Specifically, they worried that South Africa's unrelenting war against FRELIMO was likely to push Mozambique further into the Soviet camp at a time when FRELIMO appeared willing, in the wake of the veto of its membership in Comecon, to make a rapprochement with the West. Of course, it should be recalled that it was the Pretoria-sponsored RENAMO insurgency that had rendered FRELIMO increasingly amenable to closer relations with the West.

On the surface of things, Washington's limited support for FRE-LIMO and its mild rebukes of South Africa provide the exception to its policy of constructive engagement, which entailed the prioritizing of South African security concerns above all other U.S. interests in southern Africa. But a closer look at this exceptionalism reveals a different story. While the

U.S. and South Africa diverged on methods to bring Mozambique under Western control—what Saul calls the "recolonization" of the country—Washington and Pretoria ultimately shared the same overall goal, that is, the undermining of the SADC's efforts to reduce regional economic dependency on the apartheid regime.[68] Moreover, the U.S. made its support for Mozambique contingent on FRELIMO's continuing commitment to a dismantling of its socialist economic policies.

U.S. foreign aid was key to this approach. By the early 1980s, Mozambique was one of the largest recipients of U.S. food aid, and Washington used that leverage effectively. The U.S. government was doing much the same thing individual NGOs were doing: It was establishing its own alternative administrative structure, largely under the quasi-governmental organization Cooperative for American Relief Everywhere (CARE) and other U.S.-based NGOs, in order to undermine FRELIMO sovereignty and, in Hanlon's words, "to convince Mozambicans that it was the U.S. and not FRELIMO which supported them."[69] In 1983, the Reagan administration cut off U.S. food aid to Mozambique, and pressured other governments to do so, in order to force FRELIMO to sign the Nkomati accords. This suspension of shipments, some scholars estimate, may have resulted in 100,000 deaths by starvation and disease in Mozambique. FRELIMO was constrained by U.S. policy in other ways too. Its insolvency in 1984 gave the U.S., via the IMF, inordinate power over FRELIMO policy.

Meanwhile, IMF and World Bank policy can best be understood by their reaction to economic reforms undertaken by FRELIMO. In 1983, Maputo embarked on its agricultural reforms. These involved a loosening of central planning in the countryside and experimentation with market incentives to increase production. Rather than coercing farmers to grow commercial crops through cooperatives and forced villagization, FRELIMO decided to offer more consumer goods to encourage production on small, privately leased plots. The government had to borrow further to finance the imports, but it was hoped that increased production would offset the debt. By all accounts, the policy worked and a spurt in production was registered in 1985. But the IMF would have none of it. Claiming it was only interested in FRELIMO's macroeconomic balance, that is, the valuation of its currency and the immediate national debt-income ratio, it demanded a cut in debt-financed imports, and this for a program that encouraged the very market reforms the U.S. and the IMF were supposedly trying to promote.

By 1990, FRELIMO had been forced to abandon many of its economic development programs, accept the hegemony of international aid agencies and institute constitutional reforms calling for a multiparty democracy. But as Oxfam America pointed out, every reform demanded by the IMF that FRELIMO agreed to encouraged harsher ones, ultimately leading to the overturning of FRELIMO's longstanding policy of refusing to negotiate for power with an insurgency movement that the government considered to be little more than South African–financed "bandits."[70] During the Rome talks, U.S. mediators pressured both RENAMO and FRELIMO to negotiate seriously and in good faith, but the incentives it offered to each side were revealing: continued U.S. threats to cut off aid and international loans to FRELIMO, and offers of up to $15 million to RENAMO to help in its transformation from a guerrilla movement to a political party. Current U.S. relations with the now democratically elected FRELIMO government remain cordial, but pressure to push macro-economic reforms continues.

Western Europe and particularly the United Kingdom have taken a direct interest in Mozambique as well. From the early 1980s on, FRELIMO began trying to influence South African policy in a roundabout way, via Lisbon, London and other European capitals. First, it tried to use the Europeans to directly pressure South Africa to stop supporting RENAMO. By the mid-1980s, however, the FRELIMO government realized that only the U.S. was capable of exerting the necessary pressure. Machel, whose close relations with the British government dated back to the 1979–80 period when he helped move the Rhodesia-Zimbabwe settlement forward, appealed to Thatcher to convince Reagan to put pressure on Pretoria.

The new diplomatic approach had some effect. London dramatically increased its aid to Mozambique and denounced South African support for RENAMO in international forums. Thatcher did offer Machel a letter of introduction to the White House and this may have helped prevent the Reagan administration from directly supporting RENAMO, a policy advocated by many on the far right of the Republican party. But the diplomatic offensive ultimately did not have the desired effect. The Reagan administration never pressured South Africa to the degree necessary for it to feel that continued support for RENAMO jeopardized its close relations with Washington.

The other two European countries with a significant role in Mozambique have been Portugal and Italy, the latter through its hosting of the Rome negotiations between RENAMO and FRELIMO, as well as its commitment of peacekeeping troops for the cease-fire, and the former through economic investments since 1994. Most of these have come via the return of colonists who have been encouraged by FRELIMO to resuscitate commercial farming, industry and tourism.

NOTES

[1] Spikes, Daniel, *Angola and the Politics of Intervention* (Jefferson, N.C.: McFarland and Company, 1993), p. 13.

2 Davidson, Basil, *In the Eye of the Storm: Angola's People* (Garden City, N.Y.: Doubleday and Company, 1972), p. 186.

3 The coup and the subsequent war of independence are covered extensively in chapter 2.

4 Stockwell, John, *In Search of Enemies: A CIA Story* (New York: W. W. Norton and Company, 1978), p. 65.

5 Hanlon, Joseph, *Beggar Your Neighbours: Apartheid Power in Southern Africa* (Bloomington: Indiana University Press, 1986), p. 157.

6 Birmingham, David, *Frontline Nationalism in Angola and Mozambique* (Trenton, N.J.: Africa World Press, 1992), p. 49.

7 Harding, Jeremy, *The Fate of Africa: Trial by Fire* (New York: Simon and Schuster, 1993), pp. 33–34.

8 Spikes, *Politics of Intervention*, p. 63; Birmingham, *Frontline Nationalism*, p. 99.

9 Cummings, Nicholas, "Angola: A Case Study in Soviet Neocolonialism" in *Revolution*, Spring 1984, p. 46.

10 For a discussion of Soviet and Cuban involvement in Angola, see below.

11 Coulson, Anita, "Paradox of Peace" in *Africa Report*, September–October, 1991, p. 42.

12 *The New York Review of Books*, February 17, 1983, p. 7.

13 *Ibid.*

14 With its vast oil reserves, the MPLA is in a somewhat better position than most Third World countries to resist these measures, but most of the oil earnings for the remainder of the 1990s were pawned to buy weapons for the renewed war against UNITA after 1992.

15 *The New York Review of Books*, February 17, 1983, p. 7.

16 *The Economist*, September 26, 1992, p. 39.

17 For more on the Katangese rebels, see chapters 2 and 3.

18 Cummings, "Soviet Neo-Colonialism," p. 45.

19 Kaplan, Irving, *Angola, A Country Study* (Washington: American University Press, 1979), p. 186.

20 Human Rights Watch/Africa, *Angola: Civilians Devastated by 15 Year War* (New York: Human Rights Watch, 1991), pp. 8–10.

21 Bridgland, Fred, *Jonas Savimbi: A Key to Africa* (Edinburgh: Mainstream Publishing Company, 1986), p. 419.

22 Human Rights Watch, *Civilians Devastated*, p. 3.

23 Human Rights Watch Arms Project, *Angola: Arms Trade and Violations of the Laws of War Since the 1992 Elections* (New York: Human Rights Watch/Africa, 1994), p. 85.

24 Human Rights Watch, *Civilians Devastated*, p. 3.

25 Maier, Karl, "A Fragile Peace" in *Africa Report*, January–February, 1995, p. 26.

26 Hanlon, *Beggar Your Neighbours*, pp. 153–154.

[27] Nation, R. Craig, "Soviet Engagement in Africa: Motives, Means, and Prospects" in Nation, R. Craig and Kauppi, Mark, *The Soviet Union in Africa* (Lexington, Mass.: D. C. Heath and Company, 1984), p. 37.

[28] Ogunbadejo, Oye, "Soviet Policies in Africa" in Chan, Stephen (ed.), *Exporting Apartheid: Foreign Policies in Southern Africa, 1978–1988* (New York: St. Martin's Press, 1990), p. 355.

[29] Guelke, Adrian, "Southern Africa and the Superpowers" in Chan, *Exporting Apartheid*, p. 234.

[30] Nation, "Soviet Engagement," p. 49.

[31] Bridgland, *Jonas Savimbi*, p. 223.

[32] Gunn, Gillian, "Cuba and Angola" in Fauriol, Georges and Loser, Eva, *Cuba: The International Dimension* (New Brunswick, N.J.: Transaction Publishers, 1990), p. 153.

[33] Spikes, *Politics of Intervention*, p. 228.

[34] Cummings, "Soviet Neo-Colonialism," pp. 43–44.

[35] Gunn, "Cuba and Angola," p. 184.

[36] Bayer, Tom, *Angola. Presidential and Legislative Elections, September 29–30, 1992. Report of the IFES Observation Mission* (Washington: IFES), p. 6.

[37] Benemelis, Juan, "Cuba's African Policy" in Loser and Fauriol, *Cuba*, p. 126.

[38] LeoGrande, William, *Cuba's Policy in Africa, 1959–1980* (Berkeley: University of California Press, 1980), p. 9.

[39] Szulc, Tad, *Fidel: A Critical Portrait* (New York: William Morrow and Company, 1986), p. 639.

[40] Gunn, "Cuba and Angola," p. 160.

[41] Stockwell, *Search of Enemies*, p. 172.

[42] Bridgland, *Jonas Savimbi*, p. 159.

[43] Gunn, "Cuba and Angola," p. 185.

[44] Cummings, "Soviet Neo-Colonialism," p. 47.

[45] Newitt, Malyn, *A History of Mozambique* (Bloomington: Indiana University Press, 1995), p. 521.

[46] Mondlane, Eduardo, *The Struggle for Mozambique* (New York: Penguin, 1969), p. 130.

[47] Newitt, *History of Mozambique*, p. 525.

[48] Mondlane, *Struggle for Mozambique*, p. 214.

[49] Minter, William, *Apartheid's Contras: An Inquiry into the Roots of War in Angola and Mozambique* (London: Zed Books, 1994), p. 98.

[50] Birmingham, *Frontline Nationalism*, p. 57.

[51] Abrahamsson, Hans and Nilsson, Anders, *Mozambique, The Troubled Transition: From Socialist Construction to Free Market Capitalism* (London: Zed Books, 1995), p. 27.

[52] Mondlane's marriage to a white American also angered black nationalists within FRELIMO.

[53] It is said that Machel's gregariousness was a major factor in preventing Reagan's support for RENAMO, after the former made a visit to the White House in 1985. In fact, Reagan was alleged to have said that he couldn't believe such a warmhearted man could be the leader of a Marxist government.

[54] Mondlane, *Struggle for Mozambique*, p. 165.

[55] Saul, John, *Recolonization and Resistance in Southern Africa in the 1990s* (Trenton, N.J.: Africa World Press, 1993), p. 10.

[56] Hanlon, Joseph, *Mozambique: Who Calls the Shots?* (Bloomington: Indiana University Press, 1991), p. 220.

[57] *Ibid.*

[58] Mondlane, *Struggle for Mozambique*, pp. 153–154.

[59] Saul, *Recolonization and Resistance*, pp. 4–5.

[60] Finnegan, William, *A Complicated War: The Harrowing of Mozambique* (Berkeley: University of California Press, 1992), p. 57.

[61] Africa Watch, *Conspicuous Destruction: War, Famine and the Reform Process in Mozambique* (New York: Human Rights Watch, 1992), pp. 64–65.

[62] *Ibid.*, p. 85.

[63] Vines, Alex, *Renamo: Terrorism in Mozambique* (Bloomington: Indiana University Press, 1991), p. 72.

[64] Hume, Cameron, *Ending Mozambique's War: The Role of Mediation and Good Offices* (Washington: United States Institute of Peace Press, 1994), pp. 106–115.

[65] Jackson, Steven, "China's Third World Foreign Policy: The Case of Angola and Mozambique, 1961–93" in *The China Quarterly*, June 1995, pp. 420–421.

[66] The Reagan administration's only direct aid to RENAMO was the 1982 decision to allow the organization to broadcast its message over the Voice of America.

[67] Hanlon, *Who Calls the Shots?*, p. 3.

[68] Saul, *Recolonization and Resistance*, p. 10.

[69] Hanlon, *Who Calls the Shots?*, p. 171.

[70] Seidman, Ann, *The Roots of Crisis in Southern Africa* (Trenton, N.J.: Africa World Press, 1985), pp. 135–137.

6

ISSUES, TACTICS AND NEGOTIATIONS

We don't know how to describe this war. We just know that we are dying and we have to eat.
    —Angolan Civil Defense Worker

In [Mozambique] war is like a terrible accident. It must be as if you were driving in an ambulance toward that accident. You must write what you saw when you arrived, but do not ask why.
    —FRELIMO official

ANGOLA: POLITICAL ISSUES

DOMESTIC POLITICS AND GOVERNANCE

THE MPLA perspective

From its very beginnings, the Popular Movement for the Liberation of Angola (MPLA) was pegged as Marxist-Leninist. So John Stockwell, the CIA's point man in Angola in 1975, called it, though with a hint of admiration at how its ideology gave it a unity of vision and strength of organization absent from the CIA's ally the National Front for the Liberation of Angola (FNLA). The label was also applied to the MPLA by its post-independence rival, the Union for the Total Independence of Angola (UNITA). In fact, despite the MPLA's willingness to include multiparty elections in its 1990 constitutional reforms and then holding such a national political contest, UNITA leaders maintain their convictions that an essential Marxist-Leninist perspective guides the MPLA. "The MPLA is internationalist," argues a UNITA spokesperson in the U.S. "[They] approach the world from a socialist perspective and put ideological interests above national interests. And they are not Africanist. An MPLA man feels better having lunch with a North Korean than he does with a Zambian."[1]

Arguable as the accuracy of the label might be today, the question remains: Was the MPLA ever a genuinely Marxist-Leninist party by any commonly accepted definition of the term? True, all other political organizations and parties were banned in Angola shortly after independence and the MPLA attempted to rein and/or discipline dissident elements within its own ranks through purges and rigorous ideological policing. In addition,

the ranks of party and national leadership largely overlapped, and governmental decision-making was a reflection of MPLA Central Committee
thinking. In short, the MPLA saw itself as a vanguard party whose duty it
was to politicize, educate, and galvanize the Angolan people through a
variety of organizations of workers, women, youth and others led by and
subordinated to the will of the party.

The MPLA leaders had their reasons for taking this political approach.
First, like many African countries, but with an urgency almost unique to
Angola, the nation confronted the specter of ethnic conflict. Like governments of varying ideological persuasions throughout the continent, the
MPLA believed that multiparty democracy was inappropriate to a political
context where parties were likely to devolve into ethnic fronts. National
identity was weak, and nearly 400 years of Portuguese divide-and-rule
policies had seeded interethnic distrust and animosity, though scholars
continue to disagree over how deep and lasting those divisions are. Even
more importantly, Angola has been a nation at war with itself and outsiders,
including regional power South Africa and superpower America, since
before independence. The MPLA would not be the first or last government
in modern times to abandon the luxury of Western-style democracy in the
face of such a threat.

Despite this historical record, the Marxist-Leninist label does not do
the subject justice. For one thing, those who claim the label themselves
hesitate to apply it to the MPLA. In fact, one of the great ironies and
tragedies of the Angola conflict is that the U.S. and South Africa justified
their anti-MPLA actions as a reaction to Moscow's expansionism even
though the Soviets themselves distrusted the MPLA and its commitment
to their style of communism. As political scientists R. Craig Nation argues,
the Soviets had two important reservations about the MPLA and Angola.
First, Soviet leaders questioned the revolutionary credentials of the MPLA
leadership, often regarding them as little more than "bourgeois nationalists" who simply wanted to Africanize the existing political structure in
Angola. Second, and more broadly, Moscow's political theoreticians questioned whether African countries generally and Angola specifically, lacking
as they did a significant industrial proletariat, were at a historical stage where
genuine revolution was even possible.

A number of non-Soviet scholars concur on the first caveat, though
for very different reasons. Anti-Soviet communists like historian Nicholas
Cummings argue that the MPLA did, in fact, represent an African version
of the Soviet political mode, which rendered it, ipso facto, a kind of "state
capitalism" very distant from a genuine Marxist-Leninist party. Cummings
says that in a country like Angola true revolution has to be nurtured among
the peasantry and the MPLA failed to do this.

Other scholars cite a different, though related, characteristic of MPLA
rule. According to journalist David Birmingham, Angola's history rather

than Marxist ideology offers the key to the MPLA. "The bureaucratic tradition in Angola," he writes, "was a deeply entrenched one, and has been intimately linked with each stage of the country's twentieth-century political evolution."[2] Specifically, he cites the consolidation of an *assimilado* and mestizo power elite around the turn of the century, and the bureaucratic inheritance of Portuguese-style fascism. Together the two resulted in a class of leaders interested primarily in assuming control over the colonial bureaucracy with only superficial alterations. And he adds,

> The survival of an over-staffed bureaucracy was only partly explained by the needs of an inherited colonial system rooted in Portuguese fascism and serving the new Marxist concept of a centrally planned society and economy. It was also due to the political ability of the bureaucrats to defend their positions and salaries[3]

In general, the MPLA has eschewed dictatorial rule. Party leaders have ruled through persuasion. The Central Committee, representing the various power bases within the party and nation, usually reaches its decisions by consensus, though it has often promoted its policies by party diktat rather than popular choice or even ratification.

The only significant change acknowledged by Birmingham in 15 years of MPLA rule (as he wrote in 1991) was the rise of the military as "the main rival to bureaucratic power in the central councils of the ruling party."[4] Still, more recent events indicate the army remains subject to civilian decision making. When war and negotiations resumed in the wake of the 1992 elections, the army advocated a final push against UNITA but was overruled by President José Eduardo dos Santos, who sought a renegotiated settlement. On the other hand, Angola has been a nation at war. Large sections of the country remained for years under the authority of the military, which, naturally enough, tended to subordinate the MPLA's political and economic agenda (such as the late 1980s emphasis on privatized farming) to military necessity (including a continuation of the forced villagization of the population into garrisoned state farms).

In fact, it is precisely this relationship between the central government and the provinces that remains the most contentious issue concerning the MPLA's politics. UNITA head Jonas Savimbi, for one, argued that the MPLA's style of rural governance was based on a "Russian" model and hence was alien to and inappropriate for Angola. "The MPLA killed a lot of chiefs because they thought that to make a revolutionary movement they had to get rid of the chiefs so that they could build up the youth to become revolutionaries," he told his biographer in 1983. "They said the heads of villages were feudalists. But by doing so they turned the people against them."[5] Others disagree, though not with Savimbi's assessment of the chiefs. Quoting an MPLA leader, Cummings argues that the MPLA's goal was not to replace the chiefs but rather to place them under the authority of the MPLA without disturbing the "feudal and semi-feudal [political] relations" in the countryside.

> The activist does not try to take the chief's authority away from him. The activist tries to raise the chief's consciousness and to make him understand the goals of the revolution . . . The important thing is that the chief should be made to understand that the Party is there not so much to act against him and his authority, but to improve the conditions of the people and the chief himself.[6]

Still, most scholars and critics of the MPLA argue that the party did try to impose its political sway over the countryside by replacing a traditional—or, at least, colonially created pseudo-traditional—leadership with administrators dispatched from the capital. Indeed, the MPLA believed many local rulers were imposed by the Portuguese and had to be removed from power, though it is unclear how many were removed and how many were reinstated by UNITA, which had a policy of working with leaders ousted by the MPLA.

The UNITA perspective

If Savimbi's harshest critics are to be believed, UNITA has no ideological basis and no real political program outside of Savimbi's own personal ambitions and demands that his Ovimbundu followers get a share of the power that their numbers (some 40 percent of the population and the largest ethnic group in Angola) indicate they should have. Nevertheless, Savimbi personally, and the organization officially, have on occasion elaborated their vision for the future of Angola. And at times, they have also put their ideas into practice in areas under their control, at least to the extent possible in a country at war.

Savimbi's emphasis on the central role of the peasantry owes less to the Maoist ideas picked up during his young adulthood than it does to the Ovimbundu traditions he absorbed in youth. "No ideological system exists in a vacuum," Savimbi argued in 1979.

> And you cannot hurry people along a road that they do not want to follow. That is why a genuinely African revolution requires a willingness to learn from the peasants, and a patience as well, because . . . peasants are naturally *reluctant* . . . They are afraid to change because they say the future is unknown. So if you want to transform their lethargy into action you must understand their aspirations.[7] (Emphasis in original.)

If this prescription for revolution seems a bit reactionary, it is because Savimbi and UNITA usually defined themselves by what they were against rather than by what they were for, a political program that, say some critics, has rendered them singularly unable to adapt to democratic politics. As *Africa Report* concluded in 1993, "[UNITA] lacks ideological coherence, and political maturity."[8] As late as the 1992 elections, Savimbi consistently railed against what he saw as the new colonization of his country by Cubans and Soviets, although this was probably inspired as much by conviction as by his frustration that these foreigners served his opponents. Savimbi, after all, worked closely with South Africa, an outside power most observers of Angola would argue was a far greater and more immediate threat to the nation's sovereignty than any socialist bloc country.

Unquestionably, Savimbi was a fierce anticommunist and probably was so even when training in China in the early 1960s. He seems to have gleaned from Maoist thought its lessons on guerrilla tactics independent of its political, social and economic program, a distinction Mao himself would have said was impossible to make. In fact, Savimbi's ideology was a jumble of contradictions: He wanted to fight a revolution to preserve tradition. "Political and economic theories which are supported in atheistic attitudes," he argued as early as the mid-1960s,

> do not fall in line with the feelings of Africa. The African believes in a higher Being, whatever his name may be or whatever the place where he is worshipped. There is an ancestral force which transcends men.[9]

UNITA's traditionalism occasionally bordered on xenophobia and anticosmopolitanism. Savimbi's rhetoric often lumped together the Soviet hierarchy in Moscow, Cuban advisers in Angola and the MPLA leadership as a monolithic entity occupying the country and enforcing its own ideological program onto an unwilling people. And while he was often careful to avoid such rhetoric in speeches and writings intended for an international audience, at home he often cited the numerical preponderance of mestizos and *assimilados* among the leadership in Luanda, hinting to his Angolan audience that *assimilados* were out of touch with the needs and aspirations of the peasantry.

But Savimbi's leadership and political program often failed to transcend the personal. While rarely elaborating on how a UNITA government would rule Angola, except to say it was committed to democracy, he used his own lifestyle to make his case. Indeed, Savimbi had always lived in the bush with his soldiers, established close relations with traditional leaders and, according to some journalists who made the long trek to his headquarters, lived modestly, sharing the hardships of his supporters and doing without the trappings and material goods he certainly could have had. But this same emphasis on personal leadership remained rife with contradictions. Savimbi brooked no dissent, as his executions of close advisers, who had pushed for a negotiated settlement in the early 1990s, indicated. UNITA, wrote longtime Angola observer Chris Simpson in the wake of the post-1992 election fighting, "suffers, above all, from being identified with a leader incapable of playing by the rules of the democratic game."[10]

FOREIGN RELATIONS

The MPLA perspective

As in many other newly emerging states in the 1960s and 1970s, Angola's foreign policy presents scholars with a chicken-and-egg dilemma. Was its alliance with the Soviet bloc the source of Western hostility, or vice versa? At the time of independence, the media focused on one narrow aspect of this question: Did the presence of Cubans and Soviets trigger the South African invasion, or was it the other way around? Like any analysis that abstracts one issue from history and geopolitics, the media's focus obscured a much more complicated scenario.

During the struggle against Portugal, the MPLA clearly leaned toward the Soviet Union. This was due to a number of factors including the Soviet foreign policy of the Khrushchev and Brezhnev eras, the pro-Soviet tendencies of the Portuguese Communist Party—where many of the MPLA began their political careers while studying and working in Lisbon—and the fact that the U.S. and NATO were supporting and supplying the Portuguese military in its colonial wars.[11] The Soviets did maintain a steady supply of weaponry to the MPLA through much of the war (estimates run as high as $100 million annually by the early 1970s), though nothing approaching the flow of arms after independence. Relations were cordial, but Brezhnevian conservatism obviated a full embrace of the MPLA. Early Cuban/MPLA relations were more volatile, ranging from outspoken support to adventuristic and potentially threatening contacts between Che Guevara and Jonas Savimbi. By the time of independence, however, the MPLA's relations with Havana were extremely close.

As discussed in chapter 2, Soviet arms and Cuban troops were critical to the MPLA's independence victory over the FNLA, UNITA and the South Africans. However, the defining moment in the MPLA's relations with its Eastern Bloc patrons came during the 1977 Alves coup. While MPLA leader Agostinho Neto was unaware of it at the time, he later learned that the Soviets had known of the coup attempt and chosen not to inform him. While the arms flow from Moscow, which was quite lucrative for the Soviet Union given the MPLA's oil wealth, continued, the episode curdled relations between the two governments. But the Angolans were desperate. Always fearing a South African/UNITA/U.S. coalition effort to topple it, they signed a 20-year friendship treaty with the Soviet Union in 1979.

In fact, the MPLA never entirely trusted the Soviets, especially after relations between the Soviets and Americans began to thaw with the accession of Gorbachev in Moscow. Their fear of betrayal was rooted in the belief that a socialist Angola ran against the geopolitical arrangements made between Washington and Moscow at independence, arrangements that placed Mozambique in the Soviet orbit and Angola in the Western one. As one MPLA official rhetorically asked in 1986, "Did it never occur to the Americans that one of the reasons we are so reluctant to send the Cuban troops home is that we want them as a balancing force to the Soviets? After all, we all remember 1977."[12]

As this quote illustrates, the MPLA considered Cuba a more reliable ally, for both ideological and strategic reasons. Castro had been so outspoken in expressing his long-term support for the Angolan cause that even the MPLA's anxious leaders knew a Cuban retreat would have represented an unacceptable loss of face for Castro in the Third World he aspired to lead. As negotiations to remove Cuban troops from Angola, in exchange for a South African withdrawal from Namibia, proceeded in the late 1980s, the MPLA worked closely with the Cubans to make sure that Havana's pullout would not jeopardize Angolan security.

Like many other African nations, however, the Angolan government was aware that the Eastern Bloc could not provide the capital necessary to develop the country's export economy, and the MPLA's strategy was clear from the beginning: Economic development would undercut support for UNITA. Thus, while the MPLA insisted on minimum wages and benefits for Angolan workers in the key oil sector, it never threatened to nationalize American and Western oil companies. While the MPLA's rhetoric in the early years emphasized a gradual training and accumulation of capital that would allow the government to take over the business entirely, the war and, as some scholars say, the limited radicalism of the MPLA leadership rendered that policy null and void.

On the other hand, the MPLA was never successful at winning Washington's recognition, and hence was unable to gain the full support of other Western powers in its war against UNITA and South Africa. This, of course, had much to do with unrelenting hostility of the Reagan/Bush administrations, a hostility illustrated by the fact that even after the MPLA rewrote the nation's constitution and agreed to multiparty elections, Washington refused to offer official recognition. But the hostile relations between the MPLA and Washington were also a result of the Angolan government's singular failure to effectively air its case in the West. As historian William Minter points out, the bipartisan "UNITA juggernaut" in Washington probably doomed any efforts to balance the scales in the MPLA's favor.

> But the contest was made even more unequal by the failure of the Angolan government to make significant countervailing linkages in the U.S. . . . Even critics of U.S. policy had only infrequent access to usable information from Angola. In most Washington contexts UNITA's version of events went unchallenged.[13]

Only with the successful implementation of the 1988 New York accords, concerning the mutual pullout of Cuban and South African troops, did the MPLA attempt a "diplomatic offensive" in the West, an effort motivated by the government's realization that Moscow was increasingly withdrawing from the world stage and that it needed all the friends it could get in its continuing war with UNITA.[14] Added to this was Angola's growing economic plight, especially after oil prices dropped in the mid-1980s. By 1990, the MPLA was in desperate financial straits and its efforts to win Western support were part and parcel of its going, "hat in hand," to international banking institutions to arrange new loans and reschedule old ones.[15]

UNITA's post-election behavior and the collapse of the Soviet Union have helped the MPLA's cause in the West, leading to the Clinton administration's decision to establish diplomatic ties with Angola in early 1993. Yet, according to Victoria Brittain, a journalist who has covered Angola extensively for years, the international community, as represented by the UN, continues to bend over backwards to meet Savimbi's demands and has turned a blind eye to his violations of the Bicesse accords of 1991. These have included his failure to demobilize in preparation for the 1992 elections as well as his continuing demands for a national unity government, a demand that undermines the foundation of the 1991 agreement.[16]

In Africa, the MPLA struggled for recognition and acceptance, and it used a mix of power politics and appeals to solidarity to achieve them. It leveraged its geographical position and transport system against landlocked Zambia and nearly landlocked Zaire. It offered facilities in Luanda to Namibia's South-West African People's Organization (SWAPO) in Namibia, drawing it away from its pre-independence alliance with UNITA and laying the foundations for friendly relations after Namibia achieved independence from South Africa in 1989–90. With African countries and the Organization of African Unity farther afield, the MPLA appealed to their common concern about South African aggression.

As for the apartheid regime itself, Luanda continually tried to strike agreements but, as it quickly recognized, the impetus would have to come from Pretoria. The 1988 New York accords on Namibia and Angola, as well as the accession of the de Klerk administration in 1989, ratcheted down tensions between Angola and South Africa, cutting the flow of arms from Pretoria to UNITA to a trickle. But friendly relations had to await the election of Nelson Mandela and the African National Congress (ANC) in 1994.

The UNITA perspective

"No Portuguese!" Savimbi told CIA officer John Stockwell during their 1975 discussions about American aid to UNITA.

> We need help, but not from *any* Portuguese! My men will work with Americans and Canadians. Maybe French. South Africans can help. But never Portuguese!![17]

It was, says Stockwell, "the only hostility I ever saw in him."[18] Savimbi's remarks were an understandable response to centuries of Portuguese oppression and years of colonial war. But they were also disingenuous, since it has been well-documented, from no less an impeachable source than Lisbon's own military archives, that Savimbi actively cooperated with the Portuguese during the war of liberation.[19] The revelation did not help Savimbi's reputation in country. In fact, both Savimbi's covert acceptance of Lisbon's help and his public denials of it reveal much about UNITA's foreign policy, a policy marked by opportunistic short-term alliances that produced long-term public relations problems.

South African assistance provides an even more glaring example of this. "We cannot fight enemies on two fronts [with the MPLA and South Africa]," Savimbi told biographer Fred Bridgland in 1981. "We don't have any interest at all in having the South Africans come to bomb our areas."[20] Again, the UNITA leader's remarks can be charitably interpreted. Fighting a combined Cuban/MPLA front, no guerrilla commander in his right mind would want to risk provoking an attack on his rear. But the statement, implying a cool neutrality between Pretoria and UNITA, was misleading. By 1981, Savimbi was not only receiving a vast array of weaponry from Pretoria but was actively coordinating his military strategy with the South African Defense Forces (SADF). During the 1980s, it is arguable that UNITA survived and prospered via its alliance with the apartheid regime. This alliance, critical as it was, also alienated Savimbi from other African regimes, even conservative ones that shared his dislike for MPLA radicalism. More importantly, many Angolans viewed his cooperation with Pretoria as a pact with the devil, a view that no doubt contributed to Savimbi's loss in the 1992 elections.

On the other hand, Savimbi was a master at winning U.S. support. Virtually every analyst agrees that UNITA's public relations efforts in Washington were superb, both in maintaining diplomatic support during the years from 1976 to 1986 when the Clark amendment made overt aid to UNITA illegal and, in the wake of its repeal, opening up the arms pipeline from Washington. Not only did UNITA pay a lobbying firm $600,000 but Savimbi himself was adept at gauging the mood in Washington and customizing his rhetoric to exploit it.[21] As media analyst Elaine Windrich notes, Savimbi played the anticommunist, anti-Soviet expansionist card adroitly.[22]

There were, of course, ups and downs in UNITA's relations with the Reagan/Bush administration. Savimbi's triumphant coming to America in the wake of the repeal of the Clark amendment represented the zenith of Savimbi's relations with the Reagan White House. A more contentious visit in 1988 represented the nadir. In the midst of a heated presidential campaign, a growing antiapartheid movement, and disagreements between Washington and UNITA over Namibian-Angolan linkage, Savimbi was not a welcome guest.

Yet this public drubbing by the Reagan/Bush administration never threatened U.S.-UNITA relations, and arms continued to flow to UNITA throughout the Bush years. In fact, say many journalists, Bush's continuing support for Savimbi, as well as his administration's unwillingness to afford recognition to Luanda, even after the MPLA agreed to democratic elections and negotiated a peace settlement with UNITA, contributed to Savimbi's decision to return to war after his electoral defeat in 1992. As the *Economist* pointed out in May 1993, the Clinton administration's decision to recognize Luanda "probably came too late to influence Savimbi. Had the Americans acted sooner, they might have been able to squeeze concessions from UNITA.[23]

Nevertheless, the end of the Cold War left cold warriors like Savimbi exposed. As strategic considerations diminished and were replaced by new international emphases on democracy, human rights and famine relief, Savimbi's contentious relations with Western governments and international organizations could no longer be effectively offset by respect for his fierce anticommunism. Since the late 1980s, charges that Savimbi has harassed and even stymied international relief efforts have received a great deal of publicity in the Western press.

On the other hand, relations with the UN, in the wake of the 1991 Bicesse accords, have been cordial. In its efforts to score a victory in Angola, after the less-than-glowing successes in Somalia and Cambodia, the UN took a neutral position in the UNITA/MPLA conflict, which, say some journalists, actually aided UNITA. The UN ignored the reports of human rights organizations that singled out UNITA as the main violator of human rights, the chief obstacle to peace in Angola (through its reluctance to demobilize on schedule) and the most frequent violator of the country's election laws (specifically, by not allowing MPLA campaigners to enter UNITA-controlled territory). The UN's neutrality lent UNITA credibility. Some journalists have gone so far as to label the UN's approach to UNITA "appeasement."[24] "Through much of 1993," Brittain writes,

> UN planes were shot at by UNITA, UN staff killed, UN equipment stolen and UN access denied to most of Angola, but still the efforts to placate the killers with a political dialogue went on.[25]

THE ECONOMY

The MPLA perspective

Angola's mixed economy has been the result of both ideological conviction and historical necessity. The MPLA's policies have included heavy doses of state planning, state-run farms and agricultural marketing boards, a wholesale and retail system run by the government and many state-run industries. At the same time, however, many farmers practice subsistence agriculture, particularly in more isolated areas of the country, and numerous others farm commercial crops on small, privately leased holdings. A growing proportion of industry and marketing has shifted to private hands, especially since

IMF-dictated economic policies began to take effect around 1990. Meanwhile, an ongoing battle between wildcat diamond miners, once supported by UNITA, and government mining interests continues in the northeast, though the government has gained an upper hand as UNITA lost the military initiative in the mid-1990s.

Most significantly, the oil industry, far and away the most important source of foreign earnings in the country (an estimated 90 percent), remains in the hands of multinational corporations. In short, like much of the ex-communist world, the MPLA's economy is a mix of the old and the new, a continuing commitment to state planning and necessary adjustments to a world economy dominated by the multinational corporations and international financial institutions of the West. The sources of this mixed economy vary. On the one hand, Cuban and Soviet training, education and advisers had a powerful impact on the MPLA leadership. In addition, the sudden exodus of Portuguese farmers and businesspeople necessitated that the post-independence government take over state enterprises. On the other hand, the desperate need for foreign capital to pay for the weapons of war led the MPLA to seek compromises with Western capital, especially in the critical oil industry, from very early on.

But while oil may be the government's main source of revenue, it is not a labor-intensive industry. Far more Angolans were affected by the MPLA's agricultural policies. From the very beginning, the government in Luanda emphasized the agricultural export sector, and the effects were telling. While Angola was forced to import well over 50 percent of its food by the early 1980s, the production of cotton, coffee, and bananas was fast approaching colonial-era levels, until the war made it difficult to grow and transport these crops effectively. The Angolan government did not force most peasants to grow commercial crops, as the Portuguese did, but the MPLA reestablished a similar marketing scheme in the countryside. Export crops grown by peasants could be bartered, at below-market prices, for the goods that were available only through state-run marketing and distribution centers. In addition, hundreds of thousands of peasants were coerced, by civilian administrators and the military, to live and work on state farms.

At first, the MPLA argued that these policies were necessary to overcome Angola's lack of capital, which hindered government plans to create import-substitution industries. Later, of course, the money was required for defense. According to a number of economists, the MPLA seemed intent on reproducing the Stalinist path to industrial development and economic modernization, sacrificing the countryside for the needs of state-owned and -managed industry, though there was a substantial effort to rectify the grossly neglected colonial rural health care and primary education system. Indeed, hundreds of clinics and schools were established in the first years of independence, many of them staffed by Cuban doctors and teachers.

Still, unable to buy much through the production of export crops, peasants resisted agricultural collectivization in the traditional way: They retreated further into the bush or moved to the cities, a process accelerated by the violence and disruptions of the war. Agricultural production fell, and by the mid-1980s, it was estimated the country was importing as much as 90 percent of its food needs, a result both of production disincentives and war.

Corruption at the top and black-marketeering throughout the economy began to flourish. Political scientist Anthony Pereira describes a new class of industrial bureaucrats within the ranks of the MPLA. "This new party-state class," he writes,

> developed chains of clients in the public and parastatal sectors, with interests in both formal and informal economies. Concurrently, international economic linkages allowed the MPLA regime to disengage from most of its own population and to profit from corruption . . . The state virtually abandoned the peasantry and agricultural production, while the cities subsisted as best they could on imports.[26]

As war engulfed the country in the 1980s, the military began to get into the act as well, often acting as middlemen between foreign and domestic businesses and retailers, a trade that occasionally included food donated by foreign governments and international nongovernmental organizations (NGOs).

In addition, the MPLA always seemed more concerned with the cities, partly because they believed industrial workers were more essential to the economy and partly because they feared social unrest there. To that end, the government maintained subsidies on an array of basic foodstuffs and necessities and, to keep imports cheap, maintained the country's currency, the kwanza, at a level far above its black-market price. As the war escalated, things got worse and the basic safety net of the immediate post-independence period unraveled. As services broke down, says Pereira, "the MPLA leaders turned to providing solutions for individuals and/or groups that were either privileged or considered to be strategically important."[27] Meanwhile, the rest of the country depended on the black market.

In desperate need for additional defense revenues, the MPLA was compelled to seek loans from international banking institutions, including the IMF. Knowing the banks would demand an economic restructuring program, the MPLA took the initiative and at its 1987 congress introduced the Economic and Financial Restructuring Program (SEF), which included privatization of industries and business, removal of state subsidies and a radical devaluation of the kwanza.

The hardships imposed were keenly felt as wages fell, prices rose, and real hunger began to appear in the overcrowded cities for the first time. Critics sympathetic to the MPLA say the program was drastic; international business and financial sources argue that it hasn't gone nearly far enough, with large sectors of the economy still controlled by the government and the kwanza overvalued. But most observers agree that the restructuring of the Angolan economy has had an adverse impact on the MPLA itself, reversing whatever efforts it has made to develop the economy along socialist lines, as well as corrupting the leadership. After describing a litany of corrupt deal-making by MPLA leaders as the 1992 elections approached, an *Economist* reporter writes, "Now that the MPLA has abandoned Marxism, ideology plays little part in the campaign."[28]

The UNITA perspective

UNITA has been harshly critical of the MPLA's economic policies, even as the rebels made infrastructure and other economic improvements a specific target of their military strategy. Obviously, as an organization seeking to overthrow an existing government, UNITA has been clearer about what it opposes in the MPLA's economic policy than what it proposes to substitute it with. Savimbi has made his opposition to state farming a theme of his political rhetoric and military tactics, often targeting such farms and evicting or kidnapping the peasants who work them. In addition, because Savimbi sought the support of the ardent market-oriented Reagan and Bush administrations, he emphasized UNITA's commitment to free enterprise. Part of this, of course, is a product of Savimbi's well-honed instinct for striking the right chord with his international mentors. And it clearly worked, both in Washington and, as Birmingham writes of the independence period, in South Africa as well.

> UNITA was seen [in South Africa] as the most likely movement to form a pragmatic government of the Malawi or Gabon type which could do business with South Africa, or at least South African business corporations.[29]

On the other hand, as historian Gerald Bender points out, UNITA's commitment to peasant commerce was a direct result of Ovimbundu historical experience. The people of the central highlands, he says, were more rudely introduced to the colonial market economy than other ethnic groups. As Angola's richest agricultural region, the highlands were more thoroughly colonized, leading to peasant displacement, soil depletion and other external factors that broke down communal land patterns. "In other words," says Bender, "social and economic organization had become more individualized—more Portuguese as it were—with the breakdown of clan or village-bound society."[30] While a one-to-one equation between private farming by Ovimbundus and UNITA's anticommunism is too simplistic, it does offer hints about why many Ovimbundu resisted forced settlement on MPLA state cooperative farms so vehemently. It also offers a key to Savimbi's own thinking on peasant economics. Above all else, he understood his people's determination to farm land of their own, and he frequently placed the small land-holding peasant at the center of his economic agenda.

Opportunistic or historically rooted, Savimbi's own vision for a modern Angola remains muddled, with scholars and journalists grappling with what a UNITA-run Angolan economy might look like. In his classic book on the Angolan revolution, historian John Marcum argued that the MPLA and UNITA represented two different kinds of economic nationalism: The MPLA stood for an "anti-systemic" ideology that stood outside and even opposed the "logic of the capitalist world-system," while UNITA accepted it.[31] Pereira disagrees, citing the MPLA's close cooperation with Western oil companies. "Rather than system versus anti-system," he writes, "the continuing conflict in Angola should be seen as a state-led, inclusive nationalism clashing with a particularistic nationalist movement trying to seize the state."[32] In other words, the differences between the economic programs of the MPLA and economic rhetoric of UNITA have been exaggerated. Yet the question remains, What, in fact, does UNITA propose for the Angolan economy? According to journalist Jeremy Harding, the answer is a mix of purposeful ambiguity and wishful thinking. "Savimbi's vision of a civilized El Dorado still presupposed two nations," he notes,

> a peasant nation gradually restoring its land and a nation of money spinners rapidly founding a modern economy . . . On this new frontier, what recourse would the one nation have against the bustling depredations of the other? . . . [A]s a likely president of peacetime Angola, he could not produce the bold, imaginative outlines of a new African polity that extended rights and respect to the peasant majority and wealth to the country as a whole. The best he could envisage was an African version of Brazil.[33]

Given wartime conditions, the actual practices of UNITA and MPLA share certain resemblances, including forced expropriation of peasant agricultural surpluses and exploitation of mineral resources to buy weapons, with little consideration for ideological rigor as long as the flow of revenues continued. As one foreign oil worker explained in 1994, "This war is between Angola's two main tribes: oil and diamonds."[34]

A final note should be added about the Front for the Liberation of the Enclave of Angola (FLEC), an armed separatist movement in the geographically separate and oil-rich province of Cabinda to Angola's north. The organization, based among the largely Kikongo-speaking people of Cabinda, has existed since shortly before independence. Rising and falling on the fortunes of the MPLA—that is, whether or not the MPLA is distracted by the war against UNITA—FLEC seeks an independent state for the enclave or, short of that, more control over and benefits from the Angola oil industry, over 50 percent of which is based there. In late 1995, an agreement offering more jobs, revenue and administrative input to the Cabindans was signed between FLEC and the MPLA.

RELIGION, RACE AND ETHNICITY

The MPLA perspective

In 1983, Savimbi biographer Fred Bridgland accompanied a UNITA patrol as it occupied a small town in southeastern Angola. The MPLA soldiers had garrisoned one of the local churches as a barracks, he noted, and the place looked it. Pews were torn up and the altar used as a galley. The UNITA guide, he wrote, "ranted tedious propaganda about how we were the first Western journalists to see how the MPLA desecrated and violated the sanctity of churches." But Bridgland noted a few discrepancies in the story.

> Though the MPLA's constitution had anti-religious clauses, there were several Bibles in tribal languages among the abandoned possessions of the "Marxist" soldiers. It was a reminder of the danger of buying "package deals" about any group in Africa.[35]

During the colonial era, the Portuguese had worked with the Catholic church to propagandize the righteousness of their regime, though the effort had never been very effective. Angolan Catholics modified the faith to their own needs, and Protestant missions, frequently offering a vigorous critique of the Portuguese regime, made inroads throughout the colony; Protestant mission schools were the incubators of nationalist leaders, philosophies and movements. Thus, the MPLA approached Christian institutions and faith with a mix of benign neglect and tolerance. The major impact of the MPLA revolution on the churches was in education. Religious-run schools were nationalized and the curriculum secularized. But the left-leaning MPLA left the church alone, as long as it stuck to purely spiritual affairs. The 1990 constitutional reforms explicitly listed religious freedom as part of their package of democratic rights.

On the other hand, the MPLA was openly hostile to the traditional animist faiths of the Angolan people religions that the country's first constitution derisively labeled "*obscurantismo*" and vowed to "combat vigorously."[36] While UNITA could hardly use this MPLA strategy as a propaganda tool with its Western backers, many of whom were connected to or influenced by Christian evangelism, Savimbi did argue that the MPLA was attacking "the essence of our [African] values."[37] As for the MPLA, it clearly saw *obscurantismo* as an obstacle to progress and a cultural brake on modernization, believing that peasant ideas about witchcraft and magic undercut the people's faith in and commitment to revolutionary transformation. In addition, Savimbi's occasional use of "witchcraft" charges against political dissidents was exploited by the MPLA as an example of how *obscurantismo* continued to be used to exploit the Angolan people.[38] Nevertheless, traditions die hard, especially during times of duress. In the war of liberation against the Portuguese, MPLA guerrillas, though officially discouraged from it, sought out spiritual leaders for "medicines" to make them immune to the "white man's bullets." This practice continued throughout the war with UNITA, though unlike Savimbi's organization, it never became a routine part of the soldiers' indoctrination.[39]

As for racial and ethnic inclusiveness, most scholars agree that the MPLA scores well, certainly more so than UNITA. Not only is the MPLA leadership multiracial and somewhat multiethnic but its politics and propaganda are infused with an inclusive Angolan nationalism. During the war of liberation, the MPLA included many Portuguese dissidents as well as a disproportionate number of mestizos, and it boasted of this fact in its communiqués. According to Minter, the MPLA (as well as UNITA) "defined their objectives in centralizing national terms, rather than in terms of ethnic or local patronage networks."[40]

Has the MPLA's official position on a multiethnic party and government registered with the Angolan people? The answer depends on how one reads the 1992 election results. According to Ohlson and Steadman, the election results clearly indicate that the MPLA's strength remains in the cities and Kimbundu heartland of Angola, though how much this had to do with efforts by UNITA to prevent MPLA campaigning in Ovimbundu-land is open to debate.[41] Still, Pereira and other scholars disagree with the Ohlson/Steadman assessment.

> [The] evidence that regional and ethnic particularism is rather less strong in modern Angola than might be imagined is reinforced by the 1992 electoral data, which in my view, are relatively credible . . . It is thus difficult to deny that the 1992 elections reveal strong cross-ethnic support for the MPLA. Particularly striking is the fact that the party won a majority of the valid votes for the National Assembly in 13 of 18 provinces, including two—Kwanza Sul and Huila [in the Central Highlands]—claimed by Savimbi as belonging to "his" people.[42]

On the other hand, the MPLA has emphasized a general anti-tribalism, which, like its hostility to religious obscurantism, is an important part of its political agenda and propaganda. Arguing that the Portuguese had used tribalism to divide the Angolan people, the MPLA at independence "explained that any program that stressed going back toward tribal allegiances would divide the people, making them more vulnerable" to dissident political ideologies and foreign invaders.[43] This policy, says Pereira, has characterized the MPLA ever since. Writing in 1994, he argued that the party "has worked hard, and relatively successfully, to overcome ethnic imbalances whereas the UNITA continues to be primarily an Ovimbundu organisation."[44]

Still, the war has clearly had a deleterious effect on ethnic animosities. "Although UNITA and the MPLA did not have their roots in ethnic politics," note historians Thomas Ohlson and Stephen Steadman, "the last fifteen years have reinforced ethnic tendencies in the two parties."[45] Savimbi has made Ovimbundu solidarity and MPLA pro-mestizo favoritism key parts of his political message, while the MPLA has been guilty of Kimbundu ethnocentrism, as when it attacked Ovimbundu population centers that it viewed as inadequately loyal to the government.

The UNITA perspective

UNITA, of course, is largely an Ovimbundu political movement. Savimbi founded it as such, though he claimed it was open to Angolans of all ethnic groups. But while there have been non-Ovimbundu members of the organization's leadership, they have proved exceptions to the rule. UNITA's military and political base has always been in the Ovimbindu heartland of the central highlands, and in the 1992 elections, UNITA garnered approximately 80 percent of the vote, but fell far short of that mark elsewhere. Yet, the equation that Ovimbundu equals UNITA and vice versa can conceal as much as it reveals.

The sources of Ovimbundu identity, however, are as much a product of history as they are of culture. Their economic experiences under the Portuguese were especially disruptive of traditional village and clan cohesion, both in Ovimbunduland and in the Ovimbundu diaspora on the plantations of the north, where they served as laborers on lands taken from the Kikongo and Kimbundu. There they encountered other tribes who were not so much hostile to them as they were condescending, although many Kikongo, themselves displaced by the Portuguese, took out their anger on the Ovimbundu who worked for the colonists.

By independence, these opinions had hardened into stereotypes, and Savimbi played on them effectively. On numerous occasions both before and after independence, he lashed out at the MPLA for what he saw as anti-Ovimbundu exclusionism. But the rhetoric also bordered on racism. Savimbi, though denying such accusations, often employed a tribal-populist message in which he attacked the MPLA for not being African enough. Before independence, he claimed this was due to the dominant role of mestizos and whites in the MPLA. Later, he modified the charges, labeling the Luanda government as too elitist and too enamored with European ideas like internationalism and socialism.

The rifts between the Ovimbundu and other ethnic groups are also based on religious differences. Savimbi, of course, often complained about what he saw as MPLA "atheism," but that was only part of it. The Protestant missions laid much of the foundation for subsequent Angolan nationalism, as well as its tripartite division. Savimbi was the product of the U.S. and Canadian Congregational missionaries who made southern and central Angola their field of evangelization. American Baptists proselytized among the Kikongo of the north, and English Methodists focused on the Kimbundu of Luanda and its environs. "Each created a network of school-leavers," notes historian David Birmingham, who knew each other intimately and could travel with confidence through the length and breadth of their own mission fief. They rarely, however, crossed the boundaries into the other zones and had little or no contact with other Protestant churches. Indeed, they were more likely to be acquainted with local Catholics than any Protestants from other regions.[46]

Ultimately, though, Savimbi's ethnic politics were largely about getting a fair shake and a fair share for the Ovimbundu people and, of course, for himself as their leader. According to Minter, Savimbi employed a simple political logic recognizable to any urban American politician. "Since southerners [Ovimbundu] were the largest group [in Angola], UNITA implied, their party had the right to a dominant share in power."[47]

Yet, Minter also questions the tendency of journalists and scholars to overemphasize the ethnic component of Angolan politics. Ethnicity, he says, plays a major role in the upward mobility of party members and leadership, particularly in UNITA. But he also notes that the kind of "ethnic cleansing" notable in the former Yugoslavia is largely absent from Angola. Only the FNLA made it part of its strategy and tactics, to their detriment. The atrocities committed by UNITA and the MPLA, he says, had less to do with ethnicity than with political affiliation.[48]

MOZAMBIQUE: POLITICAL ISSUES

DOMESTIC POLITICS AND GOVERNANCE

The FRELIMO perspective

While riddled with ideological divisions during its first decade or so of existence, FRELIMO had, by the time of Samora Machel's accession to the presidency of the organization in 1970, settled on a coherent political program. This program would serve as a blueprint for FRELIMO during the final years of the war of liberation, the first decade of independent rule, and, arguably, in an adulterated version, during the period of retrenchment after the government's default to its international creditors forced a restructuring of government finances in the mid-1980s.

In its early years, the party was dominated by nationalist politics, not unlike those in other African countries, except for the obvious fact that due to Portuguese intransigence FRELIMO could not put them into practice. This nationalism was marked by a desire for self-determination, neutrality in the Cold War, and a desire to rectify and move beyond the dependency model of economic development whereby African countries felt locked into a relationship with the West in which cheap raw materials from mines and plantations were traded for manufactured goods at a distinct economic disadvantage. FRELIMO was also marked during this period by a modernizing urge that saw in traditional political and religious institutions a backwardness that had to be overcome in order to modernize the nation. Still, the question of whether these goals would be achieved through multiparty politics, market economics or a one-party state and socialist planning went largely unexamined.

By the mid-to late 1960s, FRELIMO was beginning to adopt a more radical political ideology that saw in capitalism and multiparty politics an ideology ill-suited as a model of rapid modernization. Like the MPLA, FRELIMO was heavily influenced by the thought and writings of Amilcar Cabral, the leader of the resistance in the former Portuguese colony of Guinea-Bissau and arguably the most important political theorist to emerge from Lusophone Africa. Cabral advocated what he called a "pragmatic" Marxism, by which he meant one adapted to the peculiar circumstances of an Africa long dominated politically and economically by European colonizers. According to Cabral, an African vanguard party had to promote political organizations based on class rather than ethnicity while, at the same time, constructing an entirely new nationalism in place of traditional and colonial models, though absorbing the best elements of each.[49]

Unfortunately, as far as FRELIMO's political agenda was concerned, its limited ability to establish liberated areas before independence required that it move very quickly to build national and party institutions after it took power in 1975. Symbolically, it relabeled itself a Marxist-Leninist vanguard party in 1977, while restricting membership to a small coterie of like-minded individuals. While the party had previously emphasized the peasantry as the most important revolutionary cohort, it shifted to a new emphasis on the relatively small Mozambican proletariat, a class it believed was more politically advanced.

These shifts toward tighter leadership cadres became evident in the way decisions were reached. Previously, FRELIMO had solicited popular input through mass meetings of the peasantry. After it took over the government, these democratic forums were drastically cut back as the ultimate decision making devolved on the central committee and was administered by party regulars in the countryside. As historian Malyn Newitt writes, "Party members gradually changed their role from dynamising, motivating and creating political consciousness in a newly liberated people to issuing orders and carrying centrally decided party diktats to the provinces."[50] Not surprisingly, the lines between party and state began to blur. Both at the national and local levels, FRELIMO leaders wore two hats: party chairpersons and governmental administrators. This had several unfortunate consequences. First, much of the FRELIMO leadership, imbued with the ideological teachings of the party, were wont to act on political theory rather than direct experience of Mozambican conditions when carrying out policies.

More dangerous to the FRELIMO program, however, was the host of local traditional leaders and entrepreneurs who remained committed to the old order established by the Portuguese but adopted the rhetoric of FRELIMO in order to advance their own interests. "The more articulate and educated members of the petty bourgeois," writes political scientist Barry Munslow,

> were quick to present themselves as longstanding sympathisers. Within the colonial hierarchy, they occupied junior grades but still enjoyed a social superiority in relation to the overwhelming proportion of black Mozambicans who were workers or peasants. The latter let them take over control of many [dynamizing groups] in part as a result of deference to their superior wealth, education and social standing.[51]

FRELIMO's leaders, however, were not unaware of the potential for misrule and authoritarianism. To counter these tendencies, they maintained a pyramid of popularly elected assemblies at the national, provincial, district, city and village levels, over 1,300 in all. FRELIMO would nominate the candidates, while the people would debate the merits of each, gradually striking off unpopular and unsuitable names from the list. FRELIMO, however, refused, as a matter of policy, to nominate traditional leaders, the so-called *regulos*, even where they were popular and effective. This created tensions and disenchantment among the people.

FRELIMO also encouraged self-examination of its methods and goals. At all assemblies and congresses, party regulars would stand up and admit to their mistakes, though this was often used to focus attention on minor details rather than overall policy. At the national policy-making level, Machel launched several "presidential" campaigns. These were not elections, but efforts, directed from the office of the presidency, to formulate and publicize national goals, such as building party organization in the mid-1970s or increased production in the 1980s.[52] Through these various methods, say some scholars, FRELIMO was effectively able to change direction in policy without losing internal cohesion.

Probably the greatest such change and challenge concerned the decision to accept multiparty democracy and elections in the early 1990s. These two primary demands of RENAMO—and key parts of the negotiations in Rome—were resisted by FRELIMO for a time out of ideological conviction and self-interest. Like many other ruling organizations in African one-party states, FRELIMO believed that internal tensions would be exacerbated by multiple parties as they became political vehicles for different ethnic groups. FRELIMO leaders also believed that a multiparty democracy would undermine the nation's revolutionary program.

Finally, FRELIMO believed that caving into RENAMO demands for multiparty elections, demands that were seconded by the international mediators of the talks, meant caving into an illegitimate group of "bandits" and surrendering its sovereignty to foreign governments.[53] Nevertheless, FRELIMO once again transformed itself, this time into a Western-style party, and campaigned as such in areas under its control, winning a majority of seats in the assembly, all the provincial governorships and the presidency. In the years since, FRELIMO has adjusted to its role as the party of government in a multiparty democracy by using its absolute majority to control the political agenda and marginalize the opposition. Many of the most important decisions emerge from the so-called presidential commissions, manned entirely by members of FRELIMO.

FOREIGN AFFAIRS

The FRELIMO perspective

FRELIMO has always taken a pragmatic approach to relations with the superpowers and, unlike the MPLA, has been notably successful in promoting its message in the West, though to do so it has had to shift with the geopolitical winds. During the war of liberation, FRELIMO was understandably hostile to the West. NATO heavily supported the Portuguese, and the ideology of liberation saw the U.S. and Western Europe as the bastions of political reaction, though the party had already adopted a studied nonalignment between East and West before independence. On the other hand, FRELIMO accomplished the nearly impossible within the socialist camp, obtaining limited military and diplomatic support from both Moscow and Beijing.

At the same time, FRELIMO was an outspoken proponent of Third World liberation and decolonization, especially in neighboring Rhodesia. At enormous economic expense to itself—estimates place it as high as $550 million in direct and indirect costs—Mozambique enthusiastically applied international sanctions against the white-ruled regime by cutting off railroad shipments to the landlocked country and providing bases for Zimbabwean guerrillas. As noted in chapter 3, this solidarity resulted in the establishment of RENAMO, a factor that steered Mozambican foreign policy toward the socialist camp, since it alone agreed to supply Maputo with the arms it needed to defend itself. RENAMO's rather sordid reputation in the West helped counterbalance this tilt to the East. As Hanlon writes, FRELIMO enjoyed "good relations with the USSR and acceptable ones with the U.S. and Britain."[54] On the whole, however, Mozambique emphasized good relations with the smaller socialist regimes like Cuba and more progressive Western governments like those in Scandinavia.

The early 1980s, however, saw several about-faces in Mozambique's foreign policy. The inauguration of the Reagan administration in 1981, and its tacit encouragement of South African aggression, made it more difficult to play both international camps against the middle. Then in 1982, the USSR failed to push through Mozambique's membership in the communist economic organization Comecon, probably because of pressure from Eastern European states who didn't want to support an economically backward member. This decision forced FRELIMO to make several changes vis-à-vis the West and South Africa. First, it appealed to the Thatcher administration, which owed FRELIMO a favor for its cooperation in the British-sponsored peace talks on Zimbabwe in 1979. The overture met with success, and Thatcher took on the duty of persuading the Reagan administration to avoid support for RENAMO. The appeal, aided by Machel's own diplomatic talents, bore fruit. In virtually the only exception to the Reagan doctrine, Washington refused to aid an insurgency that advocated free market reforms and that was fighting against a self-proclaimed Marxist state.

These overtures to the West were accompanied by a diplomatic offensive against the apartheid regime. The growing severity of South Africa's destabilization campaign and support for RENAMO forced Mozambique to ignore the wishes of its frontline state allies and sign the 1984 Nkomati accords with Pretoria, calling for a mutual cutoff of South African support for RENAMO and FRELIMO protection of the ANC. Paradoxically, FRELIMO's increasingly friendly relations with the West were accelerated by two of FRELIMO's most important diplomatic and economic setbacks. First, Pretoria's brazen disregard for its obligations under Nkomati tilted the U.S. and the West away from tacit support of South Africa. More importantly, FRELIMO's default on its international financial obligations in 1984 forced the government to approach the West as a mendicant, allowing international financial and aid institutions to dictate terms and thus proclaim that FRELIMO was abandoning its anti-Western and anticapitalist programs.

In Africa, FRELIMO used both political and military pressure and appeals to solidarity to help isolate RENAMO. In the mid-1980s, it effectively pressured Malawi to stop aiding the rebels. While RENAMO adjusted to this exile by shifting its training and logistical bases to Kenya and using Malawi only for clandestine transit, the rebels could not penetrate Mozambican territory as effortlessly as they once had. On the other hand, FRELIMO effectively solicited a solid military commitment from Zimbabwe, which felt it owed Mozambique a favor for its help during its own war of liberation and needed to secure its non–South African rail connections to the sea from RENAMO sabotage.

Despite these troops and the lessening of South African support for RENAMO under the F. W. de Klerk administration, which came to power in Pretoria in 1989 and was increasingly pressured to consider ANC foreign policy input, FRELIMO was in desperate straits and was forced to accept negotiations with RENAMO under international auspices. Nevertheless, FRELIMO refused to accept Kenyan mediators, as RENAMO demanded.

FRELIMO negotiators also rejected rebel demands for an internationally run transition government in Maputo.

An arguably greater threat to FRELIMO's sovereignty since the 1980s has come from the international aid agencies, who continue to provide a substantial proportion of the Mozambican gross national product. The war against RENAMO and South Africa not only bankrupted the FRELIMO government, but it also placed large sectors of the populace under immediate threat of famine, a situation made worse by the severe drought of the late 1980s and early 1990s. While FRELIMO has had some success in balancing the country's desperate need for aid with a determined effort to counter NGO attempts to undermine its sovereignty, Mozambique continues to be governed both by FRELIMO and the major international relief organizations. That is to say, either through well-intentioned paternalism or racism, many of the larger NGOs, such as CARE and Save the Children, have made it a policy to establish their own administrative networks in Mozambique, believing FRELIMO is either too incompetent to do the job or too biased against RENAMO-controlled areas to do it fairly.

In the late 1980s, FRELIMO began to establish its own administrative clearinghouse to retain some control over these international aid efforts and to prevent the organizations, which are often very jealous of their administrative bailiwicks, from duplicating one another's efforts. In addition, by abandoning its role as the vanguard party of the Mozambican revolution in the late 1980s, FRELIMO has directly and indirectly encouraged the establishment of Mozambican-based and -run NGOs and civic organizations to promote education, health, democracy and economic development in the countryside and cities.

THE ECONOMY

The FRELIMO perspective

As with those of the MPLA, FRELIMO's economic ideas and practices have been the result of both ideological conviction and administrative necessity. During the war of liberation, FRELIMO formulated a rigorous critique of the existing colonial economic order. It denounced a system in which peasants were forced to grow crops and sell them at colonial marketing boards for below-market prices, or work on the large plantations that occupied the most productive land in the colony, particularly in the fertile Zambezi River valley. In urban areas, FRELIMO envisioned state-owned industries and a limited private sector, this latter policy bordering on black nationalism as it promoted the idea of replacing the existing Portuguese and Indian retailers with African ones.

A decade in the making, these plans had to be put into practice precipitously when most of the colony's Portuguese entrepreneurs and managers fled during the independence period, a situation exacerbated when impoverished peasants began flocking to the cities looking for employment once colonial restrictions on internal migration were lifted. FRELIMO's commitment to rapid industrialization and modernization, and the fact that it was forced by necessity to place industrial and agricultural enterprises into inexperienced FRELIMO managerial hands, led to a series of economic mistakes and setbacks. In addition, under socialist bloc tutelage, central planning and an emphasis on high-tech factories were rapidly adopted, resulting in both inefficiencies and a drain on state revenues.

In the hopes of following the counterdependency Third World model of utilizing peasant surpluses to accumulate capital for the creation of import-substitution industries, Frelimo continued the Portuguese practice of inadequately compensating farmers for their commercial crops, though there were some important modifications. Peasants were not so much exploited through low prices as through a dearth of consumer goods to buy. In addition, FRELIMO used coercive methods to keep colonial-era laborers on existing export-crop plantations and even increased their numbers through coercive recruitment. The policy known as villagization also had its positive side. It allowed FRELIMO to make educational facilities, literacy campaigns and health clinics widely available to the peasantry.

Foreign affairs also dictated economic policy. The application of sanctions against Rhodesia, along with the loss of Portuguese technicians, cut seriously into the revenues Mozambique obtained through railroad transit and port traffic. Beira, the country's main port, for instance, became an economic backwater during the 1970s and 1980s. In addition, the growing hostilities with Rhodesia and South Africa virtually destroyed the lucrative tourist industry of colonial times. By the mid-1980s, Mozambique was facing bankruptcy and was becoming increasingly dependent on foreign aid, to the point where it represented well over half the country's GNP by the latter part of the decade.

FRELIMO responded to the crisis with its characteristic mix of revolutionary commitment and pragmatic adjustment to international demands. At its Fourth Congress in 1983, Machel launched one of his so-called "presidential campaigns," around the theme of enhanced productivity. This entailed shipping thousands of idled urban workers into the countryside without adequate preparation at the urban end or the necessary infrastructure in the countryside. As Hanlon comments, "These authoritarian measures were not even effective; forced villagization and Operation Production only created recruits for [RENAMO]."[55] At the same time, FRELIMO rigorously combated the black market, which flourished due to the party's refusal to import consumer goods. In 1983, the government went so far as to execute an Asian prawn dealer for illegal economic activities.

Several years later, FRELIMO changed tacks again, this time to a more market-oriented approach, but only after a lengthy struggle within the central committee. At first, those officials prevailed who argued that previous policies, including heavy investment in modern industry, simply needed more time to reach fruition. The problem, said this faction, was not in central planning per se, but in the inexperience of government administrators, which, it was presumed, would be overcome as the managers gained more expertise. Still, there was widespread consensus that the government's agricultural policies were not working. But rather than shifting resources from revenue-draining state industries, the government decided to add to its strained budget the import of consumer goods and simple tools, while speeding up their distribution to state-run retail outlets in the countryside.

Despite the deficits it produced, the policy was actually quite successful, and Mozambique experienced a mini-boom in production in 1985 and 1986. Commercial crop output jumped as peasants now had an incentive to produce and were allowed to farm land leased directly to them. Several years of adequate rainfall helped as well. FRELIMO hoped that it had initiated a self-sustaining economic cycle in which rural production would increase revenues, which, in turn, would allow the government to sustain both its older industrialization program and its new emphasis on consumer imports and distribution. Unfortunately, two things interceded. First, of course, the war made both rural production and distribution increasingly chancy. Second, FRELIMO went broke before it could reap the benefits of its new policy.

FRELIMO's need to reschedule its loans came with a price, and the leadership knew it. The government decided to get a jump on international lending institutions and their inevitable demands for restructuring by launching its own program, the Economic Rehabilitation Program (PRE). In fact, Maputo and the international banking institutions were not that far apart in their thinking. FRELIMO understood the importance of the agriculture to the country's economic well-being and had always advocated a mixed economy, both of which were elements of Cabral's pragmatic, African-based Marxist legacy. But, as FRELIMO pointed out to international lenders, it faced both historical and current constraints in implementing market reforms. First, the party had been forced to take over many state enterprises because of Portuguese flight and a lack of local capital. Furthermore, as the war escalated, the local entrepreneurial class was unwilling to invest in risky rural enterprises, preferring the cities for their safety and the custom that came from the growing number of international aid agencies that set up offices there. Thus, by necessity, FRELIMO argued to its international lenders, the government had to take a leading role in economic planning, development and management.

Nevertheless, FRELIMO abandoned its previous revolutionary commitment to improving the economic conditions of the people at whatever cost and began to emphasize macroeconomic stability. This, of course, meant a serious devaluation of the metical—Mozambique's currency—a drying up of credit, and cutbacks in subsidies on basic goods. The safety net was tightened as fees were imposed for basic health and education, though on a graduated scale. The hardships were felt in both the cities and the countryside, as the supply of consumer goods dried up and prices rose. This, in turn, resuscitated the black market, crime, and RENAMO's fortunes.

In recent years, the government has maintained its commitment to central planning, but has restricted it largely to monetary measures and larger state projects. In the latest five-year plan, announced in March 1995, FRELIMO introduced a new tax code to encourage private enterprise, announced a project to exploit newfound gas reserves in the southern part of the country, and streamlined rules on foreign investment, including a controversial program to allow South Africans to establish export-crop farms. While FRELIMO insists that fair prices will continue to be paid to farmers, it has also accepted IMF advice that the growth in the money supply is the main cause of inflation and thus economic stagnation. The plan, therefore, advocates a more restricted supply of credit aimed at providing capital to the most productive sectors of the economy rather than the neediest.

FRELIMO, however, has not given up on some of its early economic goals, despite the restrictions placed on it by international lenders and aid programs. In 1995, when the IMF demanded that FRELIMO further cut back on subsidies and social services from the bare minimum they had already been reduced to, FRELIMO demurred, appealing to the governments that foot the IMF bill. In a rather remarkable turn of events, most of the Western ambassadors in Maputo, including that of the U.S. who had previously urged the IMF to impose harsh restrictions, signed a letter criticizing the tactics of the IMF, forcing the institution to back down. Victories of this kind have been rare in Mozambique since the mid-1980s. As political scientist Merle Bowen wrote in 1992,

> The basic problem in Mozambique has been that the socioeconomic base of the state has been changed by the international donor community and by foreign private capital. At the same time, the dominant force is no longer the peasantry (as it was during the war of liberation) or the modernising state bureaucracy (as during the subsequent phase of attempted socialist transformation), but the private sector, albeit dependent upon the resources made available by external forces: the World Bank/IMF, multinational enterprises, and NGOs. In this context, the most serious threat to ordinary Mozambicans in the approaching era may be the need for an increasingly repressive state to guarantee the smooth performance of the "triple alliance."[56]

POLITICS AND THE ECONOMY

The RENAMO perspective

To many observers of the war in Mozambique, the notion of a RENAMO political and economic program is an oxymoron in and of itself. Indeed, during its Rhodesian tutelage, the organization admitted it had no program. As RENAMO leader Andre Matsangaissa explained just before his death in 1979, RENAMO was "not interested in policy making . . . later we will have to work out politics but first communism must go from our country."[57] As numerous observers to the peace talks in Rome a decade later asserted, RENAMO had to invent its political, economic, and social agenda on the spot.

RENAMO's efforts to formulate a political and economic ideology or program for Mozambique have been desultory at best. In 1982, the organization issued a "Manifest and Programme," which included vaguely worded demands for multiparty democracy, a private enterprise economy, civil rights and social services. By the mid-1980s, RENAMO felt called upon to justify its activities to the Mozambican peasantry through leafleting and rallies. According to Vines, the leaflets, usually in cartoon form for their largely illiterate or barely literate audience, included a "vague anticommunism and anti-Frelimoism, with a promise for a better future once the war is won by RENAMO.[58]

While RENAMO has made an issue out of "foreigners in our own country," meaning Russians, it undermines this message with a rather strange appeal to colonial-era nostalgia. After occupying a FRELIMO stronghold in Mozambique's far north in the mid-1980s, says political scientist Tom Young, guerrilla commanders promised the local peasantry that RENAMO would bring back whites "to govern and that people would be supplied with basic necessities."[59]

Abroad, RENAMO has tried to tailor its message to its intended audience. In Europe, where many expatriate Mozambicans live, it emphasizes its commitment to the original ideals of FRELIMO founder Eduardo Mondlane, which, RENAMO says, have been compromised by the present Marxist-oriented leadership in Maputo, though the group is vague about what those original ideals were. In the United States, where RENAMO aims at winning support from extreme anticommunist and evangelical Christian organizations and individuals, the emphasis is on RENAMO's anticommunism and its respect for religion.

RELIGION, RACE AND ETHNICITY

The FRELIMO perspective

Mozambique is a religiously diverse country, and its politics reflect that. Two major faiths, Christianity and Islam, share about 40 percent of the country, the former divided into a predominant Catholic church and a host of Protestant sects. The other 60 percent practice animist faiths of a bewildering variety. Complicating the picture is the fact that many Mozambicans, particularly in rural areas, do not see any contradiction in calling themselves, say, Catholics but participating in the rituals of animist faiths.

Like any revolutionary regime, FRELIMO's leaders realized they had to come to terms with organized religion and popular faith. According to historian Alex Vines, FRELIMO was remarkably tolerant of the latter but hostile to the former. Organized religion, especially Catholicism and Islam, were the new nation's only supra-ethnic civil associations and thus rivals to the revolutionary organizations FRELIMO was trying to establish, especially in the educational field. In addition, the Catholic church "represented considerable networks of patronage" extended across urban-rural, ethnic and even racial divides. "In its early hostility to the Catholic Church," he concludes, "FRELIMO was in conflict with a social force stronger than anything the party had to offer."[60]

Other scholars agree with Vines' overall portrayal of the relationship between FRELIMO and organized religion, though they emphasize that FRELIMO, despite its ideological atheism, established particularly warm relations with Protestant sects and individual mosques and Catholic churches that had supported the war of liberation against the Portuguese and shared FRELIMO's economic and political goals for post-independence Mozambique. Whatever the degree of initial hostility, relations with the Catholic church warmed during the 1980s, as even conservative Catholics became horrified with RENAMO tactics. Still, most Catholic priests endorsed RENAMO in the 1994 elections, though there was no embrace of Dhlakama himself. As for Islam, FRELIMO maintained relatively good relations with the network of mosques in the north. Most Mozambican Muslims live in towns and cities along the seaboard, which remained areas of support for FRELIMO throughout the war.

FRELIMO's approach to animist faiths has been more ambivalent. Clearly, its modernizing agenda made little room for traditional beliefs in magic and the power of spirit doctors. This was reflected in its policy of removing traditional village authorities, many of whom acted as both secular and spiritual leaders. The obvious contempt for such leaders that FRELIMO administrators displayed alienated many villagers, and RENAMO exploited this discontent in two interconnected ways. First, its destructive, murderous and arbitrary attacks on civilians created a feeling of insecurity and powerlessness among the peasantry that led them to search for answers and solutions to their problems in the traditional spiritual realm. Second, RENAMO made a point of executing FRELIMO administrators and returning local power to traditional spiritual and secular authorities. Unfortunately for RENAMO, many of these traditional leaders had not been popular and even those who were found it difficult, in the face of continued warfare and famine, to deliver the spiritual goods, that is, protection, security and freedom.

What arose out of the confusion of war was an extraordinary movement known as the Naparama (named after the region where it began). A blend of animist spiritualism and New Testament theology, Naparama offered the peasantry of central and southern Mozambique a sense of security and protection that more traditional faiths could not muster. Its founder, Manuel

Antonio, a traditional healer from Nampula province, convinced local peasants that he had died of measles as a young man, been resurrected, and was now ready to share his secret with others. By rubbing the excretions of a secret plant, people could render themselves immune to bullets.

More anti-RENAMO than pro-FRELIMO, the Naparama guerrillas, numbering some 20,000 by 1990, had swept large areas of central and southern Mozambique free of RENAMO forces. Part of the movement's success came from Antonio's shrewd battlefield tactics, including the removal of all Naparama dead in order to maintain the illusion of magical protection. RENAMO forces, largely rural and uneducated, grew increasingly reticent about attacking Naparama positions. FRELIMO meanwhile established increasingly close relations with Antonio and his guerrillas, and the two began to coordinate their strategy. Some FRELIMO units even began to use Naparama magic themselves. In 1991, Antonio was killed in a RENAMO ambush and the movement did not survive his death, though rumors persisted during the rest of the war that he had been resurrected yet again and was waiting for the right moment to rejoin his troops.

FRELIMO's initial hostility to traditional faiths was exceeded by its hostility to traditional or, more precisely, the quasi-traditional leadership that arose under the Portuguese. As Mondlane wrote in 1969, the power of tribal chiefs and tribalism in traditional Mozambican society was based on "a popular conception of legitimacy, not on force . . . and in its precolonial form . . . [it] served its purpose quite well within a limited area, providing an adequate form of organization in the interests of the majority." But, he added, it could not form "a satisfactory foundation for the needs of a modern state," especially since the effect of colonialism "was to pervert all traditional power structures, encouraging or creating authoritarian and elitist elements."[61]

This conviction was reinforced by experience, especially the divisions during the 1960s between traditionalist northerners versus revolutionary southerners that contributed to Mondlane's own assassination in 1969. In addition, the ethnic groups of central Mozambique, who had more directly experienced colonial exploitation on the plantations there, tended toward a black nationalism unacceptable to the urban leadership that included mestizos and whites. Still, ethnic hatreds were largely absent from FRELIMO. Internal conflict was more regionally based and concerned racial and political disputes rather than ethnic ones. In addition, the wholesale destruction of paramount chiefs by the Portuguese since the early 1900s, that is, those institutions and individuals who commanded respect and obedience over a largely decentralized and dispersed ethnic group, meant that FRELIMO's assault on traditional local leaders did not galvanize broad ethnic movements against the government. Peasants in a particular village might resent the Frelimo administrator, but there was no supra-ethnic authority to appeal to except, perhaps, RENAMO, whose tactics usually proved even more offensive than the government's.

The elections of 1994 proved the lack of ethnic tensions in Mozambique. While many Ndau, whose members predominate among the RENAMO leadership, voted heavily for Dhlakama, they were the exception to the rule. As Minter writes, "The link between ethno-regional divisions and political allegiance fell far short of an exact correlation."[62] Where politicking and campaigning could be conducted in an atmosphere relatively free of intimidation, most voters opted for FRELIMO or minor parties. Only in areas of RENAMO control, where voters either feared retaliation or believed that by voting for the party they were voting for peace, did RENAMO win a majority. Since RENAMO's areas of control were concentrated in the central provinces, it created voting patterns that could be interpreted as regionally or ethnically based.

The RENAMO perspective

RENAMO has made religious freedom an important element in its hastily formulated political program and in its previous appeals to its one major foreign constituency outside of South Africa, the evangelical Christian community. These appeals are at once genuine and misleading.[63] On the one hand, the organization has gone out of its way to depict itself as a protector of all faiths. Numerous accounts of RENAMO-destroyed villages noted that often the only building left unlooted was the church or mosque.

Unlike many of FRELIMO's leaders, who were educated at Protestant missions, RENAMO's leadership is largely Catholic, reflecting its rural origins where that church enjoys much of its strength. In addition, RENAMO makes much of what it says is the antireligious bias of a Marxist-oriented government, though FRELIMO has backed away from its original hostility to the Catholic church since a 1983 visit by the pope demonstrated the tremendous sway the church held over Mozambican Catholics. On the other hand, RENAMO's association with American evangelicals is also a bit deceptive in that the organization's main religious appeal is to the traditional and neotraditional faiths of approximately 60 percent of the Mozambican people. Like the Naparama and some of the FRELIMO soldiers, RENAMO guerrillas utilized magic as part of their spiritual preparation for battle.

During colonial times, many religious healers and spiritual leaders gained prestige by their principled resistance to Portuguese rule. With local political leaders often compromised through their association with the hated colonial regime, spiritualists often rallied the support of the peasantry through ceremonies and "magic" aimed at the Portuguese. After independence, many local FRELIMO administrators failed to make the distinction between these genuine spiritual leaders and the local political leaders who had worked for the Portuguese. That failure, along with their strongly modernist outlook, led many such administrators to exile or shame local healers. As noted above, when Mozambique slid into warfare, many peasants rallied to these traditional spiritualists as a means of personal and communal empowerment. RENAMO, then, made it a point to show these leaders respect and give them back their central role in village life. Those who have observed Mozambican village life directly have noted the importance of traditional faith, RENAMO's use of it, and the fact that FRELIMO's early antitraditionalism was a major source of peasant discontent with the regime.

Ethnic politics, though important to RENAMO, is not as significant as with UNITA. Many of RENAMO's leaders, including Dhlakama, come from a subgroup of the Shona tribe known as the Ndau. While most Shona people live across the border in Zimbabwe, the Ndau people generally inhabit those portions of Mozambique adjacent to that country. The Ndau have a military tradition and the Portuguese often employed them as local gendarmes, an especially opportune choice given the fact that the Ndau largely felt excluded from FRELIMO leadership. While there are non-Ndau people in the leadership of RENAMO, they are forced to learn the tongue since it has become the lingua franca of the movement. Portuguese is frowned upon as antinationalist. Many of the guerrilla recruits, of course, are not Ndau, but RENAMO maintains all-Ndau elite battalions.

RENAMO insists that it is not an ethnic-based movement and that all Mozambicans are welcome. But there was a pattern of preferential treatment of Ndau-speaking civilians by RENAMO as it conducted its raids in the countryside. That may have something to do with ethnic solidarity and bias, or it may be due to the fact that most Ndau people lived in RENAMO's "control" zones and therefore were not subject to frequent RENAMO attacks. Still, as noted above, while voting patterns from the 1994 elections did not necessarily follow ethnic lines, there is some evidence that RENAMO is becoming what FRELIMO feared: an ethnic and regional party with a power base among the Shona and Ndau peoples of central Mozambique.

TACTICS

ANGOLA

The MPLA

For more than 30 years, Angola has been at war. During this time, the conflict has taken almost every conceivable form: guerrilla warfare in the bush, house-to-house fighting in urban areas, set land battles involving tank warfare and air support, and lengthy urban sieges. Aside from the massive death of combatants and the awesome destructive force of the weaponry employed, the only constant has been civilian suffering. It is often said that civil wars and insurgencies are won or lost in the hearts and minds of the populace. In Angola, this truth was reduced to its essential: which side could effectively foment fear and which side could offer protection from it. And because Angola experienced so many different kinds of war on so many different terrains from 1961 onward, virtually no citizen has been exempted from it.

During the anticolonial phase of the Angolan war, the MPLA operated as a classic guerrilla force, at least according to its supporters and sympathizers. As Africanist Basil Davidson notes, the MPLA was the organization most feared by the Portuguese, both because its guerrillas were the "most resilient fighters" and because they offered the peasantry a sense of protection. "To these simple people," said a white South African journalist covering the war in the late 1960s, according to Davidson, "young MPLA guerrilla trainees are more reliable than both the Portuguese officials with whom they have fleeting contact and the grab-all UPA (later FNLA) terrorists."[64] To MPLA detractors like Bridgland, the MPLA enjoyed "limited success in winning local support . . . What support they did get came mainly as a result of the peasantry being thrust into the MPLA's arms by the fortified villages programme and the brutality of the Portuguese army."[65]

With the Portuguese retreat, the war's venue and tactics changed. In the capital, the MPLA unleashed armed civilian committees against FNLA supporters, then forcefully disbanded them when the leadership feared they were no longer under its control. At the same time, the MPLA joined forces with the highly disciplined and conventional Cuban armed forces in pitched land battles with South African forces and their UNITA/FNLA allies. According to Bridgland, whatever loyalty was enjoyed by the MPLA was lost by its post-victory arrogance of the mid-1970s. "They told us UNITA was finished," he quotes a local chief as saying. "They said theirs was the only real liberation, but they were thieves."[66] As Bridgland concludes, "Angola was now into that cycle of horrific violence which civil war breeds, for the guerrillas too admitted killing unarmed civilians, often accidentally, but sometimes with callous deliberacy."[67]

Angola's escalating war effort of the 1980s was marked by both traditional conventional military strategy and counterinsurgency techniques. Beginning in 1981 with Operation Askari, South African forces joined UNITA in great offensives in the southern half of the country, launching invasions every two years. While Pretoria claimed the attacks were directed at SWAPO bases fighting for the independence of Namibia, most observers agree that the real mission was to relieve MPLA pressure on UNITA. These operations culminated in the great land battles around Cuito in southeastern Angola in 1987–88, and were essentially won through superior Angolan air power (due to the international embargo, South African planes were antiquated and no match for Luanda's modern

MiGs) and conventional flanking moves by Cuban forces that isolated the SADF and forced it to retreat from Angola for good.

Long before the South African defeat and the end (until the post-1992 period) of conventional warfare in Angola, much of the rest of the country was embroiled in guerrilla fighting where the MPLA used classic counterinsurgency methods to combat UNITA forces. To prevent peasant support for UNITA, the government used the classic method, employed in wars from Vietnam to the Kurdish insurgency in Turkey, of forcing country folk into garrisoned villages where they could be both protected and controlled by the military. Not all peasants were coerced into the villages by the MPLA. Some came voluntarily, and many more were driven there by war and UNITA atrocities. Whatever the reason, the villages offered only limited security, as they were specifically targeted by UNITA forces.

According to Human Rights Watch, the MPLA was not entirely innocent of atrocities either. The MPLA often used the villages as both a civilian shield and a pool of potential recruits for the army, including teenagers as young as 15. In order to protect its bases and villages, the MPLA sowed antipersonnel mines along paths and roads likely to be used by UNITA forces. In the early and mid-1980s, these counterinsurgency methods were largely employed in Ovimbunduland. But with South Africa's retreat, UNITA flanked the MPLA and spread its forces into the north and east. "Now the fronts were nominal," writes Harding.

> In fact, they had blurred beyond recognition. This loss of definition meant more torment for civilians, especially in the North, where UNITA was heavily armed and fighting wherever it saw the chance. Reports coming in from Uige suggest that the province was ravaged.[68]

The spread of the war was a great disappointment both for civilians and for the MPLA's military strategists. Just when they thought they had achieved an unassailable position, with South Africa out of the picture and UNITA isolated, Savimbi outmaneuvered them. Perhaps more than anything else, it was this growing sense of futility that led the MPLA to seek negotiations and eventually demobilization and elections. But, as will be discussed in chapter 7, the MPLA was tricked by UNITA and demobilized without getting assurances that its moves were being reciprocated by UNITA. Thus, when war commenced again in late 1992, the MPLA suffered immense military setbacks, including the loss of some 70 percent of the countryside and a number of provincial capitals, including the Ovimbundu "capital" of Huambo, Angola's second-largest city.

Thus began the final and most brutal campaign of the entire 30-year Angolan conflict. After going on a major weapons-buying spree (hocking several years' future oil earnings to do it), the MPLA launched a massive offensive against UNITA, first sweeping it from the countryside and then besieging cities like Cuito and Huambo, which were largely destroyed by house-to-house fighting, UNITA and MPLA artillery, and government bombing raids. In other cities, the MPLA, armed civilian militias, and the so-called "ninjas" or security police rampaged through the streets, attacking both UNITA guerrillas and civilians they suspected of collaborating with the enemy, as well as engaging in extensive looting of property. With the fall of Huambo and Cuito in 1994, Angola has largely returned to peace, though sporadic attacks and counterattacks by UNITA and MPLA forces, largely in more isolated areas of the countryside, show up from time to time in wire service reports.

UNITA

From one perspective, Jonas Savimbi appears the masterful guerrilla leader and tactician of guerrilla warfare. After his defeat by the MPLA in the mid-1970s, he led his followers on a "long march" into the bush, where he rebuilt his army. He kept the vastly superior forces of a Soviet-armed and Cuban-aided MPLA off balance during the 1980s, and he came close to defeating Luanda altogether in the early 1990s. Equally important, he has managed to win support from powerful international allies, first from South Africa and then the U.S. When he found himself bereft of this financial and military support, he cannily moved his forces into northeast Angola, where he could exploit the income from the diamond industry.

A more critical eye, however, sees weaknesses and flaws. South African military aid helped him resurrect his army in the 1970s and rescued him from defeat at least several times in the 1980s. But his victories of the 1990s owed much to the continued flow of American arms and a willingness to dupe the MPLA and the international community into thinking he had demobilized his forces when, in fact, he had not. A more critical analysis also reveals the horrible cost the Angolan people have had to pay for UNITA's military success. Virtually every human rights organization has singled out UNITA as the worst abuser of civilians in Angola. Even Fred Bridgland, Savimbi's laudatory biographer, eventually turned against his subject in the late 1980s, exposing Savimbi-directed atrocities of civilians and murderous purges of UNITA ranks. According to Minter, Savimbi's military strategy can be summed up in one brief statement: "Making life physically impossible for civilians . . . in government areas."[69]

To that end, UNITA employed a variety of tactics. It targeted garrison villages where peasants had gone to escape its attacks in the countryside. It destroyed government infrastructure, including transport, hospitals, farms and schools. It forcibly recruited peasants to work on farms that supplied food to its forces and demanded that others serve as porters and servants in the camps. It strewed millions of land mines haphazardly on paths, roads and fields to render them useless and limit the ability of civilians to migrate to MPLA-controlled areas. As Harding writes, "Neither side was fastidious about civilians, but for UNITA soft targets such as schools or clinics were a strategic imperative, for they were symbols of the government's effort, however cursory, to manage and develop the country."[70] But mostly, UNITA tried to sow terror that would render the civilian population pliable and undermine their faith in the government's ability to protect them. As one former UNITA soldier explained as early as 1981,

> [Savimbi] had given instructions to all leaders of bases to open a "surprise offensive" against people who refused to work with UNITA. This "surprise offensive" was cutting off the noses, cutting off of breasts, raping women, and above all killing those who didn't accept UNITA policy.[71]

By the end of the 1980s, HRW reported, UNITA was even using famine as a tool of war, denying international access to regions under its control in order to force concessions from the MPLA.[72] And as Minter points out, until the broadening of the war in the late 1980s and early 1990s, all of this was largely conducted in areas of the country populated by the Ovimbundu people who, supposedly, represented UNITA's most loyal supporters.[73]

Only in the 1990s, with the waning of international support for UNITA, did these tactics receive significant play in the mainstream press, largely because the organization had begun to target UN officials and other foreigners and turned to the use of terrorist bombings in Luanda and other cities. Under the limelight of negative publicity for the first time in the early and mid-1990s, Savimbi has equivocated, either denying the charges, citing similar MPLA actions, or saying he is no longer in control of his officers and men in the field.

MOZAMBIQUE

FRELIMO

Unlike the war in Angola, the conflict with RENAMO rarely, if ever, transcended its insurgent roots. There were virtually no major land battles and most fighting was done when battalions (rarely numbering more than 200 to 300 soldiers or guerrillas) encountered one another in the field. This is not to deny the violence and destructiveness of the war, but simply to point out that it boiled at a lower temperature, largely because outside forces were absent and Mozambique's more impoverished and resourceless economic base made it impossible to conduct warfare on an Angolan scale.

Like those of the MPLA, FRELIMO forces were guilty of atrocities and human rights violations, especially concerning the government's policy of forcing peasants into garrisoned villages and then using these as a pool of captive recruits and a shield against attack. "Throughout the war, a basic aim of both the FRELIMO government and the RENAMO rebels has been to control as many civilians as possible," a 1992 HRW report noted.

> Both government forces and RENAMO have practiced scorched earth methods and used military force to move hundreds of thousands of civilians into their respective areas of control. Once a civilian settlement is established, the local military force, either the FAM [Mozambican Armed Forces] or

RENAMO, mounts control posts to ensure that civilians do not flee into enemy territory.[74]

Still, like most observers of the conflict in Mozambique, HRW makes it clear that the vast majority of human rights violations and atrocities have been committed by RENAMO forces. FAM's negative impact on the vast majority of Mozambican peasants has been the result of inefficiencies, lack of discipline, and tactical errors. As noted in chapter 3, FRELIMO failed to anticipate the kind of insurgency it had to face after independence, allowing RENAMO to conduct its brutal campaign largely unopposed for years. While some observers, like anthropologist Christian Geffray, have asserted that peasant support for RENAMO was the result of the agricultural and political policies of FRELIMO, others argue that the situation in the countryside was more nuanced than that. The peasantry were not driven into the RENAMO camp because of the policies of FRELIMO, says Minter, but because the government did not adequately defend them, nor did it provide them the tools to defend themselves. The military was along conventional lines and military authorities approached the problem of attacks on the peasantry from a conventional perspective, that security would be provided strictly by formal forces.[75]

RENAMO

A discussion of RENAMO tactics is not recommended for the squeamish. Regardless of their previous ideological convictions, virtually anyone who returns from Mozambique, having seen the results of RENAMO raids, comes to the same conclusion: RENAMO is a terrorist organization. Its strategy is actually quite simple. It relies on random acts of destruction and death to make life unbearable for the living. It does this by destroying both private and public property and instilling the maximum amount of terror in the populace. RENAMO's human rights violations include murder, rape, looting, arson, sabotage, forced portering, servitude and recruitment, as well as the total disruption of economic activity.

Journalist William Finnegan described a mid-1980s tour of a town in Zambézia that had recently been attacked by RENAMO forces.

> Every window, every window frame, every door, every doorframe, every piece of plumbing or wiring or flooring had been ripped out and carried away. Every piece of machinery that was well bolted down or was too heavy for a man to carry—water pumps, maize mills, the generator in the power station, the pumps outside the gas station—had been axed, shot, sledgehammered, stripped or burned . . . There were few signs of battle . . . but a thousand relics of annihilative frenzy; each tile of mosaic smashed, each pane of glass-block wall painstakingly shattered. It was systematic, psychotically meticulous destruction.[76]

Railroads, a particularly important part of the Mozambican infrastructure, were especially hard-hit by RENAMO. "RENAMO," says Harding, took a dim view of mechanical motion . . . Having no use for vehicles themselves, their work was primarily destructive. The roads and railways of Mozambique were RENAMO's broadsheets. Here the rebels scrawled their objections to FRELIMO in a profane vocabulary of sabotaged track . . .[77]

To undermine support for FRELIMO, RENAMO especially targeted the health and educational facilities established in the early years of independence. According to UNICEF, more than 1,800 schools had been destroyed by 1985—affecting over 300,000 students—as well as 25 percent of the clinics. Robbery and theft were as endemic as vandalism. RENAMO had a well-established network for removing property and transferring it over the border to Malawi, where it was used to purchase luxuries for the officers, necessities for the soldiers, and arms for the movement. Moreover, the same peasants who were being robbed were forcibly recruited as porters to carry the loot.

The other RENAMO strategy was terror. The group committed a host of brutal atrocities to demonstrate FRELIMO's inability to protect the Mozambican people. "In the early 1980s," notes Human Rights Watch/Africa, "RENAMO acquired its reputation for savagery. It became particularly well-known for a policy of mutilating civilian victims, including children, by cutting off ears, noses, lips and sexual organs."[78] It also forcibly recruited soldiers, some as young as 10 years old, and then trained them in the most brutal forms of aggression. One of its methods, according to Magaia, was to force children and others in the villages it attacked to murder family members in order to cut them off from their previous lives and initiate them into RENAMO's ranks. After forcing a railroad worker in Manica province to kill his own brother-in-law before his sister's eyes, a RENAMO officer allegedly pronounced: "Now you're one of us. You've been baptized. You can come with us."[79]

NEGOTIATIONS

ANGOLA

Not surprisingly in a war that has lasted more than 30 years and has involved at least five major foreign players (the U.S., USSR, Cuba, Zaire and South Africa), the history of peace negotiations in Angola has been both complex and drawn out. And as in many conflicts, particularly civil ones, negotiations in Angola have often risen and fallen with the tides of war. Diplomacy, it has often been said, is war by other means. In Angola, the adage has often worked in reverse: war as a way of setting the possibility, pace and agenda of negotiations.

The 1988 New York accords

The New York accords were, perhaps, the most complicated of the several sets of arrangements that have attempted to settle the war in Angola. The accords were based on an idea known as *linkage* that was conceptualized in the Reagan State Department. It was a simple idea in theory, the mutual withdrawal of South African forces from Namibia and Cuban forces from Angola, but it was painstaking in practice and took nearly a decade to bring about. To make linkage work, several significant obstacles had to be overcome. They included, on the one side, MPLA fears of abandonment by the Soviet Union and Cuba, Castro's commitment to the MPLA and Third World solidarity in general, and the pre-Gorbachev Soviet leadership's determination not to lose Angola to the Americans. On the other, linkage author Chester Crocker, Reagan's undersecretary of state for African affairs, had to fight off the administration's pro–South African right wing, Pretoria's determination to impose a military solution on Angola, and Savimbi's fears that, with South Africa out of the picture, he would be left to fight the superior forces of the MPLA alone.

Gradually, then with increasing momentum after 1986, each of these obstacles was overcome, some by diplomacy, others by events on the battlefield, while still others evaporated due to circumstances that had little to do with Angola itself. The accession of Gorbachev, for example, included a dramatic internal reassessment of both the Soviet Union's capacity to influence world events and its reconceptualization of its relationship with the U.S. in less confrontational terms. Also, UNITA was brought on board with promises of military aid from the U.S., though the 1986 overturning of the Clark amendment that banned U.S. aid to UNITA so angered the MPLA that it walked out of the talks for some 18 months.

But the most important reason for the implementation of the linkage idea was the result of the historic battlefield losses inflicted on the South Africans by the combined forces of Cuba and the MPLA in 1987–88 (see chapter 3). More than a military setback, the 1988 battle of Cuito Cuanavale, which resulted in the MPLA-Cuban entrapment of tens of thousands of crack South African troops inside Angola, threatened South Africa's hold on Namibia, destroyed the SADF's reputation for invincibility, and undermined domestic support for the hard-line Botha regime. The victory also supplied a shot in the arm for the MPLA, which, in turn, allowed Cuba to retreat from Angola without seeming to abandon its ally. In short, all sides had come to the conclusion, some more reluctantly than others, that the proposed agreement did not represent a catastrophic loss to them, that is, a loss so threatening that continued war seemed a better option.

As in any successful negotiations, all sides were forced to make significant but not life-threatening concessions. South Africa accepted the idea that an independent Namibia did not endanger its own security. Cuba adjusted to the concept that its retreat from Angola did not jeopardize the security of the MPLA regime, while the MPLA accepted the continued existence of an apartheid regime in South Africa, but one that promised to be nonaggressive. Significant pressure was exerted as well by the superpowers, though it took different forms with each. The Soviet Union made it clear to the MPLA that continued resistance to an agreement that left UNITA intact might jeopardize Luanda's relations with Moscow. And America's assurances of continued support for UNITA brought Savimbi on board, though not until after he had tried and failed to persuade his allies on the South African and U.S. right to scuttle their respective countries' commitment to linkage.

In the end, after an eight-month marathon series of negotiations that took place on three continents, the accords were signed in New York City on December 23, 1988. South Africa and Cuba lived up to both the spirit and letter of the agreements. Free elections were held on schedule in Namibia in 1989, leading to the expected overwhelming victory of SWAPO leader Sam Nujoma as president, and independence in March 1990. Cuban forces withdrew from Angola on or ahead of schedule, with the last troops leaving in May 1991, just a week before the signing of Angola's next major agreement, the Bicesse accords.

The 1991 Bicesse accords

The negotiations leading to the Bicesse accords were both less complicated and more intense than New York, shorter in duration but more acrimonious in spirit. The greater simplicity of the issues involved had an equally simple reason: only two players, the MPLA and UNITA, were directly involved. Their intensity and bitterness are not hard to understand: more was arguably at stake. Both sides had to abandon the fears and aspirations that had accumulated for over a decade and a half. Unlike the New York accords, both sides could more easily interpret the negotiations as a zero-sum game, in which one side or the other would lose all. This kind of thinking is, of course, a diplomatic dead end. Making things worse and different from the earlier talks, which involved sovereign states, neither side accepted the legitimacy of the other, so that even willingness to talk to each other was a hurdle to be overcome.

In one way, however, the negotiations leading to the Bicesse accords were much like those leading up to New York: Battlefield events determined the pacing. Between 1989 and 1991, UNITA and MPLA forces were engaged in a seesaw battle for Angola (see chapter 3), each made negotiation-killing demands to stop the talks when they felt it was in their interest to do so, that is, when their improving military position might lead to an enhanced negotiating position. But for all the concessions made by both sides, none was as important as sheer battlefield exhaustion and the realization that a final military solution was unavailable to either party.

Still, one can be too evenhanded in this. Most observers say it was UNITA that was largely responsible for keeping the talks on hold. First, for much of the 1989–91 period it held the battlefield advantage. That is to say, it was not about to defeat the MPLA and take over the government by force of arms, but it was effectively demonstrating that it couldn't be beaten, and in a conflict between governments and insurgencies, most diplomats and military strategists agree, that represents a victory. Even more important a reason for UNITA's intransigence was its internal politics. While the MPLA coalition contained a hard-line faction within its ranks, the Savimbi-controlled UNITA was a hard-line faction through and through. One U.S. mediator involved in the negotiations became so frustrated that he violated diplomatic niceties and publicly called the UNITA representatives "compulsive liars."[80]

The Bicesse accords represented a last diplomatic gasp for the Soviet Union. During the ceremonies marking Namibian independence in March 1990, Soviet foreign minister Eduard Shevardnadze and U.S. secretary of state James Baker agreed to pressure their respective clients in Angola to reach a peace agreement, and brought the Portuguese on board as mediators. Five sets of inconclusive talks followed over the next year. The major obstacles included mutual recognition by UNITA and the MPLA, the formation of a national army out of both forces, and the timing of elections.

Under pressure from the Soviet Union, the MPLA rewrote the country's constitution in 1990, legalizing opposition parties, lessening government control of the economy, and establishing freedoms of press, speech and religion. While these constitutional reforms met most of the conditions Washington had set for recognition of the government in Luanda, the Bush administration continued to hold out. As Elaine Windrich notes, this continued support allowed Savimbi to ignore international and African pressure to negotiate.[81]

Savimbi's ploy was a clever one. Arguing that the international community was biased against him, he insisted that the U.S. serve as mediator and implementer of the peace accords. As the U.S. was UNITA's main supporter, this was clearly unacceptable to the MPLA and kept a final commitment to achieve a peace treaty on hold until January 1991. Only after a major UNITA offensive failed in the spring did Savimbi finally agree to sign the Bicesse accords, which called for legalization of UNITA, multiparty elections to be held within 18 months, full demobilization of forces under UN auspices, and the establishment of a 50,000-man Angolan military force composed of equal numbers of MPLA and UNITA combatants. On May 31, 1991, MPLA president José Eduardo dos Santos and UNITA chief Jonas Savimbi signed the accords.[82]

Comprehensive as the Bicesse accords seemed, there were many important political and military elements left out. Either by omission or commission, the parties to the agreement, as well as the U.S. and Soviet observers and Portuguese mediators, remained silent on the postelection period, assuming that Angola could immediately function as a multiparty democracy after more than 30 years of war and 15 of one-party government. In addition, because the UN played a minimal role in the talks and because it felt strapped by commitments elsewhere (including Somalia and Cambodia), the UN committed a limited number of peacekeepers.[83]

Not only was the number of blue helmets below the minimum most outside observers said was needed, but they were given an extremely limited mandate. The UN Angolan Verification Mission (UNAVEM) was not allowed to prevent human rights abuses, nor even make them public. As a 1994 Human Rights Watch report concluded, "This contributed to both sides increasingly feeling confident enough to violate the peace accords by intimidating suspected opposition sympathizers."[84] Even more importantly, the hands-off policy encouraged Savimbi to keep large numbers of his best troops away from the demobilization centers, while the limited number of observers allowed him to dupe the UN into thinking that he was. Following his defeat in the September 1992 elections, Savimbi used his non-demobilized troops to launch a major offensive against the MPLA that, in a matter of weeks, seized about 70 percent of the countryside and many provincial capitals that he had never captured before. The MPLA, which some observers estimated had demobilized more than 60 percent of its troops by election day, was caught unprepared.

The Lusaka accords

Within months of the outbreak of renewed warfare in Angola, the UN, the U.S. and various African countries tried to step into the diplomatic breach and halt the fighting. Talks were arranged in the capitals of Ethiopia and the Ivory Coast in January and March of 1993, respectively. While both the MPLA and UNITA sent representatives, the two sets of talks were failures. This was largely because UNITA, enjoying an overwhelming military edge and confident that it could either win the war or extract major concessions from the MPLA, did not negotiate in good faith. Once again, Savimbi believed that military might allowed him to flout international condemnation. This time, however, he miscalculated.

For one thing, U.S. policy on Angola had shifted. Savimbi supporter Bush had lost to Clinton, and the new administration quickly recognized the government in Luanda. Not only did the U.S. lift its sanctions against selling military hardware to the MPLA, but it advocated a UN embargo against UNITA. By November 1993, the UN was ready to act. And while Savimbi knew he could partially get around the embargo by utilizing revenues from the diamond fields he controlled in northeastern Angola and a sympathetic regime in neighboring Zaire, he also realized that he could not match the massive arms shipments the MPLA was purchasing with money borrowed against future oil earnings.

By March 1994, exploratory talks between the MPLA and UNITA had begun in Lusaka under Zambian mediation. The talks, which lasted eight months, bogged down over two interrelated issues: a power-sharing agreement demanded by UNITA, the terms of a cease-fire, and which of these two should proceed the other. Adding to the stalemate was the war itself. While the MPLA had gained the military advantage by early 1994, the international community, including Angola's arms suppliers and financial lenders, was putting immense pressure on the regime to reach an agreement with Savimbi. The result was an intense debate within the MPLA ranks over whether to pursue the war to the end or seek a negotiated settlement. As the factions contended in Lusaka, the military continued to press UNITA, increasing Savimbi's sense of desperation and leading him to threaten in autumn 1994 to "return to the bush" and fight on as a guerrilla force.[85]

This threat and the above-mentioned international pressure forced the MPLA to concede, though its offer of power-sharing fell far short of what Savimbi desired. While the MPLA offered UNITA three of the nation's nineteen provincial governorships and four cabinet posts, the former were scattered around the country and did not include the Ovimbundu "capital" of Huambo (the MPLA feared giving Savimbi a coherent power base), while the latter did not include key posts like interior (police), defense or the treasury. On his part, Savimbi agreed to a schedule in which a cease-fire would precede political and constitutional change. Since Savimbi has long believed that the only way to influence the government was through the threat or application of military resistance, this represented a significant concession. Both sides agreed to put off discussion of more delicate and complicated matters—including a shared executive branch, along the lines of post-apartheid South Africa—until later.

Meanwhile, the UN, having learned its lesson from the disaster of 1992, in which commitment to a fixed election timetable was given precedence over the pace of demobilization, showed a willingness to let the talks go on as long as necessary. In addition, the UN agreed to augment its peacekeeping efforts in Angola, committing a billion dollars and several thousand mediators who would now have a broader mandate to intervene when the accords were violated. Despite this apparent evenhandedness, some observers have argued that Savimbi has emerged the winner from these talks, since he has been able to gain a share of power, even though the previous Bicesse accords offered no power-sharing to the loser of the 1992 elections. In either case, Angolans remained wary, given the failure of the Bicesse agreement and the fact that Savimbi failed to show up in Lusaka for the formal signing ceremonies in November 1994. Despite these fears, the accords have largely held, though each side accuses the other of violations and the UN has lodged formal complaints against UNITA for attacks on peacekeepers and foreigners.

MOZAMBIQUE

The history of negotiations in Mozambique is quite different from that in Angola. First, with no major non-African regimes involved in the conflict, the negotiations were simpler and less drawn out, though the agreement reached between RENAMO and FRELIMO was several years in the making. Secondly, FRELIMO was forced to negotiate with two antagonists who enjoyed little support from outside: South Africa and RENAMO were both pariahs. Yet this did not necessarily give FRELIMO an edge. Because of their outsider status, both South Africa and RENAMO were relatively immune from international pressure. In the case of the Nkomati accords, this meant Pretoria felt free to violate them even as they were being signed. As for the Rome accords, it was the insurgents' very isolation, and the paranoia and fear it engendered among their leadership, that made RENAMO such a difficult party to negotiate with.

The Nkomati accords

When delegates from South Africa and Mozambique sat down together in late 1982 at Komatipoort, a small border town in the Transvaal, South Africa, the two sides had been at war for almost two years, albeit without formal declarations of belligerency. But it was a peculiar and very unequal kind of war. South African troops were not in combat and the fighting occurred entirely on Mozambican territory, with occasional firefights between RENAMO and the various armies of Mozambican border states like Malawi, Zambia and Zimbabwe. Moreover, for South Africa, the war represented a mere blip on the military and economic radar. This is not to say the war was not important to Pretoria. Indeed, it was a key to South Africa's larger destabilization policy against the frontline states. But it cost the military and economic giant little in the way of resources or public unrest at home. On the other hand, the war was devastating the Mozambican countryside and putting a fantastic strain on the nation's economy and military.

Thus, each came to the talks with different fears, hopes and objectives. For South Africa, a diplomatic arrangement with Mozambique offered several advantages. First, it would help eliminate an important and geographically contiguous base for ANC operations. However, as most experts have noted, South African intelligence knew as well that the ANC did not operate major bases in Mozambique, though it transited the country. Instead, Pretoria hoped formal diplomatic relations, and an agreement with a radical black African state, would open other doors on the continent and in the West, helping to alleviate the apartheid state's isolation and the growing pressure for sanctions in the international community. However, not everyone in the Botha regime agreed with this strategy. Destabilization was working, and why fix something that's not broken or, in this case, fix something that's supposed to be broken?

For FRELIMO, the choices were more stark. It did not want Mozambique to be the first radical state in Africa to open relations with the apartheid regime, nor did it want to abandon its close friends in the South African liberation movement. (Its costly commitment to Zimbabwean rebels in the 1970s indicated the importance FRELIMO placed on solidarity with other radical African movements.) On the other hand, ending the crippling war had to be a top priority. Machel had little room to maneuver as he sold détente with South Africa to the South Africans themselves, to other black African states and to critics within his own party. He did this by arguing that he was not abandoning the ANC, since Mozambique had never offered it permanent sanctuary in the first place, and that he was not surrendering Mozambican sovereignty. As the government-owned Radio Maputo said in December 1983,

> Mozambique cannot stop attacking South Africa because it never started . . . To achieve the modus vivendi that Machel spoke of calls for a new attitude on the part of South African authorities. This attitude would reflect an awareness that aggression against neighboring states is not going to extend the life of apartheid. The struggle against apartheid is waged from within . . . Mozambique is always ready to talk. But, as the South Africans were told in advance, Mozambique was not going there, [Nkomati] to recognize apartheid or destroy the ANC.[86]

Set back by the SADF's raids against alleged ANC bases in the suburbs of Maputo in October 1983, the talks continued in December. On March 16, 1984, Machel and Botha signed the Agreement on Non-Aggression and Good Neighborliness, which called for an immediate cessation of aid and arms to guerrilla movements in each other's countries. South Africa closed RENAMO training centers and foreign affairs offices on its bases, and FRELIMO shut down ANC liaison offices in Maputo.

Signed with great pomp and ceremony, the agreement soon showed its limitations. The South African military, which had opposed the agreement all along, airlifted a six-month supply of military hardware to RENAMO in preparation for the treaty. A bigger problem, however, concerned RENAMO itself. Excluded from the talks, Dhlakama said he had no intention of heeding them, and, to reinforce his point, he walked out of the RENAMO-FRELIMO talks that had begun in October, calling them "games of FRELIMO." As he described later,

> [FRELIMO] only wanted to eliminate, force RENAMO into an unconditional ceasefire, and then RENAMO to disappear. We said we were not prepared for that . . . Because RENAMO is strong militarily and politically, which the people support. [It is] independent, nationalist, and is installed in Mozambique. It is there. We are not going to accept to disappear. So I sent in order to stop the talks.[87]

The continuing war led to another series of negotiations between South Africa and Mozambique in fall 1984. The Pretoria declarations, also known as Nkomati II, reinforced the earlier agreement by getting each side to acknowledge the legitimacy of the other's government and committing both to establishing peace throughout the region. While most observers agree that Mozambique largely honored the spirit and the letter of both accords, South Africa did not, a fact revealed by documents uncovered in a Frelimo raid against Renamo's headquarters at Casa Banana and admitted to later by Botha himself (see chapter 3).

The Rome accords

Like the Bicesse negotiations between the MPLA and UNITA in Angola, the Rome talks between FRELIMO and RENAMO involved the participation of major international players like the United States and the mediation of third parties, in this case the Vatican's Sant'Edigio Catholic community and the Italian government.[88] The international community, including the U.S. and South Africa, applied selective pressure, particularly on RENAMO. Similarly, the talks were drawn out as both sides, and particularly RENAMO, tried to use the threat of war and battlefield advantage to win time and gain more concessions. Like Bicesse, the Rome talks involved issues of life and death for the two participants, and the intensity of the negotiations reflected that.

Talks involving Catholic mediation, specifically the Mozambican see, date back to 1984. FRELIMO resisted the idea for five years, largely because it refused to accept RENAMO as a legitimate and indigenous political movement. Arguably, in its heart of hearts, FRELIMO still does not. But by the end of the decade, it had increasingly come to the realization that it could not defeat RENAMO militarily. In 1989, South Africa's newly elected President, F. W. de Klerk, broached the subject of outside mediation to Mozambican president Joaquim Chissano, suggesting the U.S. as a possible candidate. While Chissano rejected the idea, he accepted the U.S. as an observer. Meanwhile, FRELIMO had been putting out feelers to the heads of the Mozambican Catholic church, which then contacted the Sant'Edigio community. In July, at FRELIMO's Fifth Congress, Chissano persuaded the delegates to open negotiations with Renamo, via Sant'Edigio. With its close ties to the church, RENAMO accepted an invitation to negotiate the following month.

The talks, which would continue for more than three years, involved a host of delicate and complicated issues. Mediators tried to keep the schedule and agenda flexible, trying to set limited goals for each of the eventual ten rounds of talks, hoping that ratification and implementation of limited steps would build the cooperation and confidence necessary to keep the negotiations moving forward.

The main obstacle to this approach was RENAMO. Isolated internationally and increasingly abandoned by its South African patrons, the RENAMO leadership was fearful for its own safety. Thus, throughout the talks, it insisted on getting wide-ranging concessions from FRELIMO in writing, an approach rejected by the more sophisticated and experienced FRELIMO delegates and international mediators. During numerous phases of the talks. RENAMO delegates delayed or threatened to walk out altogether. These kinds of setbacks, of course, are not unique to the Rome talks. But the reasons behind them often were. Unlike with most negotiations, internationally accepted diplomatic norms and procedures in Rome had to be worked out before issues of substance could be dealt with. For instance, in most peace talks, it is the mediators who set the agenda for the talks, albeit it with input from negotiating partners. But RENAMO had a habit of insisting that it set the day-to-day agenda, demands that of course were rejected by FRELIMO and the mediators themselves.

Early obstacles to a settlement included the subject of foreign troops in Mozambique, specifically the Tanzanians and Zimbabweans who were defending the rail corridors, and whether a cease-fire would precede constitutional and political change, as FRELIMO insisted, or the other way around, as RENAMO wanted. While FRELIMO rewrote the Mozambican constitution in 1990 to allow for multiple parties, elections and basic freedoms, RENAMO demurred. Arguing that FRELIMO was not a legitimate government, even though each side had accepted the legitimacy of the other as a negotiating partner early on in the talks, RENAMO insisted that it would only sign an agreement that required any future assembly to consider further constitutional reforms before it turned to any other legislative business. FRELIMO, extremely sensitive to the issue of sovereignty and intending to rule Mozambique until elections were held, refused.

Gradually, two outside forces began to have an impact. On the one hand, the continuing drought in Mozambique was making mass starvation a real possibility. While U.S. diplomat Cameron Hume writes that both sides acted as if there was no urgent need to reach a settlement that would allow the country to better cope with the crisis, the specter of famine clearly forced FRELIMO to concede major points, including limitations on the movement of foreign troops within Mozambique and an acceptance of a dual administration of the country until elections could be held. That is to say, FRELIMO agreed that aid and election preparations would be arranged through RENAMO in areas controlled by the insurgents. For their part, RENAMO's delegates accepted the idea that a cease-fire would have to precede longer-term constitutional and political reform. On the other hand, international assurances of support for RENAMO, including pledges of millions of dollars to help the organization convert to a political party, as well as FRELIMO guarantees of security for RENAMO and offers of offices and homes for RENAMO officials, helped overcome the rebels' fears that they would be annihilated by FRELIMO once they disarmed.

The final accords, signed by Chissano and Dhlakama on October 4, 1992, bore a striking resemblance to the Bicesse accords. Both included a UN-mediated period of demobilization, leading to the formation of a joint 30,000-man army and elections within one year. Signed just one week after the Angolan elections, the shadow of the events on the other side of the continent hung over Mozambique for years. Realizing that its failure to commit enough money and personnel had partially led to renewed fighting in Angola, the UN committed several hundred million dollars and more than 7,000 blue helmets to monitor the peace process and the elections. And when demobilization failed to move according to schedule, due to RENAMO fears and delays in the establishment of demobilization canton-ments, all parties to the negotiations agreed to delay national elections for another year.

This more flexible strategy appears to be working, though it may have to do with other factors as well. Even by Angolan standards, Mozambique has been totally exhausted by war. Without the oil resources available to Luanda, FRELIMO could not afford a further round of fighting. More importantly, RENAMO's leaders knew that they would be abandoned by their new international supporters if they chose to return to the bush. Despite numerous minor setbacks and delays, both RENAMO and FRE-LIMO lived up to the terms of the agreements and demobilized their forces.

NOTES

[1] Samondo, Marcos, interview with author, November 21, 1995.

[2] Birmingham, David, *Frontline Nationalism in Angola and Mozambique* (Trenton, N.J.: Africa World Press, 1992), p. 101.

[3] *Ibid.*, p. 103.

[4] *Ibid.* As Birmingham points out, the army represents a new, more African-based elite against the older mestizo leaders of the MPLA's civilian wing.

[5] Bridgland, Fred, *Jonas Savimbi: A Key to Africa*, Edinburgh: Mainstream Publishing Company, 1986, p. 83.

[6] Cummings, Nicholas, "Angola: A Case Study in Soviet Neocolonialism" in *Revolution*, Spring 1984, pp. 35–36.

[7] Cited in Bridgland, *Jonas Savimbi*, p. 290.

[8] Simpson, Chris, "The Undemocratic Game" in *Africa Report*, July–August, 1993, p. 50.

[9] Cited, *ibid.*, p. 68.

[10] *Ibid.*, p. 50.

[11] For more on Soviet foreign policy, see below. Though both the Kennedy and Johnson administrations gently urged the Portuguese to decolonize, they refused to push the issue, fearing it might jeopardize key U.S. bases in the Portuguese-owned Azores.

[12] Gunn, Gillian, "Cuba and Angola" in Fauriol, Georges and Loser, Eva, *Cuba: The International Dimension* (New Brunswick, N.J.: Transaction Publishers, 1990), p. 165.

[13] Minter, William, *Apartheid's Contras: An Inquiry into the Roots of War in Angola and Mozambique* (London: Zed Books, 1994), p. 153.

[14] Venancio, Moises, "Angola and Southern Africa: The Dynamics of Change" in Rich, Paul (ed.), *The Dynamics of Change in Southern Africa* (New York: St. Martin's Press, 1994), p. 178.

[15] Saul, John, *Recolonization and Resistance in Southern Africa in the 1990s* (Trenton, N.J.: Africa World Press, 1993), p. 47.

[16] Brittain, Victoria, "Savimbi, Bloody Savimbi" in *The Nation* July 11, 1994, pp. 50–53.

[17] Stockwell, John, *In Search of Enemies: A CIA Story* (New York: W. W. Norton and Company, 1978), pp. 153–154.

[18] *Ibid.*, p. 153.

[19] See chapter 2.

[20] Bridgland, *Jonas Savimbi*, p. 330.

[21] The firm, Black, Manafort, Stone & Kelly, included principles Christoper Lehman and Lee Atwater, who managed Reagan's and Bush's presidential election campaigns, respectively.

[22] Windrich, Elaine, *The Cold War Guerrilla: Jonas Savimbi, the U.S. Media, and the Angolan War* (New York: Greenwood Press, 1992), pp. 6–7, 11.

[23] *The Economist*, May 29, 1993, p. 45.

[24] *New Statesman and Society*, October 16, 1992, p. 20.

[25] Brittain, "Bloody Savimbi," p. 51.

[26] Pereira, Anthony, "The Neglected Tragedy: The Return to War in Angola, 1992–3" in *The Journal of African Studies*, Winter 1994, p. 12.

[27] *Ibid.*, p. 13.

[28] *The Economist*, September 26, 1992, p. 39.

[29] Birmingham, *Frontline Nationalism*, p. 51.

[30] Bender, Gerald, *Angola Under the Portuguese: The Myth and the Reality* (Berkeley: University of California Press, 1978), p. 180.

[31] Cited in Wallerstein, Immanuel, "On the Interpretation of Nationalism in the Periphery: Marcum's Angola" in *Africa Today*, Fall 1979, p. 71.

[32] Pereira, "Neglected Tragedy," p. 17.

[33] Harding, Jeremy, *The Fate of Africa: Trial by Fire* (New York: Simon and Schuster, 1993), p. 77.

[34] *Washington Post*, July 28, 1994, p. A20.

[35] Bridgland, *Jonas Savimbi*, p. 373.

[36] Harding, *Fate of Africa*, p. 61.

[37] Bridgland, *Jonas Savimbi*, p. 290.

[38] Windrich, *Cold War Guerrilla*, pp. 147–149.

[39] Davidson, Basil, *In the Eye of the Storm: Angola's People* (Garden City, N.Y.: Doubleday and Company, 1972), pp. 15–18.

[40] Minter, *Apartheid's Contras*, p. 103.

[41] Ohlson, Thomas and Stedman, Stephen John, *The New Is Not Yet Born: Conflict Resolution in Southern Africa* (Washington: Brookings Institution, 1994), pp. 192–193.

[42] Pereira, "Neglected Tragedy" in *The Journal of African Studies*, Winter 1994, p. 23.

[43] Peoples Press Angola Book Project, *With Freedom in Their Eyes: A Photo-essay of Angola* (San Francisco: Peoples Press, 1976), p. 23.

[44] Pereira, "Neglected Tragedy" in *The Journal of African Studies*, Winter 1994, p. 17.

[45] Ohlson and Stedman, *The New is Not Yet Born*, p. 192.

[46] Birmingham, David, *Frontline Nationalism*, p. 24.

[47] Minter, *Apartheid's Contras*, p. 217.

[48] *Ibid.*, pp. 103–105.

[49] Newitt, Malyn, *A History of Mozambique* (Bloomington: Indiana University Press, 1995), p. 542.

[50] Newitt, *History of Mozambique*, p. 543.

[51] Munslow, Barry, *Mozambique: The Revolution and Its Origins* (Harlow, England: Longman Group, 1983), p. 153.

[52] Newitt, *History of Mozambique*, p. 545.

[53] *Africa Report*, November–December, 1992, p. 32.

[54] Hanlon, Joseph, *Mozambique: Who Calls the Shots?* (Bloomington: Indiana University Press, 1991), p. 28.

[55] *Ibid.*, p. 27.

[56] Bowen, Merle, "Beyond Reform: Adjustment and Political Power in Contemporary Mozambique" in Rich, *Dynamics of Changes*, p. 144.

[57] Cited in Vines, Alex, *Renamo: Terrorism in Mozambique* (Bloomington: Indiana University Press, 1991), p. 76.

[58] *Ibid.*, p. 78.

[59] Young, Tom, "From the MNR to Renamo: Making Sense of an African Counter-Revolutionary Insurgency" in Rich, *Dynamics of Change*, p. 161.

[60] Vines, *Renamo*, p. 9.

[61] Mondlane, Eduardo, *The Struggle for Mozambique* (New York: Penguin 1969), p. 164.

[62] Minter, *Apartheid's Contras*, p. 226.

[63] In the hopes of obtaining aid from wealthy Middle Eastern regimes, RENAMO representatives there have emphasized FRELIMO's alleged anti-Islamicism.

[64] Cited in Davidson, *Eye of the Storm*, pp. 218–219.

[65] Bridgland, *Jonas Savimbi*, p. 91.

[66] Cited, *ibid.*, p. 238.

[67] *Ibid.*, p. 239.

[68] Harding, *Fate of Africa*, p. 70.

[69] Minter, William, "Behind the UNITA Curtain" in *Africa Report*, May–June, 1990, p. 48.

[70] Harding, *Fate of Africa*, p. 43.

[71] Minter, William (ed.), *Operation Timber: Pages from the Savimbi Dossier* (Trenton, N.J.: Africa World Press, 1988), p. 115.

[72] Human Rights Watch/Africa, *Angola: Civilians Devastated by 15 Year War* (New York: Human Rights Watch, 1991), pp. 2–3.

[73] Minter, *Operation Timber*, p. 27.

[74] Africa Watch, *Conspicuous Destruction: War, Famine and the Reform Process in Mozambique* (New York: Human Rights Watch, 1992), p. 70.

[75] Minter, *Apartheid's Contras*, pp. 207–209.

[76] Finnegan, William, *A Complicated War: The Harrowing of Mozambique* (Berkeley: University of California Press, 1992), pp. 11–2.

[77] Harding, *Fate of Africa*, p. 212.

[78] Human Rights Watch, *Conspicuous Destruction*, p. 27.

[79] Magaia, Lina, *Dumba Nengue: Run for Your Life, Peasant Tales of Tragedy in Mozambique* (Trenton, N.J.: Africa World Press, 1988), pp. 31–34.

[80] Minter, "Behind the UNITA Curtain," p. 46.

[81] Windrich, *Cold War Guerrilla*, p. 119.

[82] The town of Bicesse is part of a larger urban area known as Estoril, hence the treaty is sometimes referred to as the Estoril accords.

[83] The UN sent 576 officials and committed \$132 million to monitor the demobilization of troops and the elections. By comparison, it sent 7,150 officials to Namibia in 1989–90, at a cost of \$430 million, in spite of the fact that Angola, with 12 million people, has approximately 10 times the population of the former South African colony.

[84] Human Rights Watch Arms Project, *Angola: Arms Trade and Violations of the Laws of War Since the 1992 Elections* (New York: Human Rights Watch/Africa, 1994), p. 16.

[85] *Ibid.*, pp. 21–22.

[86] Cited in Khadiagala, Gilbert, *Allies in Adversity: The Frontline States in Southern African Security, 1975–1993* (Athens: Ohio University Press, 1994), pp. 185–186.

[87] Cited in Human Rights Watch, *Conspicuous Destruction*, p. 30–31.

[88] Sant'Edigio's connections to Mozambique date back to the mid-1970s, when one of its members, Jaime Goncalves, became archbishop of Beira. At first an outspoken critic of FRELIMO's policy toward the church—he was jailed for six months at one point—Goncalves' relations with FRELIMO subsequently warmed. By the early 1980s, Sant'Edigio was a major aid donor to Mozambique. A charitable organization with offices around the world, Sant'Edigio first became involved in mediation in the early 1980s, when it negotiated a treaty between the Catholics and Druzes of Lebanon.

Now I just want to go home.
> —Demobilized Angolan child soldier

We've done it. We've finally done it!
> —Mozambican Electoral Commission
> president Brazao Mazula

ANGOLA

DEMOBILIZATION AND THE 1992 ELECTIONS (1991–92)

If writing a peace treaty for adversaries at war with each other for more than fifteen years was difficult, implementing it proved impossible. Between the signing of the Bicesse accords in May 1991 and national elections in September 1992, a multinational UN peace team was expected to establish a secure and democratic environment, demobilize two well-armed military forces, register millions of voters, and establish some 6,000 polling stations, all in a country nearly twice the size of Texas. And they had do all of this according to a rigid schedule (the formation of a joint-army command was formally established just forty-eight hours before the elections), on a shoestring budget of about $130 million, and with less than 500 blue helmets whose mandate prevented them from interfering in human rights violations and political infractions.

The consequences of their failure proved a catastrophic return to war that killed half as many people in two years as had been lost in battle in the previous fifteen. In hindsight, there were plenty of warning signs and plenty of blame to share around. Depending on one's perspective, the Union for the Total Independence of Angola (UNITA), the UN and even the Popular Movement for the Liberation of Angola (MPLA) were largely responsible for the disaster. First, UNITA did not live up to the mobilization protocols of Bicesse. It held back thousands of its best soldiers and cached weapons throughout the country. And according to journalist Victoria Brittain, UNITA acted arbitrarily in its areas of control, refusing to allow the MPLA and other minor parties to campaign there and ejecting MPLA administrators who were not sufficiently pliant. Furthermore, this did not go on in secret, as several high-level UNITA officials later testified in Luanda.

Nevertheless, Brittain says, the UN team turned a blind eye. Thus, according to Brittain and several other observers, the UN was not just guilty of maladministration by omission, but by commission as well.[1] Trying to achieve such immense goals with such a limited mandate and limited commitment of resources and personnel, observed Margaret Anstee, the UN's British point person in Angola, "was like trying to fly a 747 with fuel for a Cessna."[2]

The UN, however, was not solely responsible. Like UNITA, the MPLA and most news organizations, the UN believed Savimbi would win the elections, which, it felt, made his failure to abide by the accords and demobilize irrelevant. Moreover, say political scientists Christine Knudsen and I. William Zartman, "it was the MPLA which insisted on a weak international monitoring presence out of concern for its own sovereignty."[3] The election forecasts, of course, proved mistaken. Despite widespread violations of the free election protocols of the accords and the limited UN presence, an extraordinary 90 percent of the Angolan electorate was registered to vote. The MPLA won 129 of the 220 seats in the assembly, UNITA garnered 70 and small parties took the remaining 16. MPLA president José Eduardo dos Santos won 49.6 percent of the vote for president to UNITA chief Jonas Savimbi's 40.1 percent. (In the absence of a clear majority, under the Bicesse accords, the two top vote-getters were supposed to campaign in a second round of voting. But due to the revival of hostilities, the MPLA canceled it.) While voting patterns reflected both ethnic biases and party control of the countryside, the MPLA managed to win majorities in every region of the country except the Ovimbundu/UNITA heartland in the central highlands.

These results, says international relations scholar Moises Venancio, should not seem so surprising. Savimbi had engaged in ethnocentric, racist and violent rhetoric that frightened Angola's urban, mestizo and non-Ovimbundu electorate. Nor was the MPLA's reputation as negative as observers thought. While most Angolans were well aware of its corruption and incompetence, there was a widespread feeling that it represented the Angolan people as a nation. UNITA, on the other hand, was widely seen as a tool of foreigners, particularly the U.S. and South Africa. Perhaps the best assessment of the election results was offered by one Angolan voter who said, "If I have to choose between a thief [the MPLA] or a murderer [UNITA], I will always choose the thief."[4]

Both the MPLA and the UN pronounced the elections "generally free and fair," though the MPLA's precipitate TV announcement of a landslide victory for dos Santos, even before the polls had closed on the second and final day of voting (September 30), exacerbated UNITA concerns that the elections had been marked by fraud, irregularities and voter coercion. Fraudulent or legitimate, the elections, noted U.S. undersecretary of state for African affairs George Moose, were only part of the problem.

One of the things that was clearly missing from [the UN election/demobilization] process was any meaningful discussion among the parties about what happened after the elections: what kind of a government they were going to participate in, what their respective roles were going to be post-elections, and what assurances each would have that, win or lose, they would still have a meaningful voice in the governing of the country after those elections.[5]

THE "SECOND WAR" (1992–94)

Jonas Savimbi reacted to the election results with the rhetoric of reconciliation but the actions of a man committed to renewed military conflict. During the first two weeks of October, he said he would accept UNITA's loss in assembly races in order to run in the second-round presidential elections. At the same time, however, UNITA forces began to drift out of the demobilization camps and return to their former bases, while UNITA's generals resigned from the joint army staff. On October 17, UNITA launched its first attack against a town in southern Angola. UNITA's bellicosity, say observers, was largely a result of actions taken by forces outside the country. As noted above, the UN's lenient attitude toward UNITA's preelection violations of the Bicesse accords set the precedent. More importantly, Savimbi believed the U.S. would stand by him no matter what he did. As it turns out, this was an error, but not a stupid one. In spite of the MPLA's victory in elections that received the UN's imprimatur, the Bush administration refused to recognize the government in Angola and reassured Savimbi that he would continue to receive arms from the U.S. Though usually a close observer of U.S. politics, Savimbi was preoccupied by his own elections and had not seen Bush's own political vulnerability.

By the end of October, talk of reconciliation had completely evaporated. On October 7, UNITA demanded that the National Electoral Council annul the vote-counting process, stop releasing results and acknowledge that the MPLA's recently-formed special police force (known popularly as the *ninjas*) had intimidated voters and therefore should be immediately disbanded. When Herman Cohen, the new U.S. undersecretary of state for African affairs, encouraged Savimbi to make his demands through proper UN channels, Savimbi, in an international radio broadcast, told Cohen to "go to hell."[6] By the end of the month, savage fighting had broken out in the streets of Luanda, as police and armed civilian patrols, angered by Savimbi's threats of war, attacked UNITA supporters. Over a thousand people, largely UNITA supporters, were killed in the fighting, including UNITA vice president Jeremias Chitunda, who was gunned down as he tried to escape the city. "Militarily, the government's brief counter-strike was successful," notes a 1994 Human Rights Watch report,

not only in decapitating a significant portion of UNITA's political leadership and support structure, but also in destroying UNITA's urban armed militia, known as the Special Security Corp [locals called them "*caravaneros*" after the GM trucks they drove]. The government failed, however, to weaken UNITA's regular armed forces.[7]

As for Savimbi, the MPLA claimed the citizens of Huambo had driven him into the bush, a frightening portent given the UNITA leader's record of military comebacks. What Angolans refered to as the "second war" and outside observers called "Africa's forgotten war" had begun.

It started with a nationwide UNITA offensive against towns and cities. By the middle of November, the rebels controlled 57 of Angola's 164 municipalities, including provincial capitals in Uige and Cuanza Norte in the north, Benguela in the south and the key port city of Lobito. A brief government offensive in December retook Benguela and Lobito, but by January 1993 the MPLA's previous demobilization took its toll and the offensive ground to a halt. Sensing that the tide of war was running in its failure, UNITA kept the pressure on.

The rebels' strategy, to isolate the MPLA to cities and a strip along the coast, had succeeded by March. "Ultimately," says Human Rights Watch, "it appears UNITA's aim [was] to control all areas outside Luanda and to bring the economy to a standstill—creaming off assets—especially diamonds and oil—to fund further conflict with the government and strengthen its hand in negotiations."[8] Indeed, during December 1992 and January 1993, UNITA had shipped over $100 million worth of diamonds to Europe and Israel, using that income to purchase arms via Zaire and the South African homeland of Bophuthatswana. It also captured Soyo, the main oil production and refining center outside the Cabinda enclave. This was a major feat, given that the city, in the far northwest corner of Angola, was well outside UNITA's normal area of control. While capture of the city cut off revenue to the government, most experts in the industry did not believe UNITA had the expertise to keep production going and reap substantial income. To put pressure on the capital itself, UNITA attacked the city's hydroelectric system at its source in Caxito, about 40 miles to the east of the capital, leaving Luanda without water or regular electricity for two weeks.

At the same time, UNITA was also making a major push in the south, with its ultimate goal the capture of Huambo, Angola's second-largest city and the unofficial capital of the Ovimbundu people. Backed by a heavy artillery barrage that reduced the city to rubble, 5,000 UNITA guerrillas pinned down 3,000 MPLA soldiers near the governor's palace. By the end of February, an estimated 10,000 civilians and military personnel had died in and around Huambo in what the *Economist* called "the goriest fight anywhere in the world."[9] After 55 days of fighting, the remaining MPLA forces completed a full strategic retreat to Benguela, with tens of thousands of Ovimbundu and other civilians following behind. The civilian exodus resulted from UNITA's reputation for human rights violations, a reputation that it more than lived up to in its capture of Huambo. A civilian described his own experiences to Human Rights Watch.

> The military and civilian wounded were mixed and many civilians had moved to the hospital hoping that UNITA would respect it as a neutral location. When UNITA entered the hospital they divided the walking wounded from those too ill to move. They then started to execute the badly injured. I was outside with many others less seriously hurt when we heard firing and screaming. One person covered in blood jumped from a top floor window. We fled. Although UNITA started shooting at us, we managed to escape and make the road to Benguela.[10]

As the above events indicate, the MPLA was caught almost entirely off guard by the UNITA offensive. "Between May 1991 and the elections in September 1992," says Human Rights Watch, "the Angolan government largely neglected its regular armed forces . . . [and] focused on equipping and training the Rapid Intervention Police (ninjas)."[11] While this force kept order in the cities, it was no match for UNITA's regular forces in the field. A new draft law, calling up all Angolan males born in 1974, was largely unsuccessful as well. On the other hand, the MPLA had one important resource: revenues from the more than 500,000 barrels annually pumped from the Cabinda oil fields. In April, the MPLA renounced the so-called "triple-zero" clause in the Bicesse accords, which called for a total cessation of foreign military aid to Angola. In July, the so-called "troika" of mediators at Bicesse, that is, Russia, the U.S. and Portugal, agreed to drop their embargo against arms shipments to the MPLA. Backed by substantial funds (as well as loans against future oil sales) and the lifting of the embargo, the MPLA went on a massive arms purchasing spree. In 1993, it imported $2.5 billion in artillery, tanks and small arms. In the first six months of 1994, it purchased a further $1 billion worth.

Reorganized and rearmed, the MPLA began to fight back, forcing UNITA into a stalemate through the summer and then opening a new offensive in the autumn. Sweeping east from its bastions along the coast, the MPLA cleared UNITA from the coastal provinces and laid siege to Huambo. In a 180-degree turn to the previous course of the war, the MPLA found it easier to clear UNITA forces from the countryside than from the cities. The rebels held on in both Huambo and Cuito, the other provincial capital of the central highlands. In the former, UNITA controlled the city center as MPLA artillery and aerial bombardment reduced the city to ruins, before it was looted and evacuated by UNITA forces in January 1994.

In Cuito, however, armed civilians and the ninjas never evacuated when UNITA attacked in January, and the city became a kind of African Stalingrad as the two sides fought block to block. For months, the several hundred thousand people who remained in the ruins carved holes in the walls of houses to move about without risking sniper fire. At night groups of civilians, calling themselves *batidas*, ventured into the countryside to find food. Before the city fell to the MPLA in September 1994, over 30,000 people had died from the fighting, famine or disease. The city, noted one journalist after the 21-month siege, "was hardly worth rebuilding."[12] The fall of Cuito represented the beginning of a general UNITA retreat throughout the country. Already seeing its areas of control reduced from about 70 percent to 40 percent by August 1994, UNITA was forced to pull its forces from virtually every part of Angola, except isolated regions in the northeast—where it continued to exploit the diamond resources and receive arms from neighboring Zaire—and its old stronghold in the south.

By November 1994 and the signing of the Lusaka accords (see chapter 6), the war for Angola or, at least, its most intensive phase, was over, but the costs had been appalling. During both MPLA and UNITA sieges of Angolan cities, artillery was used extensively, with little concern for whether the shells fell on civilians or combatants. While UNITA was singled out for its ruthless use of the long-range guns by human rights organizations, the MPLA did not escape censure. Its practice of bombing from high altitudes, out of range of UNITA antiaircraft guns, had an especially devastating effect since it made it impossible for pilots to differentiate between civilian and military targets.

While intensive use of firepower may be inevitable in wars of this kind, the list of human rights violations perpetrated by both sides (though, again, UNITA was especially singled out for opprobrium by human rights groups) included acts outside the pale of military necessity, including extensive looting, rape, forced recruitment, mine-laying, executions of prisoners of war and civilians and, perhaps most insidiously, the use of food aid as a weapon of war. UNITA, which was largely guilty of this last outrage, argued that denying aid to besieged cities was a wartime necessity, since the food and medicine was likely to end up in the hands of combatants who were defending the city and were therefore legitimate targets. When the MPLA tried to airdrop aid, it was shot at by UNITA, forcing the planes to fly at altitudes where pinpoint placement was rendered impossible. Many such drops simply ended up in UNITA hands and so the government cut back on them.

The UN complained that international relief flights were shot at as well. Aid transport by ground was virtually impossible. Both UNITA and MPLA soldiers, often facing hunger themselves, usually waylaid the convoys, thus ending several brief efforts by the UN and international aid organizations to bring food and medicines by truck. In its 1994 report, Human Rights Watch reported no less than a dozen incidents in which convoys were turned back by UNITA or aid flights were shot at after being given clearance to land by rebel forces. Meanwhile, old MPLA and UNITA tactics of forced displacement or villagization and forced portering and servitude were revived. Altogether, it has been estimated that at least 100,000 people died during the most intense phase of the "second war," that is, between October 1992 and January 1994. Another 600,000 people were driven from their homes, most fleeing to Luanda and the coastal enclave under MPLA control. But, noted journalist Cindy Shiner in early 1994, a city designed for 400,000 was rendered unworkable when it had to support 2 million.

> [Refugees] find little respite in Luanda, where annual inflation has hit 1,300, cholera and measles are epidemic, and the only housing available is in abandoned buildings or squalid shantytowns. The number of severely mal-nourished in at least two . . . neighborhoods is double what it was six months ago.[13]

THROUGH LUSAKA (1994–96)

UNITA's declining fortunes were reflected in Savimbi's demands and rhetoric. In the early part of 1993, Savimbi was brushing aside efforts by the beleaguered MPLA and the international community, including a scaled-back UN contingent, to negotiate an end to the fighting. Bowing to his demands, the UN replaced Margaret Anstee, its chief representative in Angola, with Malian diplomat Alouine Blondin Beye. In public, Savimbi said that Anstee, as a British citizen, was ignorant of African affairs. In private, he accused her of MPLA favoritism. As late as summer 1993, Savimbi was demanding a fully decentralized administration for Angola, a demand that the MPLA dismissed as a ploy to partition the country.

On the other hand, Savimbi's bluster hid well-founded concern that the MPLA was gaining the initiative. The international lifting of the embargo against the MPLA in July led Savimbi to resurrect the "triple zero" option that he had been violating since the end of 1992 when he established supply routes through Zaire. He also demanded that all foreign forces evacuate Angola, a reference to the several thousand black and white South African mercenaries the MPLA had hired to protect its oil fields. But it was the UN Security Council's November 1993 decision to embargo oil and arms sales to UNITA that forced Savimbi to accept international mediation. Still, with its diamond revenues, UNITA has the means to buy arms on the international marketplace. Under the Lusaka process, all mining supposed to come under the control of Endiama, the state monopoly. As of late 1996 arrangements to transfer production and marketing had failed to material-ize, though talks about sharing the diamond wealth were in the offing.

Moreover, in July 1994, both Human Rights Watch and the UN accused several African countries, especially Zaire, of participating in sanctions-busting by UNITA by allowing arms to be transshipped through their airports.[14] As recently as September, journalists were reporting Zairian-based supply flights bound for Savimbi's airbase at Negage in northwestern Angola, where UNITA patrols continue to man armed checkpoints.

Despite this ongoing evidence of UNITA violations, talks between the MPLA and UNITA began in Lusaka in December, though only after a one month delay, the result of a bomb going off at UNITA headquarters, an act Savimbi said was perpetrated by MPLA spies and aimed at himself. While the talks and the agreement are discussed in chapter 6, several key elements should be reiterated here. Generally, the Lusaka accords built upon the framework of the Bicesse agreement, especially in regard to the quid pro quo of MPLA and UNITA demobilization in exchange for a mutual role in administering the country until elections, in the case of Bicesse, or a final power-sharing agreement, in the case of Lusaka, could be arranged. This slightly modified arrangement meant, of course, that the most important result of the Bicesse accords, multiparty elections leading to a democratic government, had now been abandoned. Though not specific on the subject, the Lusaka accords accepted the idea of power sharing within the national and provincial executive branches, even though UNITA had lost the elections and therefore had no right to such a role.

In addition, the Lusaka accords were markedly different in their agenda. Having learned a lesson from the failed Bicesse accords, all parties to the Lusaka agreement, including the UN, which took a much more central role in 1994 than it did previously, abandoned the idea that the agreement could settle all future political problems. As Knudsen and Zartman write, "by avoiding a winner-take-all situation and addressing the issues of power sharing, Beye was accepting the areas of the Bicesse Accords that had worked, and he was targeting the crucial areas of failure."[15] Instead, the Lusaka agreement was intended to create an atmosphere of trust and a structure for continuing discussions.

The pacing of the Lusaka agreements was also markedly different than at Bicesse. Rather than pushing the situation on the ground to meet the timetable established by negotiators, the process would work the other way around. At the beginning of the talks, say Knudsen and Zartman, "Beye publicly announced that he was in no rush for a quick-fix formula, demonstrating a commitment to the process that was intended to evoke a like commitment from the hostile parties."[16] And while it was impossible to avoid having events in Angola complicate the talks, Beye was determined to avoid the vicious circle evident at Bicesse, in which public pronouncements by the negotiators created hostile reactions and further hostility inside Angola. To that end, he imposed a news blackout on all activities in Lusaka, in order to create "a climate of mutual confidence."[17] After almost a year of intense negotiations, the Lusaka accords were signed on November 21, 1994, amid accusations by UNITA, the MPLA, and the UN that fighting was occurring in both the north and the central highlands.

The results of Lusaka also differed from those of Bicesse. At first appearances, the almost total cessation of hostilities following the 1991 agreement seemed to indicate that Angola was on the road to permanent peace. In hindsight, of course, it turned out to be a false calm. UNITA had stopped fighting both because it expected to win and because it was preparing itself militarily for a possible political defeat, while the MPLA remained nonbelligerent in response to its adversary's seeming cooperation. The period following the signing of the Lusaka accords, on the other hand, has been marked by continuing, though sporadic, hostilities and signs of wavering commitment on both sides. A rough survey of AP and Reuters wires mentioning attacks by one side or the other between November 1994 and January 1996, and usually based on accusations lodged by either UNITA or the MPLA, reveals over 35 major violations.[18]

The state of peace and of war in Angola fluctuated throughout 1995. All during the year, and as late as 1995, UNITA accused the MPLA of attacking UNITA combatants and even civilians in both northern Angola and the central highlands. During a spate of fighting in August, UNITA said that the air force was attacking its troops in the south. Meanwhile, the MPLA, the UN, and outside observers charged UNITA with cease-fire violations, including attacks on MPLA forces throughout the country, failures to demobilize, illegal recruitment, the murder of four foreigners on a beach south of Luanda and receiving arms via Zaire. In February, one UNITA defector went so far as to say Savimbi was denouncing the Lusaka accords, sending troops to Cabinda to avoid demobilizing, and generally preparing for war.

By late 1996, however, demobilization appeared to be moving apace. The UN claims that UNITA is meeting the letter of the accords and has demobilized 80 percent of their forces, though it is still feared that elite forces and caches of weapons are being held in reserve. And as of January 1997, some 20,000 UNITA soldiers had walked out of the camps to destinations unknown. As a measure of goodwill, five UNITA generals relocated to Luanda in September to take up their posts as heads of the new joint-command Angolan army.

For its part, the UN, which began deploying the first of the proposed 7,500 troops in December 1994, acknowledged the violations, but tried to downplay their severity. According to representatives of the international organization, the biggest problems were delays in demobilization and continuing violations of the cease-fire. But the UN secretary-general tried to put a positive spin on the problem. "Some incidents may be attributable to delays in the disengagement of troops, local attempts to regain territory, increased acts of banditry and lack of troop discipline or to the establishment by UNAVEM of more effective verification mechanisms."[19]

While the UN said both sides were "living under the delusion" that they could extract further concessions by holding their troops in reserve, it acknowledged that UNITA was procrastinating. Yet, in statements from the field, UN officers maintained neutrality. After a confrontation between UN and UNITA forces in August, Uruguayan Colonel Roque Gallego told a Reuters reporter, "it's convenient to blame UNITA. But it doesn't matter to us, the UN. What we want is for the cease-fire violations to stop, so that we can commence disarming soldiers and establishing some measure of safety for Angolan citizens."[20] This kind of talk led some outside observers to accuse UNAVEM of appeasing UNITA. Part of the problem resulted from where the two sides found themselves when the ceasefire took hold. The MPLA controlled the cities, but UNITA maintained a stranglehold over the nation's roadways, thus it was more likely that as the UN moved around it was likely to come into conflict with UNITA.

Despite the continuing delays and conflict, both UNITA and the MPLA were beginning to make reconciliatory moves. In February, Savimbi overcame hardline opposition to the Lusaka accords within UNITA and got the rebels' congress to ratify the treaty. In addition, on more than one occasion, Savimbi publicly pledged allegiance to the Angolan government and swore that he would not return to war. But as for his role in future power sharing, Savimbi remained ambivalent. In August, he said he would accept the vice presidency, but then backed off later and said he would prefer to be in the opposition. A UNITA spokesperson in the United States told this author in late November that Savimbi was still unsure what his position in a new coalition government would be.[21] In late 1996, Savimbi turned down an unspecified government job that offered high pay and many perquisites. Savimbi said he was insulted by the patronizing tone of the offer.

Fear appears to be a big reason for this hesitancy. UNITA officials point out that they were attacked twice before, in 1975 and 1992, when they showed up unarmed in the capital. More significant, however, is the fear that Savimbi's movement would collapse without his immediate presence. "If we give up our army and then our president too," explained one UNITA officer, "we're nothing."[22] Under post-Lusaka arrangements, UNITA delegates to the national assembly began taking their seats in January 1997.

Savimbi's reticence may be attributed to the fact that in August 1995, the MPLA-controlled assembly reformed the constitution to include two vice presidencies, presumably in order to dilute the power of the position. The MPLA had done this once before, offering UNITA one minor cabinet post in the wake of the 1992 elections, an offer Savimbi labeled an insult. Nevertheless, the MPLA was making concessions to peace as well. In February, it committed $500 million to help fund the peace process. And, along with UNITA, it sent its first contingent of forces to the UN's demobilization camps in November 1995, symbolically on the first anniversary of the Lusaka Accords but, in fact, well behind schedule.

And while fighting between UNITA and MPLA troops has been reported as late as December 1995, dos Santos and Savimbi continue to meet. After a May session in Gabon, they jointly addressed an aid conference on Angola in Brussels. In January 1996, they met again in Luanda for the first time since the war had recommenced in October 1992 to speed up implementation of the accords, including demobilization, and to find ways to avoid further ceasefire violations. In late 1996, meetings were held to discuss UNITA control of the diamond fields of northeastern Angola. One tentative solution involves the establishment of a private corporation run by former UNITA officers named by former UNITA soldiers with profits divided between UNITA shareholders and government coffers. "Finally, the grey clouds that were hanging over the peace process are clearing," noted the state-run *Jornal de Angola* daily. "There are some who consider [the meeting] the best moment since Lusaka."[23] After a visit to Angola in late January, Madeleine Albright, American Ambassador to the UN, was optimistic, saying the two parties "just needed one final push" to make the peace process stick.[24]

THE FUTURE OF ANGOLA

It is a truism in the diplomatic community that with the Cold War over, sub-Saharan Africa has been marginalized, "fallen off the radar screen of the world's consciousness."[25] With no Soviet threat and no ideological points to score, Africa is being left to fend for itself. In the case of Angola, this may be a blessing in disguise. Few countries have suffered as much from late Cold War–era interventionism (one thinks of Afghanistan, Cambodia and Nicaragua). Angola has an especially miserable distinction. Before it was a Cold War battleground, the nation was the rear guard of European anti-decolonization and then the front line of apartheid defense.

   The cost of this triple holocaust has been horrific: an estimated one million dead over 30 years, and several million refugees. Not one but two generations have grown up with war. In fact, more than three-quarters of the population has known nothing but fighting an enemy, be it the Portuguese, Zairians, Cubans, South Africans and one another. Perhaps, most tragically of all, the wars of Angola will live on long into the peace. As many as 10 million land mines lay in wait for the unsuspecting peasant farmer to stick his or her hoe in the ground. Already, Angola may have more amputees per capita than any other country in the world, though Cambodia is giving it a run for its misery.

   It is easy to say "Enough is enough," "Foreigners out," "The West be hanged." The Eastern Bloc, Western Bloc and South Africa have brought the country nothing but trouble. Surely the Angolans, even in their worst moments, could not possibly have made such a mess of things without this dubious outside support. And while it is true that sub-Saharan Africa is being marginalized, Angola, by necessity, will remain on the world's radar screen. The country, with its vast resources of diamonds and oil, is simply too important to ignore. The Angolan people can only hope that the news coming out of their country in the future will be more prosaic and positive: a rebounding economy, gradually rising indexes of social development, and routine elections.

The radical economic ideas and programs of an earlier era are gone, but the impulses may remain. As political scientist John Saul writes, if economic restructuring and market reforms do not produce adequate improvements in the standard of living (and he is far from optimistic that they will), then the Angolan people may demand a new direction that bears a remarkable similarity to the old. And having insisted on the importance of democratic expression, how could the West demur? Nevertheless, he concludes, the current leadership is unlikely to be the "midwife" of a new socialism. Having failed to "de-Stalinize" early enough, it may not be able to accept that a more just social and economic order must arise from the grass roots rather than be imposed from the capital. Like other scholars, and particularly those on the left, Saul places great faith in the possibility of civil society, civic organizations and indigenous NGOs.[26]

It is as easy to be optimistic as pessimistic about Angola's future. True, the nation has suffered from a massive trauma that will haunt its collective consciousness for years to come. But the healing has already begun, and the prognosis is positive. In his work on nineteenth-century medicine, historian Charles Rosenburg posited that a patient's chance of recovery increased in direct proportion to the distance he or she maintained from the nearest doctor.[27] That may very well apply to Angola. With the Cold War and apartheid dead and buried, it is unlikely that the old teams of doctors, with their cures worse than the disease, will come to ply their trade.

Not that Angola will be left entirely to itself. The world's banking institutions and aid organizations will remain in Angola, and they will continue applying their Western-oriented economic nostrums. Whether they are applicable to Angola and good for the Angolan people will be seen. From the left, scholars argue that the economic reforms are tailored not only in the West's image, but in the West's interest. The international community, they say, seeks the kind of macroeconomic balance—that is, a devalued currency, lowered credit, openings to foreign investment, and market reforms—that lead to expatriation of profits and debt repayment, but not economic gains for the Angolan people. The new "internationalistas" are as rigidly driven by ideology, they conclude, as the old socialist ones.[28] For their part, the international institutions involved in Angolan economic restructuring argue that their solutions could not possibly be worse than the corruption, incompetence and stagnation produced by socialist economic planning, and will probably be a whole lot better, at least in the long run. The questions remain, however: Given Angola's current political instability, will there be a long run? Will the people patiently endure the immediate suffering restructuring brings?

The short-term future of Angola is indeed volatile. To the UN's credit, and the international community's shame, there is a widespread acknowledgment that the poorest of Angola's poor, that is, refugees and potential land-mine victims, must be taken care of first, but thus far precious little action has been taken. As of September 1995, there remained several hundred thousand refugees in Zambia and some 3 million internally displaced persons, according to the UN High Commissioner for Refugees.[29]

Between 50,000 and 80,000 Angolans, many of them children, have suffered crippling injuries from land mines. In order to carry out its work, the UN has hired international firms and trained Angolan personnel to clear the main roads, but uncounted fields, paths and minor roads remain unpassable and unusable.[30] Land mines, of course, are an especially insidious weapon. In Angola, most were strewed around the landscape with no regard for victims and no mapping. Indeed, terror is the land miner's most effective ally. A single explosion renders a field or path unusable, whether it has been nominally cleared or not. It is said even an augmented demining program will be at work for decades.

Cantonment of demobilized troops proceeds, but a final plan for a joint military force remains to be hammered out. Like land mines, ex-soldiers who cannot find work or cannot adjust to civilian society maintain their explosive potential for years to come. Crime, which has witnessed dramatic growth in recent years, will remain a serious social problem for some time to come. Again, there are positive signs. One of these is a family retracing program, instituted by an Angolan NGO, that reunites teenage soldiers with their families. While it has linked up an estimated 10,000 families, there are hundreds of thousands more in need of such help.

In the final analysis, hope lays with the Angolan people themselves, and there are signs they are rising to the immense task of nation rebuilding. When a UNITA general and an MPLA one met to shake hands on a battlefield in the central highlands in January 1995, and for the first time since fighting had recommenced in October 1992, an Associated Press reporter observed, they were "met by cheers from their troops."[31] Angola's warring factions, says Minter, have been put on notice. "The vast majority of Angolans . . . of all backgrounds, profoundly weary of war, strongly endorse . . . national unity and reconciliation."[32]

MOZAMBIQUE

DEMOBILIZATION AND THE 1994 ELECTIONS (1992–94)

While Angola had slipped back into a brutal second round of fighting between late 1992 and 1994, Mozambique was winning the peace, albeit gradually and fitfully. Indeed, the war in Angola has cast a sobering shadow on all parties in Mozambique—the Mozambique Liberation Front (FRELIMO), the National Mozambican Resistance (RENAMO) and, perhaps most importantly, the United Nations Commission on Mozambique (UNOMOZ). All have shown flexibility and a willingness to adjust the election and demobilization schedule to fit events on the ground. The cease-fire, which went into effect after the October 1992 accords were signed in Rome, has rarely been broken by either side, though FRELIMO filed a slew of accusations against RENAMO in the first several months of the truce.

If violence was generally absent during these years, fear was not. RENAMO, in particular, was concerned that giving up arms meant isolation, marginalization and even elimination. Its leaders refused to come to the capital until money was forthcoming from the international community and offices, housing and proper security guaranteed by the FRELIMO government. At the same time, however, RENAMO leaders asserted their commitment to the electoral process in no uncertain terms. "RENAMO will respect the election results, even if we lose," said Internal Affairs Director Jose Augusto Xaviere.

> We are not like UNITA, who are only after power. We fought for the principles of multiparty democracy and a free-market economy. The Chissano government [FRELIMO] has already instituted those changes, so we have already won. Even if we lose the elections, we will have won because there will be democracy in Mozambique.[33]

For its part, FRELIMO evinced a continuing resistance to accept RENAMO as a legitimate political party and worried that the party was likely to return to guerrilla fighting, a concern shared by Tanzania and Zimbabwe, which refused to leave the transport corridors they were protecting until UN troops had been fully deployed. One reporter noted of 1993, "the atmosphere between both parties was . . . one of suspicion and confrontation."[34] RENAMO was demanding the right to administer its control areas and appoint the governors of several provinces. In August, President Chissano and RENAMO's Dhlakama met for the first time on Mozambican soil. The gesture was a noble one, but the talks proved inconclusive. "RENAMO was becoming dangerously isolated," says Vines, "putting the entire peace process in jeopardy."[35] Nevertheless, the Maputo government lived up to its obligation to help RENAMO leaders adjust to life in the capital. Ensconced in a seaside villa, Dhlakama, noted an *Economist* reporter, "did not look like a man eager to go back to the bush."[36]

Thus, demobilization, which events in Angola proved to be the most important part of the peace process, moves forward at a frustratingly slow pace. Demobilization, in a case like Mozambique, involves two kinds of trust and confidence-building. Each side must accept that the other is acting in good faith and that the mediating team, in this case UNOMOZ, is competent and fair in carrying it out. Having been at war for more than fifteen years, it was not likely that the former would happen overnight. And as for the UN, despite its greatly augmented commitment to Mozambique (a result of its failure in Angola) and pleas to the international community that it live up to its financial pledges, it was often caught short, with inadequate facilities for demobilizing soldiers.

Under the Rome accords, UNOMOZ was to establish 49 demobilization camps, or cantonments. Under the original plan, these were to be run by just 21 administrators, but events in Angola forced the UN to adjust. Eventually, after many delays by FRELIMO and RENAMO over which nationalities would be acceptable, the Italian government agreed to commit 1,200 soldiers, but as Rome insisted on shipping its personnel and equipment by sea, it took several extra months to get the cantonments up to speed.[37] Further delays were caused by the joint FRELIMO-RENAMO demobilization committees, who, according to one journalist, "worked at a snail's pace," largely because RENAMO lacked qualified personnel.[38]

Though the camps offered basic and desperately needed amenities like food, clothing and beds, the first contingents of FRELIMO and RENAMO soldiers did not start showing up until December 1993. Under the Rome accords, national elections were to be held within one year of the signing, that is, by October 1993. By summer 1993, the slow pace of demobilization caught the attention of the UN Security Council, and Boutros-Ghali flew into Maputo to arrange a balloting delay of one year with the two Mozambican parties. Money for RENAMO and the new timetable for elections and cantonment helped break the logjam and, by spring 1994, the pace of demobilization was picking up. RENAMO's leadership, well-funded and comfortably housed in Maputo, felt confident; FRELIMO, on the other hand, was being pushed into compliance by a series of mutinies by soldiers eager to go home.

Unlike Angola, election campaigning in Mozambique was a quiet, even desultory affair. Human rights activist Ruth Minter, who spent time in Mozambique during the elections, said she saw little campaigning, even in Maputo—"an occasional poster and loudspeaker truck," but nothing one might expect in a nation's first election and especially one that was to determine the future of a country.[39] Moreover, the electioneering was largely negative. A RENAMO spokesperson told journalist Jeremy Harding that FRELIMO's campaign consisted of little more than a resuscitation of old and, in his mind, unfounded charges of RENAMO violence and intimidation. "Is it possible that someone wants to bring down the name of RENAMO," the spokesperson asked rhetorically, "by coming with these things?"[40] Other journalists pointed out RENAMO's appeal to ethnicity, which accused FRELIMO, among other things, of favoritism to southern

Mozambican peoples, an urban-mestizo bias, and an animosity toward the Shona and Ndau-speaking peoples in RENAMO's stronghold in the central provinces.

Ultimately, the October 28–29, 1994 elections provided a substantial victory for FRELIMO and a landslide for Chissano, albeit with a sizable minority choosing RENAMO. The government party received 44 percent of the vote, winning a slight majority of 129 seats in the new 250-seat parliament. Chissano, on the other hand, beat Dhlakama by a 53 percent to 34 percent margin. A last-minute boycott by Dhlakama—based on claims that the elections were being run fraudulently and continuing demands for postelection power sharing—fizzled, dissuading little of the nearly 90 percent of the Mozambican electorate that cast ballots. UNOMOZ was quick to endorse the legitimacy of the elections. "The United Nations observation," declared UN special representative to Mozambique Aldo Ajello,

> would not support any possible claim of fraud or intimidation, or any other patterns of incidents that could have affected the credibility of the elections. Indeed, the voting can be described as having been carried out peacefully and with integrity.[41]

But, as some outside observers noted, Ajello had to say that, given the UN's previous failure in Angola and its hankering for a success somewhere. Indeed, election violence was largely absent, but fifteen years of war and the continuing de facto dual administration of the country meant that intimidation was part of the political landscape.

Post-election assessments focused on one question: Why did RENAMO get such an unexpectedly high percentage of the vote? Needless to say, the answers vary, depending on the region observed and the perspective of the observer. Some say the church played a role. Its mixed endorsement—RENAMO for the assembly, Chissano for president—helps explain the discrepancy between the party's relative success and its leader's poor showing. FRELIMO argues that pro-RENAMO *regulos*, the colonial-era administrative class, played a decisive role.

Election results, on the other hand, showed a strong correlation between voting patterns and areas of control. RENAMO won 79 of its 112 seats in the three heavily populated central provinces that remained under its control on election day, though FRELIMO made a decent showing there, picking up more than 40 seats. In the south, however, it was the government by a landslide. In Maputo city and the three southern provinces, FRELIMO took 57 seats to RENAMO's five. Patterns like this, says former FRELIMO consultant Prexi Nesbitt, who visited Mozambique during and after the elections, suggest intimidation and fear on the part of voters.

> My take is that 20 percent of RENAMO's vote was from people who were discouraged, disillusioned or completely alienated from FRELIMO . . . corruption, blaming FRELIMO for the war . . . 80 percent were by people who had been given a message, not always hidden, sometimes explicitly, that a vote for FRELIMO meant the war would continue and the way to peace is to vote for RENAMO.[42]

Other observers claim that RENAMO's vote was due to UNOMOZ failure. Historian William Minter said that democracy and respect for human rights was more rigidly enforced in government-controlled areas than in RENAMO ones. As for the parties themselves, each filed a list of fraud charges against the other.

Still another factor was voter ignorance, not so much with the issues but with the electoral process itself. Because Mozambicans had no familiarity with formal democratic processes and a high percentage were illiterate, the contending parties had to establish nonverbal associations between their campaigns and the ballot, which included party symbols and candidate photos to help those who couldn't read. RENAMO, for example, used Dhlakama's distinctive glasses. Unfortunately for the rebel leader, a candidate for one of the minor parties wore similar ones. FRELIMO's vote totals were affected by its place on the ballot, which had been established by lottery. On the presidential side, Chissano came last. But on the assembly side, FRELIMO was in the middle of the ballot. Some observers say that voters checked off Chissano's name, then moved automatically across the ballot and did the same on the assembly side. This, they say, explains why the Democratic Union, "the least known" of all opposition groups, according to the *Southern Africa Report*, was the only party besides FRELIMO and RENAMO to break the 5 percent barrier to gain entry into the assembly. It was at the bottom of the assembly ballot next to Chissano.[43]

SINCE THE ELECTIONS (1994–97)

The elections settled who would rule Mozambique, but not how they would rule. Both at the national level and, more importantly, at the regional and local levels, disputes quickly emerged, and not just over the formulation and implementation of political and economic policy. The disputes involved basic questions of sovereignty as well. During the first session of the new national assembly in December 1994, telecast live to the nation, RENAMO delegates walked out after being outvoted on the choice of the house's speaker. As they left, members dropped hints that some kind of power-sharing arrangement would be the only thing that would bring them back. FRELIMO stood firm and the delegates returned in January.

Away from the capital, there were all kinds of disputes, especially in former areas of RENAMO control in the central provinces. In May 1995, a FRELIMO administrator's house in Maringue, Sofala, was burned to the ground. In June, RENAMO leaders in another part of the province imposed a boycott on government schools, health clinics, and shops to express their outrage at the appointment of a pro-FRELIMO administrator. All through the spring, RENAMO erected roadblocks near its old headquarters at Casa Banana both to collect revenues and protest the government's unwillingness to share state moneys. *MozambiqueFile*, the government's international newsletter, concluded, "a situation of 'dual administration' still prevails, whereby the *de facto* ruler of these areas is the former rebel movement RENAMO."[44] Perhaps the most serious clash of all occurred in Manica province in June, after an insurrection of *regulos*, aided by 'armed RENAMO troops,' led to the occupation of the local police headquarters.[45] After negotiations and an unspecified use of force, the national police reoccupied the building in September.

From FRELIMO's perspective, these disputes reflected an alliance between unreconstructed *regulo* elements and RENAMO cadres. "For *regulos* still operate on a hereditary principle, which is absolutely at odds with legitimation by democratic vote," *MozambiqueFile* argued.

> If *regulos* really feel that they represent local opinion, then they should run for office in the elections. If they won, they would have the respect and prestige they crave—but as elected representatives and not because their father or grandfather was a low level official running errands for the Portuguese.[46]

Others charged RENAMO's leadership. According to Nesbitt, RENAMO wants more than just a fair share of power.

> Dhlakama believes he should be president. It's based on ambition . . . He suffers from delusions. Four years of the negotiating process made him believe he was an equal player in the process. You have to look at his biography and RENAMO's history.[47]

RENAMO's insecurity has been reinforced by the international community's cessation of funding. In September, RENAMO warned its former international backers that unless they were willing to finance the party through the year 2000, the party would be forced to go back to fighting in the bush. Both FRELIMO and the international community dismissed the threat, and that for a good reason. Without a sufficient armed force, RENAMO is helpless. Thus, party leaders say FRELIMO doesn't take them seriously and they complain often about FRELIMO arrogance. In fact, the government has refused to appoint RENAMO people to all but the lowest posts in the bureaucracy. There are no RENAMO cabinet members and no RENAMO provincial governors.

The dispute over power is but half the story. RENAMO also feels left out of the money, not the petty funds to run the party but the real money (by Mozambican standards) that some FRELIMO officials are making from the wholescale privatization of Mozambican state assets. In power, more educated, and with better international contacts, some FRELIMO politicians represent a ruling class transforming itself from the moderately well-compensated managers of state enterprises into the well-compensated managers of foreign run corporations or even into owners themselves. Thus, the irony of the self-described free market party, i.e. RENAMO, fighting in the assembly against the once self-described "revolutionary-vanguard" party's two most controversial proposals: the privatization of industry and the invitation to South African businesses and individuals to run Mozambican farms and mines.

Nor do all the disputes in post-election Mozambique divide along party lines. Both RENAMO and FRELIMO are facing internal problems of their own. As the opposition party, of course, the stakes involved in RENAMO disputes are smaller, though they are indicative of RENAMO's problematic transition from a rebel army to the loyal opposition. RENAMO leaders made great promises to their followers and potential followers when they needed to fight FRELIMO. They recruited (voluntarily and/or by force) all kinds of people to administer their control areas and run the organization. For example, RENAMO recruited a number of young men by offering them scholarships to attend university after the war. Without sufficient funds, those scholarships are not forthcoming and the young people have disrupted RENAMO meetings to make their demands. FRELIMO's crises are more grave. Having accepted (or been forced to accept) radical economic restructuring, FRELIMO has alienated some of its core constituencies, including soldiers, police, and industrial workers, all of whom went on strike at different points during 1995 to protest inflation and demand higher salaries. In the case of some soldiers, the demands are simply to be paid at all. By late September, an estimated 35,000 jobs had been lost to restructuring, according to the Mozamibican General Trade Union Confederation.[48] Meanwhile, the government was placing its economic hopes on oil discovery. By mid-1996, American and British oil companies had committed $300 million to an oil exploration project along Mozambique's 1,500 mile coastline.

Since the elections, Mozambique has faced and continues to face a series of problems. Urban crime, though low by American or even South African standards, is growing, while banditry in the countryside remains a serious problem. The sheer volume of arms and out-of-work soldiers has led to a spate of hijackings and armed raids on rural villages and shops. Meanwhile, the country's military and police, according to the government's own spokespersons, are both incompetent and increasingly out of control. A particularly rancorous and potentially explosive issue involves the establishment of an independent military judiciary that tries, punishes and imprison civilians in clear violation, say many Mozambican parliamentarians, of the nation's constitution.

As in Angola, land mines remain a living nightmare. They were scattered around the country by both RENAMO and FRELIMO. Indeed, the UN says land mines from the Portuguese era remain. All parties, and particularly RENAMO, scattered them in haphazard fashion and did little to map their location. As in Angola (and elsewhere), mines were laid for military purposes, such as protecting garrisons, and to terrorize the civilian population. Antipersonnel land mines sowed in fields, paths, and roads were intended to obstruct civilian movement and trade and to hamper agricultural production. South Africa and RENAMO's basic objectives, to render the country politically ungovernable and economically crippled, were well served by land mines.

No one is exactly sure how many of these weapons were buried during the long years of war. In December 1992, the UN offered an estimate of two million, but, as Human Rights Watch points out, "this figure has no scientific basis."[49] As important as land mine totals are their placement. Fortunately for the country as a whole, the vast majority of mines were laid in the central provinces where the war was fiercest. But for those who live there, the toll is devastating. According to a recent article in *Lancet*, the British medical journal, land mine injuries in some areas of the country approach 2 percent of the population. "Our results," said Harvard's Alberto Aschiero, head of the team of U.S. doctors who conducted the study in 1995, "suggest that the impact of land mines is substantially higher than originally thought."[50] Osorio Severino, the head of the UN's Mozambique land mine commission, estimated that the buried weapons were still causing 40 casualties a month. He estimated that before the 10-year removal project is finished, another 5,000 Mozambicans might die.[51]

Nature has added to the country's woes. Massive flooding in early 1996 displaced over 200,000 people from their homes and farms, requiring an emergency international airlift of 12,000 tons of food. The flooding unleashing an epidemic of malaria. The Mozambican Ministry of Health reported over 7,500 cases between January and March 1996, making it the nation's number one killer again.[52]

There is some positive news emerging from Mozambique, however. By midsummer 1995, nearly all Mozambican refugees in almost every neighboring country, including the more than one million in Malawi, have returned, mostly to their villages and farms. A positive sign, says the UN, though Human Rights Watch pointed out this could mean escalating land mine casualties. The main exception to repatriation remains South Africa. Several hundred thousand Mozambicans live in the South African townships and work in the mines, most of them illegal. While some have met with anti-immigrant violence, economics keeps them from returning. The South African government is currently debating the issue, with the likely consensus being an amnesty for all Mozambicans currently residing there but heightened border security and a return of new economic refugees in the future.[53]

In August 1995, the UN High Commissioner for Refugees, having distributed seed, cooking oil, food, and farm tools, as well as sponsoring irrigation and health projects, announced success and pulled up stakes. This followed the pullout of peacekeeping troops early in the year in the face of criticisms that the volatile political situation did not justify such a precipitous move.

THE FUTURE OF MOZAMBIQUE

Unlike Angola, Mozambique may very well fade from the world's consciousness with the end of apartheid, the Cold War and the RENAMO insurgency. Indeed, it is hard to imagine the Western community being all that concerned about world supplies of cashews and prawns, Mozambique's two main exports. As economist Joan Robinson commented after the decolonization of Africa in the early 1960s, "The misery of being exploited by capitalists is nothing compared to the misery of not being exploited at all."[54] Robinson, of course, was writing long before the expansion of international lending and aid in the 1970s and 1980s. International banking institutions and NGOs are likely to play a critical role in the political and especially economic rebuilding of the country for many years to come.

After all, Mozambique is desperately poor and lacks the coveted resources of Angola. Aid made up well over half of the Mozambican GNP in 1995. As noted throughout the book, international financiers have a major influence on the country's economic decision-making, and many NGOs have established extensive administrative networks throughout the country that, in the best of cases, augment government efforts to unite the country but too often undercut and delegitimize them. In 1991, journalist Joseph Hanlon wrote,

> Mozambique is the mendicant and the donors are trying to call the tune. Nevertheless, Mozambique has retained a surprising amount of power to set policy and direct donors . . . From a position of apparent weakness Mozambique has pushed and even forced donors to follow its policy and guidelines. The government has retained an economic role in the face of near total donor opposition. It has finally convinced even the World Bank of the need to link growth with adjustment.[55]

The government and people of Mozambique will need even more of that determination and skill in the future. It may not be easy. The sense of camaraderie and shared suffering of the early years of the revolution have given way to corruption among the worst of the government leadership, and a privatization of public interest among much of the rest. In the absence of a safety net, and enticed by the wages offered by aid agencies and the opportunities of privatization, many of the best-skilled have abandoned their government posts.

Robinson's bittersweet nostalgia for capitalist exploitation has its counterparts on the left. Not only has the end of the Cold War marginalized Mozambique, notes Saul, but the retreat of the Soviet Union from Africa and the subsequent demise of the Eastern Bloc means there is no effective counterbalance to the West. The impact of these developments, he argues, will be felt in both direct and indirect ways. Military assistance will no longer be forthcoming, though, of course, it is no longer so desperately needed. In addition, despite the relative backwardness of East Bloc technology and its misplaced emphasis on bureaucracy-heavy state planning, the economic aid it offered came cheaper and with fewer strings attached than World Bank and IMF financing.[56]

As with Angola, those who wish Mozambique well are placing their hopes on the remarkable growth of civic institutions and indigenous NGOs that have marked the postwar period. "What is happening in the present crisis in Mozambique," write economists Hans Abrahamsson and Anders Nilsson,

> is that people today cannot depend on modern society's institutions (either state or market functions) for their long-term survival. Therefore guarantees for survival which have their roots in pre-modern times are acquiring greater importance.[57]

Mozambique is likely to remain a country where the overwhelming majority live in the countryside and farm. Even the most ardent centralizers within FRELIMO recognize that, at least in the short- and medium-range future, policies from the capital will have a decreasing impact on rural areas. The exception may be schools and hospitals, if these are possible under economic restructuring, but economic help is unlikely to come from Maputo. The Mozambican people will be on their own and will have to create political and economic institutions appropriate to their needs. Whether the people can overcome their recent past will depend on how they build their future. Whether the revival of the social, political and economic structures of premodern times that Abrahamsson and Nilsson talk about represent a reversion to the discredited colonial past, the establishment of an exploitative neocolonial present, or a progressive synthesis of old and new for the future is a question this book cannot answer.

NOTES

1   *New Statesman and Society*, October 16, 1992, pp. 20–21.

2   *Ibid.*, June 11, 1993, p. 11.

3   Knudsen, Christine and Zartman, I. William, "The Large Small War in Angola" in *Annals of the American Association of Political and Social Sciences*, September 1995, p. 137.

[4] Venancio, Moises, "Angola and Southern Africa: The Dynamics of Change" in Rich, Paul (ed.), *The Dynamics of Change in Southern Africa* (New York: St. Martin's Press, 1994), p. 19.

[5] Cited in Knudsen and Zartman, "Large Small War," p. 136.

[6] Meldrum, Andrew, "Hungry to Vote" in *Africa Report*, November–December 1992, p. 26.

[7] Human Rights Watch Arms Project, *Angola: Arms Trade and Violations of the Laws of War since the 1992 Elections* (New York: Human Rights Watch/Africa, 1994), p. 19.

[8] *Ibid.*, pp. 20–21.

[9] *The Economist*, March 6, 1993, p. 43.

[10] Human Rights Watch, *Arms Trade*, p. 91.

[11] *Ibid.*, p. 25.

[12] Syagues, Mercedes, "The Siege of Cuito" in *Africa Report*, January–February, 1994), p. 17.

[13] *Ibid.*, p. 16.

[14] Human Rights Watch, *Arms Trade*, pp. 47–59.

[15] Knudsen and Zartman, "Large Small War," p. 140.

[16] *Ibid.*, p. 139.

[17] *Ibid.*

[18] Based on Reuters and Associated Press online wire services, c-reuters@clarinet.com and c-ap@clarinet.com.

[19] *Angola Peace Monitor*, August 10, 1995, no pagination, actsa@geo2.poptel.org.uk.

[20] Reuters online wire service, June 25, 1995, c- reuters@clarinet.com.

[21] Samondo, interview with author.

[22] *The Economist*, September 14, 1996, p. 43.

[23] Cited in Reuters, January 14, 1996.

[24] "The News Hour with Jim Lehrer," January 31, 1996.

[25] *Ibid.*

[26] Saul, John, *Recolonization and Resistance in Southern Africa in the 1990s* (Trenton, N.J.: Africa World Press, 1993), pp. 51–53.

[27] Rosenberg, Charles, *The Cholera Years: The United States in 1832, 1849 and 1866* (Chicago: University of Chicago Press, 1962), pp. 1–9.

[28] Saul, John, *Recolonization and Resistance*, p. 54.

[29] UN Chronicle, September 1995, p. 42.

[30] Affecting, ironically, a number of South African firms that originally built the weapons.

[31] Associated Press online wire service, January 10, 1995, c-ap@clarinet.com.

[32] Minter, William, *Apartheid's Contras: An Inquiry into the Roots of War in Angola and Mozambique* (London: Zed Books, 1994), p. 105.

[33] AR Report, March 4, 1993, p. 50.

[34] Vines, Alex, *Angola and Mozambique: The Aftermath of Conflict* (Washington: Research Institute for the Study of Conflict and Terrorism, 1995), p. 17.

[35] *Ibid.*

[36] *The Economist*, March 26, 1994, p. 46.

[37] Many of these soldiers, as well as others sent to take over security in the transport zones from Tanzanian and Zimbabwean troops, had to be rotated when a particularly unsavory scandal was uncovered involving underage Mozambican prostitutes living and servicing the soldiers in their camps.

[38] *The Economist*, August 7, 1993, p. 41.

[39] Minter, Ruth, interview with author, December 2, 1995.

[40] Harding, Jeremy, *The Fate of Africa: Trial by Fire* (New York: Simon and Schuster, 1993), p. 248.

[41] *Southern Africa Report*, December 2, 1994, p. 6.

[42] Nesbitt, Prexi, interview with author, December 13, 1995.

[43] *Southern African Report*, December 1994, pp. 9–13.

[44] *MozambiqueFile*, July 1995, p. 4.

[45] *Ibid.*, October 1995, p. 14.

[46] *Ibid.*, August 1995, p. 3.

[47] Nesbitt, interview with author.

[48] Africa Information Afrique (AIA), http://web.apc.org/aiacan/, January 19, 1996, p. 1.

[49] Human Rights Watch Arms Project, *Landmines in Mozambique* (New York: Human Rights Watch/Africa, 1994), p. 14.

[50] Cited in Reuters, c-reuters@clarinet.com, September 14, 1995.

[51] Africa Information Afrique (AIA), http://web.apc.org/aiacan/, April 4, 1996, p. 1.

[52] *Ibid.*, March 27, 1996, p. 1.

[53] The border between Mozambique and South Africa represents a particularly tricky issue. Under the apartheid regime, an electric fence was constructed along much of it. After taking power in 1994, the ANC turned off the fence, though border police turned it back on in summer 1995. Followers of the South African political scene say that "Mandela hit the ceiling" when he heard of this and had the fence's electrical system disconnected. Nesbitt, interview with author.

[54] Robinson, Joan, *Economic Philosophy* (Chicago: Aldine Publishing, 1963), p. 45.

[55] Hanlon, Joseph, *Mozambique: Who Calls the Shots?* (Bloomington: Indiana University Press, 1991), p. 255.

[56] Saul, *Recolonization and Resistance*, pp. 38–39.

[57] Abrahamsson, Hans and Nilsson, Anders, *Mozambique, The Troubled Transition: From Socialist Construction to Free Market Capitalism* (London: Zed Books, 1995), p. 179.

GLOSSARY AND ACRONYMS

Ajello, Aldo Head of the UN peacekeeping force in Mozambique (see UNOMOZ).

Alves, Nito MPLA general and interior minister who led a failed coup against President Agostinho Neto in 1977 (see NETO, AGOSTINHO).

Alvor Agreement The failed January 1975 agreement between the MPLA, the FNLA and UNITA.

Anstee, Margaret Head of the first UN peacekeeping force in Angola (see UNAVEM).

Armed Forces Movement A group of left-wing officers who overthrew the Marcello Caetano government in Portugal in 1974 (see CARNATION REVOLUTION).

assimilado Assimilated. It refers to those Angolans and Mozambicans who adopted the Portuguese language and culture during the colonial era.

Banda, Hastings President of Malawi from 1971 to 1991.

Beira Mozambique's second largest city and port. Connected to landlocked Zimbabwe via the Beira corridor railway, it is the latter country's main outlet to the sea.

Benguela railway Angola's most important railroad, it connects the port of Lobito to eastern Angola, Zaire and Zambia.

Berlin Conference The 1884–85 conference at which the European powers divided Africa among themselves.

Beye, Alouine Blondin Head of the second UN peacekeeping force in Angola (see UNAVEM).

Bicesse accords The 1991 peace treaty between UNITA and the MPLA (see LUSAKA ACCORDS).

Botha, P. W. South African president from 1978 to 1989.

Bridgland, Fred Jonas Savimbi's biographer.

Cabinda An oil-rich enclave separated by Zaire from the rest of Angola (see FLEC).

Cabora Bassa Mozambique's largest dam.

Caetano, Marcello Portuguese dictator from 1968 to 1974.

Carnation Revolution The 1974–75 revolution that ended Portugal's nearly 50-year-old fascist dictatorship (see ARMED FORCES MOVEMENT).

Casa Banana Located in central Mozambique, it served as RENAMO's field headquarters for much of the war.

Chingunji, Tito A close advisor of Jonas Savimbi, he was executed in 1991 or 1992.

Chipenda, Daniel Head of the MPLA's eastern force during the colonial war, he was a challenger to Agostinho Neto (see NETO, AGOSTINHO).

Chissano, Joaquim President of FRELIMO and Mozambique since 1986.

Clark amendment The 1976 law outlawing U.S. military aid to UNITA.

Constellation of Southern African States (CONSAS) Apartheid South Africa's unsuccessful plan for a Pretoria-led economic union in southern Africa (see SADC).

constructive engagement The popular name for the Reagan administration's policy toward southern Africa (see LINKAGE).

Contact Group Including Britain, France, Germany and the U.S., it attempted to make peace between Cuba, South Africa and Angola (see CONSTRUCTIVE ENGAGEMENT).

COREMO Comitê Revolucíonario do Moçambique (Revolutionary Committee of Mozambique).

Cristina, Orlando RENAMO's secretary general and foreign minister from 1976 to 1983, he was the organization's personal link with Rhodesia and South Africa.

Crocker, Chester The Reagan administration's undersecretary of state of African affairs and author of constructive engagement (see CONSTRUCTIVE ENGAGEMENT).

Cuito Cuanavale The 1987–88 land battle between the MPLA/Cuban and UNITA/South Africa forces.

de Klerk, F. W. President of South Africa from 1989 to 1994.

degregado Degraded one. The prisoners and insolvent debtors Portugal unsuccessfully tried to settle in Angola and Mozambique in the nineteenth and early twentieth centuries.

Dhlakama, Afonso Head of RENAMO since 1979.

dos Santos, José Eduardo President of the MPLA and Angola since 1979.

dynamizing groups Local committees established by FRELIMO to promote revolutionary policies in the countryside.

Executive Outcomes A South African mercenary firm that has supplied soldiers to both the MPLA and UNITA.

FLEC Front for the Liberation of the Enclave of Cabinda (see CABINDA).

Flower, Kenn The head of Rhodesia's security forces who helped bring RENAMO into being.

FNLA National Front for the Liberation of Angola, formerly Union of the Peoples of Northern Angola (UPNA) and Union of Peoples of Angola (UPA) (see ROBERTO, HOLDEN).

FRELIMO Mozambique Liberation Front. It has been the governing party in Mozambique since independence.

frontline states An informal alliance of antiapartheid southern African states. It included Angola, Botswana, Lesotho, Malawi, Mozambique, Namibia, Swaziland, Tanzania, Zambia and Zimbabwe (see SADC).

Gbadolite   Site of a failed Angolan peace conference hosted by Zaire (see MOBUTU, SESE SEKO).

Huambo   Angola's second-largest city and cultural capital of the Ovimbundu people.

Jamba   UNITA's southern Angolan field headquarters from the late 1970s to the early 1990s (see LONG MARCH).

Katangese   A Zairian rebel movement, it fought with the MPLA in the 1970s (see MOBUTU, SESE SEKO).

Kaunda, Kenneth   President of Zambia from 1964 to 1991.

Kikongo   The main ethnic group in northern Angola.

Kimbundu   The main ethnic group in coastal Angola.

kwanza   Angola's monetary unit.

Lancaster House accords   The 1979 agreement ending the war in Rhodesia and providing for the transition to majority rule in Zimbabwe (see MUGABE, ROBERT).

Leopold II   Belgian king who occupied the Congo (now Zaire) in the late nineteenth century.

linkage   The popular term for the diplomatic initiative calling for Cuban withdrawal from Angola in exchange for South African withdrawal from Namibia (see CONSTRUCTIVE ENGAGEMENT and NEW YORK ACCORDS).

long march   Savimbi's retreat to the southern Angola bush after his defeat by the MPLA in 1976 (see JAMBA).

Luanda   Capital of Angola.

Lusaka accords   The 1994 agreement and cease-fire between the MPLA and UNITA (see BICESSE ACCORDS).

Luso-tropicalism   A term coined to explain Portugal's right to keep colonies in Africa (see NEW STATE).

Machel, Samora   President of FRELIMO from 1969 to 1986 and President of Angola from 1975 to 1986.

Makonde   The main ethnic group of northern Mozambique.

Maputo   Capital of Mozambique (known as Lourenço Marques under the Portuguese.

Matsangaissa, Andre   Head of RENAMO from 1975 to 1979, his name became the popular name for the guerrillas, or *matsangas*.

metical   Mozambique's monetary unit.

MNR   (see RENAMO).

Mobutu, Sese Seko   President of Zaire since 1961 (formerly known as Joseph Mobutu).

Mondlane, Eduardo   President of FRELIMO from 1962 to 1969.

MPLA   Popular Movement for the Liberation of Angola. It has ruled the country since independence in 1975.

Mugabe, Robert   President of Zimbabwe since 1980.

musseque   Slum or shantytown.

muzungu   Popular term for a mestizo in Angola.

Naparama   A popular, armed anti-RENAMO movement of the late 1980s and early 1990s, it relied on local religious rituals as part of its military strategy.

Ndau   A relatively minor ethnic group in central Mozambique. Ndau-speaking people dominated RENAMO's leadership.

Neto, Agostinho   Leader of the MPLA from 1961 to 1979 and president of Angola from 1975 to 1979.

New State   The official name for the fascist regime that ruled Portugal from 1926 to 1974.

New York accords   The 1988 agreement calling for a mutual pullout of South African forces from Namibia and Cuban forces from Angola (see LINKAGE).

Nkomati accords   The unsuccessful 1984 agreement between South Africa and Mozambique calling for a mutual cessation of support to guerrillas.

Nyerere, Julius   President of Tanzania from 1961 to 1985 and head of Tanzania's ruling party until 1991.

OAU   Organization of African Unity.

Operation Carlota   Official name of Cuba's military intervention in Angola.

Operation Timber   Official name for the secret agreement calling for a cessation of hostilities between UNITA and the Portuguese in the early 1970s.

Ovimbundu   Angola's largest ethnic group.

PIDE   International and State Defense Police. Portugal's security police for the colonies.

poder popular   The MPLA's armed urban committees during the war of independence.

prazo   A plantation in Mozambique.

PRE   Economic Rehabilitation Program, an economic restructuring policy inaugurated by FRELIMO in the mid-1980s.

regulo   A quasi-traditional, colonial- and postcolonial-era local leader in Mozambique.

RENAMO   National Mozambican Resistance (also known by its English acronym, MNR).

Roberto, Holden   Founder and leader of the FNLA (see FNLA).

Rome accords   The successful 1992 peace agreement between FRELIMO and RENAMO.

SADC   Southern African Development Community, an economic alliance formed to break apartheid South Africa's grip on the regional economy (formerly known as Southern African Development Coordination Conference; see CONSTELLATION OF SOUTHERN AFRICAN STATES and FRONTLINE STATES).

Salazar, António   Dictator of Portugal from the late 1920s to 1968.

Sant'Edigio   Vatican-based religious community that helped broker the Rome accords (see ROME ACCORDS).

Savimbi, Jonas Malheiro   Leader of UNITA since 1966.

SEF   Economic and Financial Restructuring Program, inaugurated by the MPLA in 1987.

Spinola, Antonio de   Portuguese general and government leader following the 1974 coup (see ARMED FORCES MOVEMENT and CARNATION REVOLUTION).

State Security Council   Executive-branch organization in charge of internal and external security of South Africa during the Botha administration (see BOTHA, P. W.).

Stockwell, John   Head of the CIA's Angola task force in the mid-1970s.

SWAPO   South-West African People's Organization. The guerrilla movement that fought against South African occupation of Namibia and the ruling party since independence in 1989.

Tsonga   The main ethnic group in southern Mozambique. Many FRELIMO officials are Tsonga-speaking people.

UNAVEM   The United Nations Angola Verification Mission. UNAVEM I administered the 1991 peace accords and UNAVEM II the 1994 accords (see BICESSE ACCORDS and LUSAKA ACCORDS).

UNITA   Union for the Total Independence of Angola.

UNOMOZ   United Nations Mozambique peacekeeping force.

Vorster, John   Prime Minister of South Africa from 1966 to 1978.

BIBLIOGRAPHY

* Abrahamsson, Hans, and Nilsson, Anders, *Mozambique, The Troubled Transition: From Socialist Construction to Free Market Capitalism*, London: Zed Books, 1995.

* *Africa Report*, New York, through 1995.

* Africa Watch, *Conspicuous Destruction: War, Famine and the Reform Process in Mozambique*, New York: Human Rights Watch, 1992.

Africa Watch, *Landmines in Angola*, New York: Human Rights Watch, 1993.

Alden, Chris, "The UN and the Resolution of Conflict in Mozambique" in *The Journal of Modern African Studies*, Winter 1995.

Angola Observer, Washington, D.C., current.

* Angola Peace Monitor, London, current.

Bayer, Tom, *Angola. Presidential and Legislative Elections, September 29–30, 1992. Report on the IFES Observation Mission*, Washington: IFES, 1993.

* Bender, Gerald, *Angola Under the Portuguese: The Myth and the Reality*, Berkeley: University of California Press, 1978.

Bender, Gerald, "Angola: Left, Right & Wrong" in *Foreign Affairs*, Summer 1981.

Birmingham, David, *Frontline Nationalism in Angola and Mozambique*, Trenton, N.J.: Africa World Press, 1992.

Bridgland, Fred, *Jonas Savimbi: A Key to Africa*, Edinburgh: Mainstream Publishing Company, 1986.

Brittain, Victoria, "Cuba and Southern Africa" in *New Left Review*, November-December, 1988.

Chan, Stephen (ed.), *Exporting Apartheid: Foreign Policies in Southern Africa, 1978–1988*, New York: St. Martin's Press, 1990.

Clough, Michael, *Free at Last? U.S. Policy Toward Africa and the End of the Cold War*, New York: Council on Foreign Relations, 1992.

Crocker, Chester, *High Noon in Southern Africa: Making Peace in a Rough Neighborhood*, New York: W. W. Norton and Company, 1993.

Cummings, Nicholas, "Angola: A Case Study in Soviet Neocolonialism" in *Revolution*, Spring 1984.

Davidson, Basil, *In the Eye of the Storm: Angola's People*, Garden City, N.Y.: Doubleday and Company, 1972.

Fauriol, Georges and Loser, Eva (eds.), *Cuba: The International Dimension*, New Brunswick, N.J.: Transaction Publishers, 1990.

* Finnegan, William, *A Complicated War: The Harrowing of Mozambique*, Berkeley: University of California Press, 1992.

Flower, Ken, *Serving Secretly: An Intelligence Chief on Record, Rhodesia into Zimbabwe, 1964–1981*, London: John Murray, 1987.

* Hanlon, Joseph, *Beggar Your Neighbours: Apartheid Power in Southern Africa*, Bloomington: Indiana University Press, 1986.

* Hanlon, Joseph, *Mozambique: Who Calls the Shots?*, Bloomington: Indiana University Press, 1991.

Harding, Jeremy, *The Fate of Africa: Trial by Fire*, New York: Simon and Schuster, 1993.

Human Rights Watch Arms Project, *Angola: Arms Trade and Violations of the Laws of War Since the 1992 Elections*, New York: Human Rights Watch/Africa, 1994.

Human Rights Watch Arms Project, *Landmines in Mozambique*, New York: Human Rights Watch/Africa, 1994.

Human Rights Watch/Africa, *Angola: Civilians Devastated by 15 Year War*, New York: Human Rights Watch, 1991.

Human Rights Watch/Africa, *Mozambique: New Constitution Protects Rights but Political Prisoners Still Suffer Unfair Trials*, New York: Human Rights Watch, 1991.

Hume, Cameron, *Ending Mozambique's War: The Role of Mediation and Good Offices*, Washington: United States Institute of Peace Press, 1994.

Jackson, Steven, "China's Third World Foreign Policy: The Case of Angola and Mozambique, 1961–93" in *The China Quarterly*, June 1995.

Kaplan, Irving, *Angola, A Country Study*, Washington: American University Press, 1979.

Khadiagala, Gilbert, *Allies in Adversity: The Frontline States in Southern African Security, 1975–1993*, Athens: Ohio University Press, 1994.

Knudsen, Christine and Zartman, I. William, "The Large Small War in Angola" in *Annals of the American Association of Political and Social Sciences*, September 1995.

LeoGrande, William, *Cuba's Policy in Africa, 1959–1980*, Berkeley: University of California Press, 1980.

Lloyd, Robert, "Mozambique: The Terrors of War, the Tensions of Peace" in *Current History*, April 1995.

Magaia, Lina, *Dumba Nengue: Run for Your Life, Peasant Tales of Tragedy in Mozambique*, Trenton, N.J.: Africa World Press, 1988.

* Marcum, John, *The Angolan Revolution. Volume 1: The Anatomy of an Explosion*, Cambridge, Mass.: MIT Press, 1969.

Marcum, John, *The Angolan Revolution. Volume 2: Exile Politics and Guerrilla Warfare*, Cambridge, Mass.: MIT Press, 1978.

McCormick, Shawn, *The Angolan Economy: Prospects for Growth in a Postwar Environment*, Washington: The Center for Strategic and International Studies, 1994.

Minter, William (ed.), *Operation Timber: Pages from the Savimbi Dossier*, Trenton, N.J.: Africa World Press, 1988.

* Minter, William, *Apartheid's Contras: An Inquiry into the Roots of War in Angola and Mozambique*, London: Zed Books, 1994.

Mondlane, Eduardo, *The Struggle for Mozambique*, New York: Penguin, 1969.

MozambiqueFile, Maputo, Mozambique, current.

Nation, R. Craig and Kauppi, Mark, *The Soviet Union in Africa*, Lexington, Mass.: D. C. Heath and Company, 1984.

Newitt, Malyn, *A History of Mozambique*, Bloomington: Indiana University Press, 1995.

Ohlson, Thomas and Stedman, Stephen John, *The New Is Not Yet Born: Conflict Resolution in Southern Africa*, Washington: Brookings Institution, 1994.

Oliver, Roland, *The African Experience: Major Themes in African History from Earliest Times to the Present*, New York: HarperCollins, 1991.

People's Press Angola Book Project, *With Freedom in Their Eyes: A Photoessay of Angola*, San Francisco: People's Press, 1976.

Pereira, Anthony, "The Neglected Tragedy: The Return to War in Angola, 1992–3" in *The Journal of African Studies*, Winter 1994.

Rich, Paul (ed.), *The Dynamics of Change in Southern Africa*, New York: St. Martin's Press, 1994.

Saul, John, *Recolonization and Resistance in Southern Africa in the 1990s*, Trenton, N.J.: Africa World Press, 1993.

Seidman, Ann, *The Roots of Crisis in Southern Africa*, Trenton, N.J.: Africa World Press, 1985.

* *Southern Africa Report*, Toronto, Ontario, current.

Spikes, Daniel, *Angola and the Politics of Intervention*, Jefferson, N.C.: McFarland and Company, 1993.

* Stockwell, John, *In Search of Enemies: A CIA Story*, New York: W.W. Norton and Company, 1978.

UN Chronicle, New York, current.

United Nations, *The United Nations and Mozambique, 1992–1995*, New York: Department of Public Information, United Nations, 1995.

Vines, Alex, *Angola and Mozambique: The Aftermath of Conflict*, Washington: Research Institute for the Study of Conflict and Terrorism, 1995.

Vines, Alex, *Renamo: Terrorism in Mozambique*, Bloomington: Indiana University Press, 1991.

Windrich, Elaine, *The Cold War Guerrilla: Jonas Savimbi, the U.S. Media, and the Angolan War*, New York: Greenwood Press, 1992.

---

*especially recommended

INDEX

Entries are filed letter by letter.
Page references followed by "g" indicate glossary.